Soldiers... in Their Own Words:

Uncut and Uncensored

"While in the Nam, a change began to occur that would continue for years afterward. I began to see how I'd been lied to, how the indoctrination had been a veiled attempt to charge us up to do the impossible for the ungrateful." —Charley Knepple (1948-1997), US Army veteran

"Combat burdens every warrior with guilt, anger and fears. The Viet Nam combat veteran is burdened also with the guilt, anger and fears of America. Sometimes he has been charged with crimes. Other times he has simply been ignored as a symbol of embarrassment. Very seldom has he been welcomed, honored and embraced. A warrior so burdened can never escape the battlefield."
—Chaplain Cephas D. Williamson, VA Med Center, Ft. Wayne, IN.

"My mind was like a blank tape on a tape recorder, with a low or underlying hum of death and destruction as the rewinding of the tape. I had no time out there to rationalize or wonder, or just scream from fear. If I would have rebelled against the war, any time in Viet Nam, any more than I did, the career officer would surely have done me in, one way or another."
—Nick Rizzo (1948-), US Army veteran.

"The ground troops in Nam were given the type of training that made them killers. They were taught to react to certain types of stimuli in a physically aggressive manner. What seems to unnerve the people of this land is that the same Nam vet is fully capable of using those same destructive skills against the general population."
—Rick Ritter, MSW, USMC veteran.

"The soldier is a non-person, an alien, a thing expected to function, while everything around him is strange and lacking in meaning. His view of his surroundings is startlingly expressed in the phrases 'The Nam' and 'The World'; Viet Nam is, in his perception and experience, someplace removed from the real world."
—Stephen Howard, M.D. US Army surgeon veteran

"Rape does not need any elaborate political or socio-economic motivation beyond a simple and general disregard for the bodily integrity of women, plain and simple. The very intensity of maleness that the military demand can only be seen as the beginnings of the power addiction that ultimately leads to female subjugation—rape." — A Woman (non-veteran)

"Torture, rape, and murder: 'Access and opportunity' are only two of the prerequisites. There has been a lot of rape in wars; I keep thinking what it would have been like to be Vietnamese. They never sold their sisters."
—A Viet Nam Veteran (male)

"On Sunday, the last day of the exhibit, during the reading of the additional 110 names for the wall, I saw a dear friend of mine crying... I too started to sob. He had a right to weep, all the rows of names on this 'WALL OF LOVE' and now more to add. *God please make us remember what happened so it is not forgotten and this horrible waste of precious human life will not happen again.*"

—Karin A. Hancuff, bereaved relative of a veteran

"The Wall is a sphinx that will endlessly pose its riddle to those who seek power and will, let us pray, devour those who cannot answer or who answer poorly. It is a sear upon the monumental landscape of our capital; like all scars, it is at once evidence of a wound's healing and a reminder of its hurt."

—Rev. Michael Scrogin

"It was a moment in time when you realize: this is it, this is the end, I am only 20 years of age and my life has been cut short. Our lives depended on God, on a platoon of protective troops, and luck. We had no weapons, but our bare hands and our courage to protect ourselves if the worst happened. And believe me, at that time you thought of only the worst."

—A Nurse veteran

"I felt that the country was embarrassed by me, that the government had used and then flushed me, that my classmates condemned me, and that my family and few acquaintances were unable to understand why I didn't act normal."

—Rev. Timothy Calhoun Sims (1949-2002)

"Survival is the reality of all war. Battlefields have no flags, only the bodies dead and wounded. High ideals have no meaning against the terror of ambush. In the final and most practical analysis, all wars are fought for the possession of dirt. Soldiers do not fight to defend god and country, but to save themselves and as many of their friends as possible."

—Roger Melton

"The first few years in the Marine Corps were filled with a sense of confidence that bordered on arrogance. By the time I got out, there was nothing inside. Not even coldness. Leaves had more sense of direction than I did."

—Paul Richard Wappenstein, Jr.

MADE IN AMERICA, SOLD IN THE 'NAM:

A Continuing Legacy of Pain

Second Edition

Ed. by Rick Ritter and Paul Richards

Book #2 in the *Reflections of History Series*

Modern History Press

An Imprint of Loving Healing Press

```
            Library of Congress Cataloging-in-Publication Data

Made in America, sold in the Nam : a continuing legacy of pain / ed.
by Rick Ritter and Paul Richards. -- 2nd ed.
        p. cm. --  (Reflections of history series ; v. #2)
  Originally published: compiled and edited by Paul Richards. Fort
Wayne, IN : DMZ Pub., 1984.
  Includes bibliographical references and index.
  ISBN-13: 978-1-932690-24-8 (casebound laminate : alk. paper)
  ISBN-10: 1-932690-24-7 (casebound laminate : alk. paper)
 1. Vietnam War, 1961-1975--Literary collections.  2. Vietnam War,
1961-1975--Psychological aspects.  3. Veterans' writings, American.
4. Vietnam War, 1961-1975--United States.  I. Ritter, Rick, 1948- II.
Richards, Paul, 1944-1984.
PS509.V53M33 2007
810.8'0358--dc22
                                                          2006030125
```

Distributed by: Baker & Taylor, Ingram Book Group
Modern History Press is an imprint of
Loving Healing Press
5145 Pontiac Trail
Ann Arbor, MI 48105
USA

http://www.LovingHealing.com or
info@LovingHealing.com
Fax +1 734 663 6861

Modern History Press

Dedicated to all the children
who will be warriors of peace
rather than of death and maiming.

Proceeds from a portion of the sale of this book will
be donated to the foodbank of the
Lincolnshire Church of the Brethren, Ft. Wayne, Indiana

Reflections of History Series

From

Modern History Press

This series provides a venue for contemporary authors who have lived through significant times in history to reflect on the impact of events and lessons they learned from them.

1. *My Tour in Hell: A Marine's Battle with Combat Trauma* by David W. Powell

2. *Made in America, Sold in the 'Nam: A Continuing Legacy of Pain* (2nd Edition), Ed. by Rick Ritter and Paul Richards

3. *F.N.G.: A Novel* by Donald Bodey

"Those who cannot remember the past
are condemned to repeat it."
George Santayana in *Life of Reason* (1905)

Modern History Press is an Imprint of Loving Healing Press.

Table of Contents

ACKNOWLEDGMENTS

An anthology such as this owes everything to its contributors. Some we can thank personally and others we can only acknowledge in spirit. Alphabetically, the contributing authors include: Don Bodey, Frank A. Cross, Jr., Bobbie Depew, R. Joseph Ellis, W.D. Ehrhart, Ed Gallagher, PhD, Sarah Elizabeth Geibel, Dennis L. Grigar, Frank Higgins, Stephen Howard MD, Lonna Kimmel, Charley Knepple, Steve Mason, Larry McFadden, Everett McKeeman, Roger Melton, Tyler Mills, Jon Nordmeyer, Doug Rawlings, Rick Ritter, Nick Rizzo, Michael Scrogin, Rev. Timothy Calhoun Sims, Terry Springer, Steve Stewart, Carol Tannehill, Jim Venable, Paul Richard Wappenstein, Jr., Candia M. Williams, PsyD., Chaplain Cephas D. Williamson, Birgit Wolz, PhD. Some additional contributors wish to remain anonymous and their works are identified only by sets of initials, but we are no less thankful for their contributions.

Several organizations helped provide reprint rights for several new articles and we wish to thank in particular the Ft. Wayne News-Sentinel, Lucy Webster (The Center for War/Peace Studies), The Christian Century, Esther Diley (Lutheran Church in America), the American Journal of Psychotherapy, and the New York Times Agency.

Bob Rich, PhD helped proof much of the new material and bring its level of quality up to meet the level of the 1st Edition text. Publisher Victor R. Volkman performed the typesetting, additional copy layout, and cover design.

A very special thank-you to the Estate of Paul Richard Wappenstein, Jr. (a.k.a. "Paul Richards") for graciously allowing us to rekindle the flame that he ignited so many years ago.

Introduction

One statement that has stood out since the end of the Viet Nam war is, "Viet Nam veterans don't seem to want to talk about what it was like." Quite the contrary. Most veterans of Southeast Asia do want to talk about their experiences. Unfortunately, the majority of Americans have not wanted to listen. Most of the people in the nation spent their time trying to turn a deaf ear to the veterans, trying to forget that our country had ever been involved in such a dirty little war. There has never been anything glorious about war, including the one in Viet Nam. Wars are not made of heroes. They are not a movie in which the good guy always wins. Wars are made up of young men and women staring at the sky with vacant eyes, their life blood mixing with so much mud and slime. Wars are the broken dreams of men and women of peace. They are families being awakened in the middle of the night only to hear their young warrior is dead in some far away place with a name so strange no one can pronounce it. War is a quadriplegic amputee who has also suffered such severe brain damage that the government warehouses him in some nursing home in Midtown, USA. It is the sound of deep sobbing tearing away at some teenage girl who sees her father's name on a wall of the dead. It is the empty desire for one more hello.

The one difference between Viet Nam and all of the other wars fought by this country had nothing to do with the individual fears and courage of the men and women who fought those wars. The difference was in those who did not fight the wars. They welcomed the victors of WW II back with parades and open arms. Those who fought in Viet Nam were spit upon. They were treated as second class citizens, or, in Harrison Salisbury's words, the "new nigger." Much of that treatment was prompted by slick Hollywood productions... productions whose only purpose were to make money. Too bad it was at the expense of men and women who wanted to do no more than what their country had asked of them. Television news also bore some of the responsibility. Viet Nam had become kind of a super soap opera, the main feature of the night. American opinion was formed against the Viet Nam veteran.

This book represents an effort by local Viet Nam veterans to speak out, to tell their side of the story. It is comprised of short stories, essays and poetry. It is the feelings of men and women who put their lives on the line, people who are, once again, trying to speak out.

Like any book, key people are involved. Two of those people are Steve Stewart and Rick Ritter. Without those two, this book would never have become a reality. Their faith and energy represent what is best about those who struggle with the problems of Viet Nam veterans today.

PAUL RICHARDS
1984

In Memoriam

It was but a few months after the release of *Made in America Sold in the Nam* in 1984 that Paul met his untimely death. As it has been with so many over the decades of my practice many vets have survived many different "hells" only to succumb to strange and sometimes even bizarre endings in this life. I vividly remember the call from the sheriff's dispatch to be with Paul's daughter for the remaining hours during the night he died. Paul had been hit by a car while changing a flat tire in the fog early in the morning.

I'm certain I don't have the chronology correct at this point in time, but I recall the drive to his house in the early morning. His other family was farther away than could provide immediate support at that time. Thoughts and memories ran through my mind during the quiet time his daughter and I had before the dawn. It took a little while for this twist on reality to really sink in to our awareness. The many details that were looked after in the preparation for the funeral and the subsequent wake sometimes just delay this reality.

Foremost was the painful realization that Paul had survived two tours in Nam with the Marine Corps and yet still had met this early demise. Perhaps the saddest recurring theme in my 25 plus years as a therapist for vets is that many vets and their families would get closer to healing and pulling their lives back together and then the veteran's life would be ended by some strange twist of fate. It's most eerie when it happens during the first real calm point in many decades. Though of course it is a bittersweet ending...

If memory serves, Billy Joel's song "Goodnight Saigon" (from *The Nylon Curtain*) was a theme for many of us leaving the cemetery that day. It was a moment that struck home the pain of losing another of our brothers.

We release this second edition of *Made in America, Sold in the Nam* with gratitude for the permission of Lisa, one of Paul's surviving children. This new and expanded edition, about four times as large as the original, is not only a tribute to the untimely nature of Paul's demise, but also a true continuation of the primary theme of the book: the journaling of my former clients from the Vet Center during the 1980s (with a few supplements). I have continued to work with veterans from other conflicts and wars, including soldiers from other countries and former enemies as well. As such, it is clear to me that regardless rhetoric or spin, the human costs of war continue to mount in an alarming measure. We remain seemingly unable to communicate or live with our fellow travelers in this life.

Therefore, it is incumbent on us all to carry on with what we have and do the best we can to not forget—it is indeed a task that is unforgiving at times, but so very rewarding in so many other ways.

Hopefully, I have done an adequate job in editing this work anew in the eyes of Paul, Charlie, Linda, Rudy, Russ, Tommie, John, Mark, Billy, Skeet, and many others.

Rick Ritter
August 25, 2006

Quick Facts: Viet Nam Veterans and Stress

Excerpt from the Executive Summary of the major findings from the Center for Policy Research (NY) on Viet Nam era veterans[*]. This study was conducted under contract with the Veterans Administration and involved a sample of 1,440 men (veterans plus nonveterans).

- Approximately two-thirds of all veterans worked full-time for the entirety of the time they were enrolled in educational training, in spite of the fact that the majority of veterans were full-time students.

- When background differences between veterans and nonveterans are statistically controlled, veterans still show some residual disadvantage in educational and occupational attainment, especially in the case of Viet Nam veterans. *This leads us to conclude that military duty in Viet Nam had a negative effect upon post-military achievement.* Duty elsewhere also has a statistically significant but substantially smaller impact on educational attainment.

- For most Viet Nam veterans, particularly those involved in heavy combat, the combat experience and the fact of survival were the most important things that happened to them during the time they spent in Viet Nam.

- Exposure to combat increased feelings of alienation.

- The main types of readjustment problems described by combat veterans are related to the trauma of combat, loss of support offered by the military milieu, lack of interest in normal activities, explosive anger, confusion, loss of confidence, recurrent memories of war in the form of nightmares.

- The incidence of medical problems during and immediately after military service increases with combat exposure.

- Although the majority of Viet Nam veterans do not believe the war had a long term negative effect on their personal development, it is clear that the impact of combat and exposure to death was profound. While the end result, such as becoming mature might be positive, many men acknowledge that pain and distress was associated with the process.

- Most Viet Nam veterans, especially those involved in heavy combat feel that their experiences in Viet Nam affected them profoundly.

- Combat veterans also report significantly more stress symptoms during the year prior to the interview. But this effect is confined mainly to veterans who served between 1968 and 1974. For this group the effect is large.

---

[*] A. Egendorf, C. Kadushin, R. Laufer, G. Rothbart, & L. Sloan (Eds.), *Legacies of Viet Nam: Comparative adjustment of veterans and their peers* (1981). New York: Center for Policy Research.

- Viet Nam combat veterans report more anger and hostility than their peers.

- The likelihood of being arrested after service was the same for men "not arrested before service" as those who "had a pre-service arrest."

- In the "after-service" period, heavy combat veterans have a higher arrest rate than any group.

- Blacks and Latinos were more stressed than whites. Relatively speaking, simply *being in Viet Nam* was as stressful for blacks as being in combat was for whites.

- Almost 70% of black veterans who were in heavy combat are stressed today; 40% of black Viet Nam veterans are currently stressed.

- Men from the most stable families are likely to develop stress reaction involved in heavy *combat*. Men from average families are likely to develop stress reactions after exposure to even low amounts of combat. Men from the least stable families may develop stress reactions simply in response to daily life stressors. Exposure to combat does not greatly affect their level of stress reaction.

- Based on a case-by-case review, Viet Nam veterans differ markedly in the extent to which they have "worked through" war experiences.

- Most Viet Nam veterans deal with war by avoiding troubling issues, blaming the unease they feel on others, or by resigning themselves to self-pity or self-blame. Those who assume responsibility for the implications of their experiences, although a minority, set an example worth communicating to others.

Reaching out to assist Viet Nam veterans may be more difficult than is often assumed. Those who are most likely to respond to offers of help frequently have problems that are more severe than many counselors and therapists may be prepared to handle. Those might be readily aided, the great majority of Viet Nam veterans with unresolved war experiences, are much less likely to accept the role of counselee or patient.

It is important for veterans to come to grips with war experiences. Programs undertaken to encourage and assist veterans in working through their experiences will not duplicate the impact of the incentives provided for higher education under the GI Bill. Working through is not an intellectual procedure and policy makers should not assume that the current GI Bill or the existing structure of higher education with its emphasis on vocational and intellectual skills will address veterans' needs for personal development.

The soldiers who carried the brunt of the battle have become the veterans who, more than most of their fellow citizens, feel the urgency of *finding meaning in the sacrifices of the war years.*

1 The Molting Dream
By Dennis L. Grigar

MARCH 1969: A week's worth of mild rain and warm winds has just about eliminated any traces of winter, but all around us tight groups of people huddle together. Perhaps they're sharing the secrets and promises that strengthen the bonds of family—I can't tell, and won't find out this time around. Mom stands nearby, torn between my nervous tension and Dad's outright impatience to have it over with. We're in Alma, Michigan, standing on the sidewalk by a squat cinder block building that houses my draft board, waiting for the busses.

When they finally arrive, twenty minutes late, Dad assumes it's time to go, so he walks up to me and pushes out his hand. I offer mine and am awed by the differences between us. He grabs me in his enormous clutch and shakes me as if to test the feel of a wrench. I don't like it but he won't let go; he's got something to say, something just for me.

"Well, good luck, and I hope they make a man out of you." His eyes bore into me, wanting to make sure I get the point. I get it alright, and it hurts. When I turn away from him to kiss Mom goodbye there are tears in my eyes. They leave soon after, but the busses don't go for another forty minutes, so already I'm on the outside looking in.

Eighteen hours later, in a cold and crummy barracks at Ft. Knox, Kentucky, a soldier stands inches away from my face screaming at me to cut my moustache RIGHT NOW! Tired and disoriented, I start to move from instinct, and luckily move in the right direction. RUN is the command, so I run, certain now of where and what I am. It's the one-sided handshake again, and I'm on the ass end. Nothing has changed.

• • • • •

NOVEMBER 1969: Hand carrying orders for Viet Nam, I check into a camp someplace in Maryland for Combat Orientation. For the next eight days the United States Army is going to convert me from a humble clerk typist into a jungle savvied warrior. I believe from the outset that this will be a large crock of shit, and I'm right.

We get up early every day and go through the motions of warming up our bodies. If it's raining (and it was for five out of the eight days) we stay indoors and do jumping jacks in front of our bunks. Some of the older fellas with three or more stripes on their arms seem disinterested by the warm-up sessions, more often than not they skip this part to go take a dump or clean up. I've noticed a lot of bars on this base, and the bedcheck at night is basically nonexistent, for obvious reasons.

By the end of the second day I've borrowed an E-6's shirt and am digging the nightlife in a lively club a few blocks away from our barracks. He's been through one tour already, and is taking the Orientation again just for the hell of it. A career man, he tells me that combat duty is a piece of cake compared to the spit and polish garbage of Europe or the States. He goes on to assure me that my coke bottle glasses will keep me out of the boondocks, so what's to worry? We have a few more beers and I leave, feeling no pain.

Outside a cold November fog shrouds the night, creating an ideal backdrop for one of the most bizarre scenes I've ever witnessed. From nowhere a bugle call pierces the silence around me, and seconds later the barracks to my front left erupts with activity.

From both stories of the building, men scramble out into the muddy street and form two perfect lines. They are dressed to the max: white belts and gloves, shiny parade helmets, jackets and pants with lots of red decorations, boots glistening with the familiar spit shine I've never perfected. This is a showboat outfit, and from the intense precision of their lineup I gather there's a show about to begin. Easing back into the cover of fog I watch and wait.

Long minutes pass, I light a cigarette and wonder if this is a waste of time. Those dudes are classy though, not a whisper, cough, or movement from anyone. A vision flashes through my mind—I once owned a set of plastic soldiers and used to line them up in formation then leave them somewhere to go off and be a kid again. Except for little puffs of hot breath, these guys could be that set of plastic soldiers, left behind and waiting for the commander to come back. A barracks door slams behind them, and suddenly the Man appears.

Wearing the standard military green uniform, I would never have guessed that he was the reason behind this show, but it's immediately obvious that God comes in many disguises. From the second he is in view of this formation every head turns to watch his movements. It's like he has forty strings tied from his body to their heads, 'cause no matter where he is, their eyes are on him. With the memory of basic training still painfully fresh, I realize that these guys are in a whole lot of trouble.

He paces the length of his formation but never looks at any of the men. When he finally talks his voice sounds tired, not the crack-your-ass bark of a basic training D.I., but there's enough poison in his words to make my ass pucker.

"You have disappointed me again, and now you're gonna pay. After this little exercise tonight I intend to let you settle the problem that's ruining your chances to be officers in the United States Army. At oh-seven hundred hours tomorrow morning some of you will report to my office for reassignment. I don't care what you look like when you get there, I don't care if you have to be carried there, but the problem IS going to be solved tonight. At oh-eight hundred hours there'll be a full dress inspection, and anyone who fails to make the grade will also be reassigned. Begin!"

The front line does a left face and moves with inhuman precision until there is only one line facing the man. Without a word they all turn face right, then the lead man double times it up to the front of their barracks, lays down on and starts to crawl around the building. Another man is right be-hind him, and in less than a minute the whole formation has formed a human snake wallowing in the cold slime.

I don't like watching people suffer so I try to slide by the Man and get to my bunk, but he spots me and asks for a light. I've got one, but hate like hell to share it with him.

"You here for the orientation?" he wants to know. I say I am and he laughs. "Just think, you might have one of these turds for your C.O."

On the last day of our training program we are taken out for a "combat simulation," complete with full backpacks and empty M14 rifles. Loaded into the back of an open truck, we travel to a scrawny wooded area and are told to pile out and patrol the place. Less than halfway into the patrol we get am-bushed. Moving around like cattle we bang into each other, dive for the same cover and fall on our weapons. I trip over no fewer than four personnel mines and am shot repeatedly by the enemy.

Riding back in the truck we smoke cigarettes and bitch about having to clean up the rifles before receiving our diplomas in combat training. I look around me and see a lot of men covered with red powder. The red powder came from those personnel mines that explode like party favors under our feet. It seems to me that if the redness were blood from our bodies then no one would be laughing, and I don't think I'm ready for the war.

$$\bullet \ \bullet \ \bullet \ \bullet \ \bullet$$

JANUARY 1970: Viet Nam smells like a garbage dump, has too many rows of barbed wire, and the Army doesn't seem to know what the hell it's doing. I arrive in country at an enormous airfield, am flown to an unnamed place and dumped in front of a corrugated metal building. No one is there to meet me, and my name isn't on anybody's roster. The men who have landed with me leave in jeeps or trucks, but I can't go with them because my name isn't on the list. When the last jeep starts its engine, I panic and jump in. The soldier laughs, says he'll take me to his camp and see if the C.O. can find a spare bunk for the night. I don't give a damn if I have to lay on the floor, just don't leave alone.

The C.O. says it's no problem; I can stay until my orders are straightened out, go find an empty bunk and relax. I find an empty bunk, lay down, but can't begin to relax. When we drove through a little village to get here I saw a lot of Vietnamese people, and they looked at us with hungry eyes. I saw tiny houses made out of coke cans that had been cut open, flattened out and somehow put together to form walls. I saw miles of barbed wire and soldiers patrolling the perimeter of this camp with vicious police dogs by their sides. This is a dangerous place, and I can't relax.

The night is dark and thick and still. It's hot, there's a rat hole in the la-trine, and the mosquitoes are out in force. I'm out of cigarettes but there's no place to get any. I lay on a mattress that smells like piss in a roomful of empty bunks and sweat from heat and the fear of being killed in my sleep. Hours later I'm jarred awake by an explosion that shakes the earth. With no weapon, no orders and no friends, I crawl under my bunk and eat dust.

There's lots of shouting and some machine gun fire, but it doesn't last long. I need to relieve my bladder so bad it makes me shiver, but I wait another minute or two before making the charge.

Hungry for news and some nicotine I leave the barracks to snoop around. Someone spots me not wearing a helmet or flak jacket and chews on my ass, but I bum a smoke anyway and he catches the scent of a "newbie."

"How long you been in country, dude?"

"About five hours. I don't like it."

"No shit Sherlock. Are you stationed here?"

"I don't know, I don't think so, but I really don't know."

"Well if you don't know then chances are you're not. It ain't likely they'd put ya here without a rifle or a helmet for Christ's sake! You better get back to your hooch 'fore the brass spots ya."

"What happened just now? Were we attacked?"

"Sorta," he drawls, enjoying my anxiety. "That was a rocket, knocked out a bunker, hit it dead center. Some guys musta been in there tokin' up, they're dead, but we don't know how many yet. I'm s'posed to be over there now hunting for body parts. You get yer ass back in the barracks and put a coupla mattresses on the top bunk. Mattresses help stop the shrapnel. Here," he throws me his pack of smokes, "you look like you're gonna need these tonight."

I do what he tells me, then sit in bed and smoke the rest of the ciga-rettes. There aren't enough of them to get me into daylight hours, but I'm not very tired anyway, so I listen to the night around me and kill mosquitoes. I think about men dying in a bunker while smoking dope, and wonder how long it will be before I get to taste the famed Nam weed. I've heard that it's some of the world's best and if tonight is any indication of the year ahead then I think I'd rather die stoned than straight .

• • • • •

After two days of waiting I am taken along in a heavily armed convoy to Saigon for reassignment. This is a no nonsense trip that reminds me of all the opportunities I had to skip across the border and go Canadian. It's hot and muggy, but I've been ordered to wear a helmet and flak jacket or pay the consequences. Beyond and behind us are jeeps with 50 caliber machine guns mounted in the backs, there are helicopters overhead and men with rifles and grenade launchers in every vehicle. Nobody's laughing at anything or anyone, the real war is all around us, and I still don't have a weapon.

We roll past man made craters in the earth, buildings that are sand-bagged so heavily you can't tell what they're hiding. Twisted, charred heaps of vehicles that have been pushed off the road. The whole damn trip I never see a stretch of road that isn't barricaded on either side by barbed wire, and I wonder where the hell I'd run to if we were hit.

Saigon is one of the filthiest and most exotic cities in the world. Gigantic pagodas stand beside modern ten story buildings, the traffic patterns are impossible to decipher, and there are literally thousands of people riding around on tiny motorcycles, bicycles, and dinky little vans. American and Vietnamese troops are everywhere, so is barbed wire and the smell of rotting garbage. We leave the convoy and proceed to an old hotel in the heart of the city. Right beside the hotel is a garbage dump, and if my stomach weren't empty I'd barf at the smell of that monstrous shit pile.

The hotel walls sweat, the lobby carpeting is moldy, and there are lizards skittering around on the walls. I'm given a room number, told not to leave the building, and left to my own devices. The room has nine foot ceilings and a paddle fan that doesn't work. The windows are open but I'm not overlooking the garbage dump, thank God! Instead, I'm overlooking the street, and it never stops being busy. At night I hear women scream, gunfire, sirens and outraged cries of men beating men. There are Reader's Digest magazines from the early Sixties lying around, and eventually I read a dozen of them. Time has no significance, I eat, shower, read pulp or watch the workings of an alien world from my fourth story window, and sleep. It seems like I should be taking lessons in the Vietnamese language or learning more about the culture or any damn thing, but I wait, another object left to rot in the relentless heat.

Five days of smelling and hearing the cesspool of Saigon makes my orders for assignment seem like a message from heaven. I don't give a damn where I go as long as I can call the pieces of ground I'm standing on my space. The days of being nowhere and nothing to anyone have already gnawed a hole in my soul—I need a spot to stand on and defend. That spot is called Nha Trang, and I'm told it's a beautiful coastal city with a fairly secure military base.

• • • • •

FEBRUARY 1970: Camp McDermitt is both clean and fairly secure, but I don't know anything about Nha Trang because it's off limits. The South China Sea is close enough to hear and smell, and there's a beach where we can swim on off days. I share a small hooch with some dude from the motorpool who drinks too much but likes Big Ten college sports, so we get along alright. I've been issued an M14 plus flak jacket and helmet, but they won't let me sight my rifle in. That bothers me, but I don't tell them about it because they wouldn't give a damn anyway. The order that prevails is don't make waves and you won't be noticed. I've been assigned to Headquarters as their clerk typist and go-fer, am now receiving mail from home, and feel as though I'm gonna be OK.

We've had four rocket attacks in four weeks, the largest one being a seven round barrage that kills three men in another company and destroys two bunkers. Rumor has it direct hits are few and far between, but the piercing shriek that gives us a second's worth of warning never fails to wrench my guts. With mountain ranges on three sides of our camp it's impossible to control or prepare for these random attacks, so I learn to live with one ear tuned to the skies.

The night hours are deceptively quiet and peaceful. There are a lot of hooches with big Japanese stereos, but everyone has headphones and usually keeps the noise down. I wonder how someone with headphones can tell when there's an attack, but don't bother asking, it's live and let live around here, no doubt I'll figure it out later. What I'm most anxious to figure out is where the dope comes from. I can smell it, can hear the results of it in laughter that fades when I step outdoors to look at the night sky, but no-body's offered to initiate me yet, so I listen and wait and hope for acceptance.

Six days a week a couple hundred Vietnamese pass through the front guard post of the camp and become barracks, kitchen, and bar help. Our barracks is maintained by two tiny women, one so old and grizzled I wonder how she keeps moving, the other a pretty young flirt with a taste for Ameri-can possessions. At the cost of forty dollars per month per man they make bunks, sweep floors, do our laundry and even shine our boots. By Vietnam-ese standards of living these women are high paid and extremely privileged personnel. I try and try to get them to teach me Vietnamese and tell me about their homes but they won't do it, they say Americans come and go so often there's no reason to waste time learning anything. I think it ridiculous that I can't speak the native tongue or at least understand it enough to ask for simple directions. How the hell can we be good allies if we can't under-stand each other?

One night Don pops his head into our hooch and tells me it's time to go out for a drive. I follow him to a covered pickup truck and jump in the back, excited by the prospect of sinning. We move a short distance, head out of the camp and into an area that can't be more than three hundred yards off the base. The truck drives behind a small hut then stops to unload about ten of us. I follow the crowd through a wrought iron gate that opens into an en-closed garden setting, and we are met by a group of women. Some of the women giggle and point to familiar faces, others hide beneath wide, cone-shaped straw hats, indifferent to the next pairing. An older woman appears to greet us formally, then collects five dollars per man and disappears as quietly as she came. It's open season now, but I'm new to the meat market game so I hang back and watch.

Though I don't say so it's not a woman I want, it's a taste of the weed. In a minute or two there's no one standing in the garden anymore except for me, and I wonder how I can get what I'm after. Mama-san comes back and spots me, so she walks over and asks me if I'd rather have a boy instead of a woman. Shocked and embarrassed I shake my head no, so she barks out a command and a woman in a cone hat appears. Taking my hand, she leads me through the garden and into a tiny room. One candle on a small table illuminates a cot, a chair and four dirty gray walls. No pictures, no mat on the dirt floor, no incense to disguise the smell of stale semen and sweat, this is a working class shelter, and my name is Joe.

I don't want this, I don't want it at all, so I light a cigarette and remain standing. She sits down on the narrow cot, takes off her hat and looks up at me, waiting. I can't tell her age, but from the calluses on her palm I guess she's used to farming, so I try to talk about farming. I ask her about the rice but she doesn't speak much American, so that goes nowhere in a hurry. She wants me to sit down beside her so I do, then let her take my arm and put it around her waist. She puts her hand on my leg, strokes my thigh a couple of times then waits for me to respond. I'm waiting too, waiting for an emotion I can't seem to remember.

I touch her hair, looking for a place to start. She sort of leans over my shoulder, perhaps grateful for some tenderness, but when I try to kiss her she turns her head away, so we're lost again, lost and desperately divided. She won't let it go though, pulling me down to lie beside her on the cot, determined to get through the act, or at least go through the motions. Despite a sense of helpless confusion I'm warmed by the length of another body near mine. Moving quickly, she lifts her feet up and separates my legs, then rubs my crotch with enough pressure to achieve the desired effect. Before I can respond though she stands up, turns her back to me and starts to undress.

Following suite, I get my boots off by the time she's undressed and hidden beneath a sheet. I didn't even notice a sheet on the bed, but seeing her peek over the thin pale cloth stimulates my hands to activity. Moments later we're lying side by side. She's slipped one hand around my waist and is urging me over, but I want to touch her first, to feel the length of smooth brown skin under my hands. I'm hard now, and it's starting to feel like something familiar, but my hand moves across her stomach and freezes in shock. Ripping the sheet back I look at her, look long and hard, and see that she is well into pregnancy.

It's wrong, it's all so fucking wrong I don't want anything to do with her, but when I jump up and grab my pants she grabs them too and tries to pull me back into bed. She cries out, still pulling on my pants, and before I can yank them out of her hands, Mamasan pulls the blanket door to one side and asks me if anything is wrong.

I'm naked and so goddamn vulnerable I don't know what to do. Without waiting for an answer, Mamasan snaps a line of abuse at the woman in the bed that sends her shuddering back under the covers. She shakes her head no no no, huddling in terror against Mamasan's attack, and suddenly I'm saying that everything's just fine, go away and leave us in peace. I rip the blanket out of her hand and slap it shut, but I'm shaking so bad I can hardly light a cigarette.

Sitting on the edge of the bed I offer her a puff, and she accepts it. We smoke in peace, then she puts her hand on my shoulder to pull me down and I fall. Lying beside her, I wonder what her husband thinks about her second job, but there's no use in asking because we don't speak the same language. She wants me to roll over and move with her, but I know it won't work. Whether or not it works doesn't matter though, she's insistent that we go through the motions, and when I lay on her, she finds enough skin to breach the sacred hollow.

I'm too heavy, she pushes me off her stomach, but I'm supposed to keep moving too, so I pull myself up and make our crotches rub. We rub for awhile, two damp sticks of wood having a dull go at the process of making fire, then I sigh and get up to put my pants on. In very broken English she asks me for three dollars. The five dollars I gave Mamasan was for the room, not the pleasure of this woman's company. Without looking to see what I've got I pull out a handful of bills and place them on the bed. She grabs them and starts counting the money, but I turn away and don't look at her again. Scrambling to get dressed, I finally leave the room to go outside and put my boots on. It's hot and still and the air is cramped with humidity, but at least I can see the stars and hope that somewhere something is going right for someone.

Later that night, a long time after taking the longest cold shower of my life, I lay in my bed and feel like scum.

· · · · ·

MARCH 29th, 1970 – EASTER SUNDAY: Just another workday by military standards, the C.O. issues orders that any man who wants to may be excused for an hour to go to church services. I thought about it but there's no fan and some asshole vandalized the air conditioner for parts. I don't bother to ask myself if anything is sacred anymore, and I don't go to the Sunday service either.

Around eleven o'clock there's a high piercing scream in the air and I hit the deck crawling. Apparently everyone around me does the same 'cause the ensuing shrapnel that tears through our West wall misses flesh. Three more drop around us in rapid succession, none of them as close as the first but still in our company area. There are shouts and the sound of boots scrambling over gravel, so I grab my flak jacket, helmet and the company radio and dash outside to the command bunker. Two of the five posts respond, we've taken a hit across the road, no sign of casualties yet, but where the hell are posts 1, 3, and 4?

More rounds drop in, another one smashes into the buildings across the road but I'm in contact with 1 through 3 now so at least we've got eyes to see. Number 2 says it's an affirmative on the hits in our buildings, but he doesn't see... yes he does, a man has walked out into the driveway, away from cover of the buildings. He looks wobbly, better send someone out there quick to pull his ass back.

I tell the First Sergeant we've got a wanderer, maybe shell shocked, and Top wants to know if I'll go out and get him. I hand Top the radio and start running. It's only about thirty yards away but before I'm half way there someone's already with him. Why the hell don't they go for cover?

Another round slams down about fifty yards to my left side, close enough to shower my low crawling ass with gravel, near enough to send me back towards the command bunker. We wait then for about five minutes but it's over, the damage is done. With everyone still on red alert, I hustle across the road to get an official word on our wanderer. The official word is that he's full of tiny shrapnel holes and no longer breathing. An ambulance hits the scene with sirens screaming but we hardly notice them, caught by the aura of fresh death. The ambulance is gone in less than a minute, and there's nothing else to do but go back to Headquarters and report a K.I.A.

I don't remember very much about the rest of Easter Sunday. Throughout the Christian world this is one of the most sacred holidays, a time to celebrate rejuvenation and the hopes of eternal redemption. Apparently nobody told Charlie Cong that this day is a good one to lay all weapons down and rest in peace 'cause he threw enough shit at us to take one away.

The Mess Hall's outdone themselves in preparing a fine Easter dinner but half the company don't even show up to eat. Men trickle in and out of H.Q. to pick up the news and it's plain to see that a haunted mood prevails. Late in the afternoon a well liked E-6 drops by, sits down and bums a smoke off me. I know he doesn't usually smoke so he must be in to talk awhile. Turns out he was the last one to see our man alive and well. Minutes before the rocket attack he'd stopped in to see if everything was OK and the dude told him he'd just received orders to leave country.

I listen but don't talk, not sure if I can keep from breaking down. As a teenager I shot two deer for food and still remember the brutality of my act against such beautiful animals. Hearing Bob talk about a man dying with two weeks left in county reminds me of those deer. Even with holes in their bodies they still ran for the woods, giving their blood to the snow in the hopes of reaching cover. From the depths of my heart comes a terrifying question: In the act of dying did that man leave his building with thoughts of walking home?

2 — Poems (i)

ALONE

The womb behind, the cord cut;
Lying in a basket... alone.
Small child, parents cannot understand,
Though they reach out... alone.
Thru the learning years, not grasping those around,
Reaches adolescence... alone.
Facing puberty, deepened feelings and new drives;
Questions afraid of the asking... alone.
Military years, prime of youth;
Cannot fit into their molds... alone.
Sees the beauty of life, the gifts of God,
Feels no lust for the world's ways... alone.
Longing for a family, fails in marriage,
Frustration, caring locked deep in the soul is not freed... alone.
Cries out, agonizes in the hurt,
Revels in the pleasures of life so many miss... alone.
The truth, communication lies in the music;
Wailing of blues, driving riffs of rock, classical serenity... alone.
If only someone knew, is there no way of finding;
Deepest feelings of love cannot be shared alone.

JIM VENABLE
August 31, 1981

GENTLE PERSON, THY CONCERT IS THERE

Gentle person
>   thy concert is there
>   Who took your brothers life?
Music was made
>   by men who know
>   How best to write the notes
A shot, a shell
>   a burst and sound
>   Whistle the song of death
The chorus is sung
>   by men who never
>   Could carry a tune before
Conductors appear
>   to lead the parade
>   But only from afar
Lest they be touched
>   with the notes of the song
>   That they themselves have wrote.

T.K.

THE JUNKYARD

I remember a child
    only six years old
    not really helpless
    just hungry and bold.

We drove by the junkyard

He took out his tin cup
    dipped it in swill
    drank from it quickly
    as if it could kill

We came to a stop
    in our traveling jeep
    he hollered from behind us
    "Hey G.I. anything for me to keep?"

He had no parents
    they had been killed
    his value for life
    was deeply instilled.

I tossed off some C-rations
    said, "this surely will beat
    anything so far you
    might have had to eat."

He looked at me kindly
    then said, "cam on ong.
    for my brothers and sisters
    I will take this on home. "

We drove down the road
    when out loud I had said
    "war is worse for the living
    than ever could be for the dead."

PAUL WAPPENSTEIN

OLD MYTHS

Citations, medals, warrants of promotion:

All the things I ever earned I framed
And tacked up in an attic room
I used to use for studying.

That was several years ago;
Before the nightmare eyes had fully set,
Before events began to show
How deeply they were etched.

Now the room is cluttered with old clothes
And broken toys and boxes.
I don't go up there anymore;
I've lived the myth,
and seen the horror of the lie.

Yet even now, sometimes I find
Faint traces of an older pride.

I guess old myths die hard.

W. D. EHRHART

FRONT STREET

His distrust of trees came in the war
he said, every night watching.
looking them over before bedding down.
Birds deceived by searchlights
perked up, sang songs
in dust covered branches.

Couldn't walk in the open
or under trees
because of snipers, and
even now refuses the sidewalk
that busy elms have made
into a tunnel on Front Street,
refuses except when walking
his four year old daughter
to the far corner and back,
returning always with a blot
of wetness on his pants
and the squealings of a child –
her hand held too tight   too tight daddy.

FRANK HIGGINS

3 Nothing Left to Give: A Journal of Viet Nam 1969–70

By Charley Knepple

"I will never romanticize war,
War is hell."

Readjustment Blues

Every vet thinks that once they get off that Freedom Bird that they can start living where they left off. So many things change while you're gone; friends move away, get married, and are busy holding down jobs, and the same goes for family. The first thing a Vet feels is separation and isolation.

Home had been my anchor. During those eleven plus months while I was 10,000 miles away, the world seemed sometimes unreal. The only contact was through unsatisfying letters, which could only hint at the changes taking place there. The military's programmed de-personalization had unleashed so unreal of a state of mind in me that I could not detect the changes in my identity. Identity, or lack of it, was only part of the problem.

The Vet vows that once home, he will never think of the Nam again, but the first newscast you see with footage of Nam grunts will take you right back. And when the radio played The Doors, Eric Clapton, Johnny Winter (etc. ad infinitum) I could practically feel the lumps of the sandbag bunker. All those lonely nights on the bunker listening to the radio was conditioning, and I could not get away from the stimuli.

Some fears creep in, ambush, and harass you. When lightning hit a flagpole one night, I responded by dressing myself and running out of the room completely confused about what had happened. Was I merely animal instinct? In a later incident, I was attending night school while there was some demolition going on nearby. With the first explosions, I wanted to tear myself out of my seat and run outside. I don't know how, but I resisted. I was gripping the desk with white knuckles and feeling very anxious and uncomfortable. When I looked up, I realized that the professor and several students were looking at me. I let it pass without comment. How could I explain, and how could they understand?

At the end of the first year back home, I had not gone a day without thinking about Viet Nam. I wasn't concerned about this except that I also talked about Nam a lot and sometimes people would say, "Well, that's over now." But when I was there I wanted to be home, and when I got home I sometimes wanted to be there.

Another year passed and I was involved in getting married and finishing school, but I still thought about the Nam a lot and talked about it less. This journal is the first time I have been willing to express some of the feelings I have held inside since my return from Nam.

About that time, the news was filled with Viet Nam as the NVA took over Quang Tri province and headed south. Eventually, Saigon fell. I knew it was coming, but I was shocked—stunned—by the pictures of that last helicopter lifting off the American embassy building. News photos had shown Russian-built tanks on the road through QTCB.

So here I am today. I'm a Viet Nam Veteran and I feel that no one cares or at least tries to understand. Not like they cared for the vets of previous wars. I have been made to feel foolish if I mouth the phrase "When I was in the Nam..." People still tell me in subtle ways that, "It's over, forget it." How can I forget? Every time a chopper goes overhead, I look up. Golden oldies can take me right back to the bunker, and its "OK Lord—lay it on me." Whenever I shower, I see that little chunk of shrapnel in my thigh that was once part of a Chinese rocket. After I'd been home eight years, I'd begun to think that it was wrong to think about the Nam. I felt that it was wrong to wonder what became of Holle's wife and especially his little girl. Sometimes worrying about my thoughts would interfere with other things and cause me to withdraw from communication. What's my identity? If I include Viet Nam Veteran, I sometimes feel guilt, like I'm asking someone to feel sorry for me.

I can't and won't deny that I'm a Vet. I'm proud of the way I performed in adverse conditions. I was awarded the Eighteenth Brigade Ring and an Army Commendation Medal because I did my job well. I have an appreciation for life and human beings that is a direct result of the death and destruction I was so near. Each Viet Nam Vet took home something from every other Vet. We were survivors, sure. But when it comes to self-esteem, I'm bankrupt. Everyone, when given a chance to prove himself, can become a hero. There were no heroes made in Viet Nam.

What I Hope to Say

I know little of politics and world affairs and I have no ability to predict the future. So as I write this in 1980, I don't know if there will be future armed conflicts. The likelihood is probably very high. There have already been two "wars to end all wars". Those occurred prior to the Korean War, and my war, Viet Nam.

I hope that this will be more than just the ramblings of a Viet Nam vet. It is meant to be a journal of my feelings and reactions to Nam. Just possibly, it might persuade someone to consider the personal aftermath of war and to think deeply about the effects of becoming a man with a rifle in your hands. Many young men growing up feel the need for some definitive act that will separate them from the boys. For many, the military will hold a certain appeal.

Personally, I was reluctant to choose the military in 1967, but as American involvement in Viet Nam increased, and more and more young men were needed to carry out 'our mission", I found myself with no choice to make. The official pronouncement came in the form of *greetings* from my local Draft Board.

What I had seen in the beginning as a chance to separate myself from the boys became an experience too difficult to endure at times. It never ceases to amaze me how the human spirit can suffer so much without complaint only to begin to fray at the edges later as remembrances of war turn into haunting.

This journal began in 1975 as notes to myself, which were eventually transferred to the pages of a composition notebook, and were finally typed into these pages. [Ed. Note: this edition contains the first-ever complete printing of Knepple's original manuscript.]

• • • • •

Shit! I can't keep my eyes open and I can't get comfortable enough on these sandbags to sleep. We've been sitting in this same CP for a month. Every night getting maybe two hours sleep here or there, then spending the whole day on the road. Why don't I just go to sleep? Fear? Paranoia? I might be the only one on this bridge still awake. It's so damn quiet! The night is so long and boring, it almost makes me wish something would happen to break the boredom. However, I've learned that there are a lot worse things than boredom. In the couple of months that I've been here, I've learned a lot. Take a little trip with me as I revisit how I got to be here in this bunker and join me in my dark night of the soul.

• • • • •

First Days

It was quiet in the plane on the way over. Very quiet. Everyone deep in thought, already missing whatever they had just left, fearing whatever they were about to experience.

There must have been some vacationing tourists in the terminal at Honolulu, although I don't remember seeing them. I guess I needed to see some indication that life goes on: I wanted to see palm trees or a beach, or something. I could have been in any airport in the world, except for the fact that I was in brand new green jungle fatigues on my way to war. Did they the tourists feel for us or were they too involved in their own good time?

We arrived at Ton San Nhut, Viet Nam airbase just after noon. My first impressions: the country is ugly, as ugly as anything I can remember; there are sandbags everywhere; it is hot; it is dusty. The bus ride from the Repl-Depl provided me a closer look at the country. The closer you look, the uglier it gets. There are screens over the bus windows: are they there to protect us, or to separate us from the Vietnamese along the road? They live in garbage; disease almost seems to be visibly carried along in the hot dusty air.

A formation after dark at the Repl-Depl, roll call directions: "Stand behind your duffle bag, dump it out, throw jackets and stateside clothing in this shed. You won't be needing those here, kiddies. You will be going to Cam Ranh Bay at 0830 tomorrow."

Cam Ranh Bay, more directions and a three mile walk across the compound to the 504th MP Group area. Cam Ranh is all white sand surrounded by hills. Someone points out that VC rockets are often dropped into the compound from those same hills.

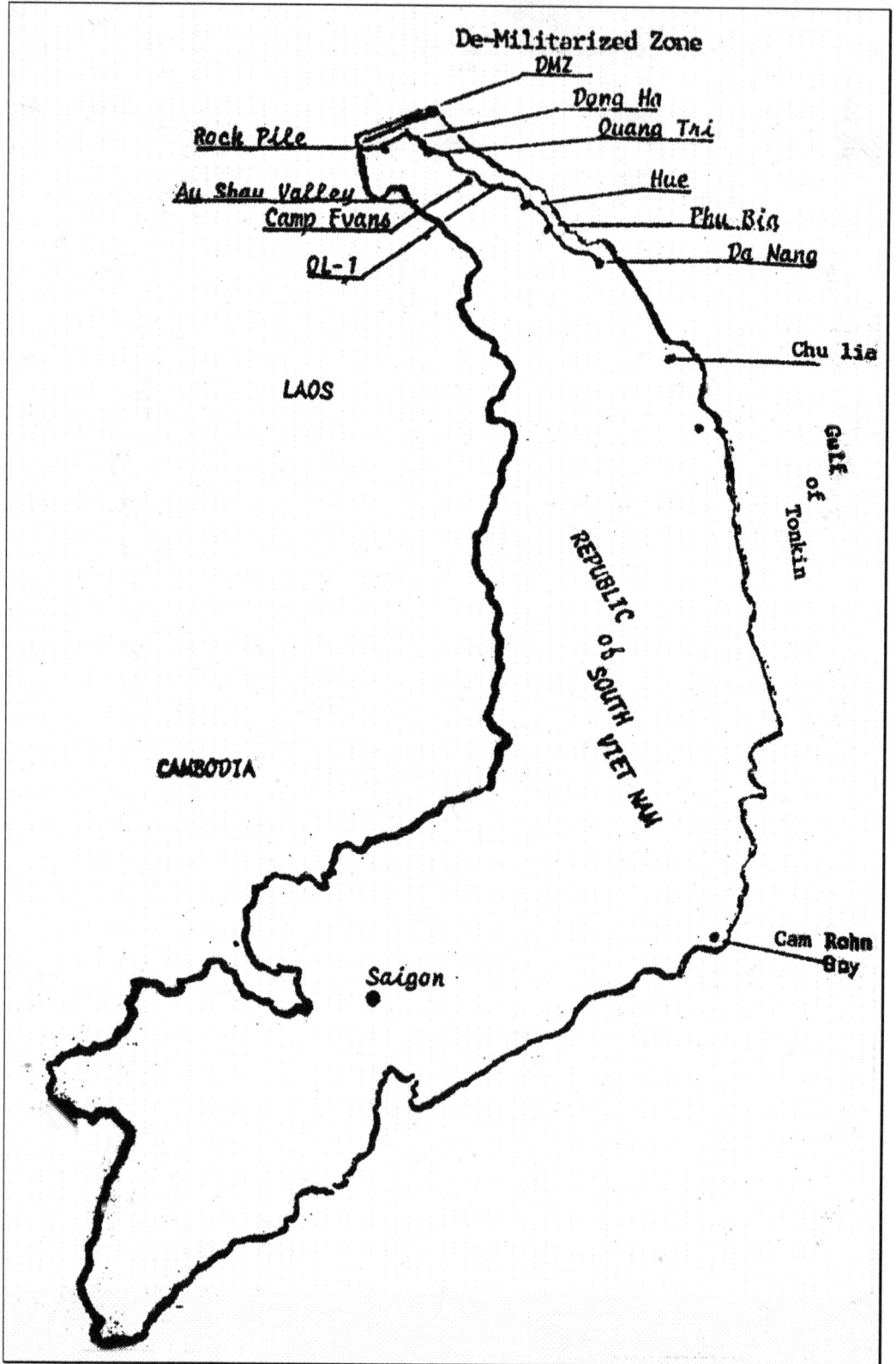

De-Militarized Zone
DMZ
Dong Ha
Quang Tri
Rock Pile
Hue
Au Shau Valley
Phu Bia
Camp Evans
Da Nang
QL-1

Chu lia

LAOS

Gulf
of
Tonkin

REPUBLIC
of
SOUTH
VIET NAM

CAMBODIA

Cam Rohn
Bay

Saigon

"Why don't they do something about that? How do you tolerate them getting that close to an established command post like this?"

That night I'm lying on the top bunk in a hooch made of 2x4s and tin, forty men are talking quietly among themselves.

"Did you hear about the tigers here?... the Montagnards?... the VC tunnels?"

Incoming! Incoming! Thuds are not too far away, rockets whistling overhead. Two days in country and we're already under attack! Fifteen minutes later, it's all over. We're in bed again, lights out, but with one eye open.

The next day it's school—desks in a portable classroom. "This is marijuana; it can be identified by this smell. I'm going to pass around this sample for everyone to examine... This afternoon we'll be talking about the black market, then we'll make assignments to "A", "B", or "C" Company and you will ship out tomorrow morning."

If I had a choice, where would I like to go? Headquarters Company is here, they say it's the best. "A" Company is at An Khe, near the jungle. "B" Company is at Phu Bai, near the coast. But, hope you don't get "C" Company, they are at Quang Tri—the DMZ.

"*Knepple*—C Company."

"*Shit*, well, goodbye Peters, goodbye Trammel. Have a good year."

Up Country

It's a long, hot drive from Cam Ranh to Phu Bai. We're traveling on QL-1, the only paved road in Viet Nam. A war has been fought over this country since before the Korean War. We pass crashed-out choppers, bombed-out buildings, and concrete pillboxes. All permanent buildings have bullet holes in the walls. The road winds through hills, jungle, rice paddies as far as the eye can see, villages, and sand dunes. At one point we pass through "Cloud's Nest", a high mountain pass that has been considered strategic by both sides for a long time. Beautiful from a distance, it is bald, shelled out, scarred, and frightening up close. You feel vulnerable, even at midday.

Finally, we arrive at Phu Bai, where I am met by the courier from Quang Tri, who will take me to my home. I take my duffle bag out of the nearly new, clean M35 "Deuce-and-a-half" truck of HQ and put it into the beat up Jeep of "C" Co. The floor of the Jeep is covered with sandbags. The courier tells me this is because the pavement runs out at Hue, a few miles ahead, and the sandbags are for protection in case of a road mine.

Hue is a beautiful, clean, modern city (all by Vietnamese standards, of course). There is a downtown area with closed-in stores and a theater looking out over a wide, clean river. At one point we pass the Catholic Church that suffered so much damage in the TET offensive of '68. It looks skeletal, buried in a ribcage of bamboo scaffolding. We cross the river on a floating bridge. At the north end of the city is a huge, walled citadel. And sure enough, after passing the Citadel, the pavement runs out and we begin thirty miles of dirt road to Quang Tri.

M35: 6x6 truck was a workhorse in Viet Nam

The country looks poorer here, flatter, but less developed than in the south. The villages are of cardboard and tin, looking mostly of a temporary nature. Farms consist of a few meager paddies and thin water buffalo. A couple of Viet Cong bodies are on display in one of the villages. The further north we get, the fewer people we see along the road.

Quang Tri is a moderately sized city on the Quang Tri River. It's dirtier and more heavily sandbagged than cities in the south. Just across the river is the ancient "Street Without Joy" that the French fought so desperately for, now the location of Quang Tri Combat Base (QTCB). This is the home of the Third Marine Division. The east side of the base is an airfield. "C" Co. area is just across the road from the landing strip. The Company area is two rows of hooches, ten in a row, two shower rooms, three latrines, a generator shed, a motor pool, and six piss tubes, all heavily sandbagged and surrounded with concertina wire.

Jarheads and Patrols

There is an old railroad bridge built by the French between QTCB and the city. The bed of the bridge had been filled in with railroad ties to carry road traffic. I'm assigned to a patrol attached to the Marines, code named "Orient 6-2". Our job is to protect the road from QTCB south to CP 42 during the day and cover the Quang Tri Bridge at night. A typical day follows a routine like clockwork:

Dawn - 0800	Make visual inspection of bridge, pilings, and area. Open road to traffic and drive patrol Jeep to QTCB.
0830-0844	Formation
0845-1200	Road Patrol
1200-1300	Lunch
1301-1759	Pick up rations; return to Road Patrol
1800-Dusk	Report to bridge to close road to traffic. Make commo checks with base, clean weapons, eat, relax (?)
Dusk-Dawn	Watch: two men awake, one asleep. Four hour shifts, one man changing each two hours.

The bridge becomes really spooky at night. There are lights under it, focusing on the pilings. Our Jeep is parked at the north end. About fifty meters down the approach, concertina wire is strung across the road. Next to the road is the Marines' tent . They have some scuba gear and periodically check the pilings and river fences.

Marines, or "Jarheads", have a certain mystique. They are very professional about their jobs. Very relaxed off duty. They possess a kind of tongue-in-cheek confidence in themselves. This lot are career soldiers, older than us, and they seem to be better trained, better prepared.

There is a mine field around the approach to the bridge on both ends. We are to maintain light discipline, flashlights forbidden, matches scorned.

What can an ingenious youth do for entertainment in such a boring situation? On military commo radios, there is a red signal on the band selector to warn that there can be no further dial rotation without damage to the set. Since there is still an open band where this occurs, ingenious yanks call this "Scarlet-O-5". Someone broadcasts on Scarlet O-5 all night with music and chatter. There are other channels on the "Bullshit Net" (network) and you can usually get on by giving your hometown as your callsign.

Nicknames

When you got to Nam, you were waiting to hear what your callsign or nickname would be. When you got it, you knew you had been accepted by your squad. Be it Moe, Cool Breeze, Pig Pen, Clutch, or whatever, it was your individuality and you had a responsibility to upload its image. Ask a Vet what his nickname was in the Nam.

It's during this bridge period that I got my first special callsign and nickname, "Scummy Wrench". It was just after dark and intelligence had put us on Condition Red, meaning that there was a pretty good chance of enemy contact in the area that night. All of us on "Orient 6-2" and our partner patrol "6-2 Bravo" were to keep watch all night. We got a call on the radio from our base. *The Company runner, Hogan, has gone into Quang Tri to take the interpreter home and hasn't returned. Is he at our location?* I radio back that he isn't with us. We try a couple of other frequencies and finally raise him.

He's in the western part of Quang Tri. His Jeep had broken down and he couldn't move it in any direction. He thought the rear end had seized. I radio that I've got tools and that I can probably get it going. The tools I had stolen from the motor pool. I get them out of my Jeep and run across the bridge. I take 6-2 Bravo's Jeep and go off in the direction of the interpreter's house, finding him a couple of blocks from there. I crawl under the Jeep, unbolt both prop shafts from the rear end and wheels, put the Jeep in four wheel drive and take off on front wheel power. When we get back to the bridge, I call base to report that the runner would be spending the night with us at the bridge, and they respond using the callsign "Scummy Wrench, Combat Mechanic." It stuck.

North and the DMZ

After about a month on the Quang Tri bridge, I was assigned to the north patrols, "Orient 6-3 and 6-3 Bravo." The job was to patrol the highway from QTCB to the Demilitarized Zone (DMZ) by day, and to protect two small bridges or CPs by night. CP 50 was a newly constructed bridge over a narrow river a few miles north of Dong Ha CB, near the DMZ. The bridge was important to the half-dozen or so firebases along the DMZ for re-supply. The Third Marine Division had been making contact with the NVA regularly in the area. They were working a massive operation called "Virginia Ridge" from the Rock Pile to the DMZ and east to the coast. Operation Virginia Ridge ran from April 1st to July 16th, 1969. For the last month of the operation, I would sit at CP 50.

The farther north you go on QL-1, the more hilly and desolate the country gets. It's lush green country, but it leaves you feeling cold, small, and vulnerable. This part of the country is still "owned" by the NVA.

Things were relatively quiet on the bridge, but every night there was contact in the area. One night, a platoon of marines ambushed a column of NVA and wiped them out. A few days later, though, the same platoon had thirteen men die when an enemy mortar hit a pallet of ammunition on their small LZ.

There are moments in every man's life which he will relive forever in slow motion. One such moment occurred on a morning about two weeks after moving onto the bridge at CP 50.

It had been a frightfully dark night. A couple of other positions had called in illumination during the night because no one could see. Not a star in the sky. Dawn had come just one half-hour before and we were brewing some instant coffee while picking up our equipment and readying our patrol. The only conversation was in low voices, not much to say; we had made it through the night: Roberts, Lias, and I. There were also a handful of ARVN on the bridge.

The muffled talk and clink of coffee cups is interrupted by the deafening crash of a rocket. It hits next to the road at the south approach to the bridge, about 35 feet from Roberts and me. We're just below road level on the other side of the road so everything's missed us. We dive for the bridge and cover ourselves the best we can next to the wooden structure. Two more

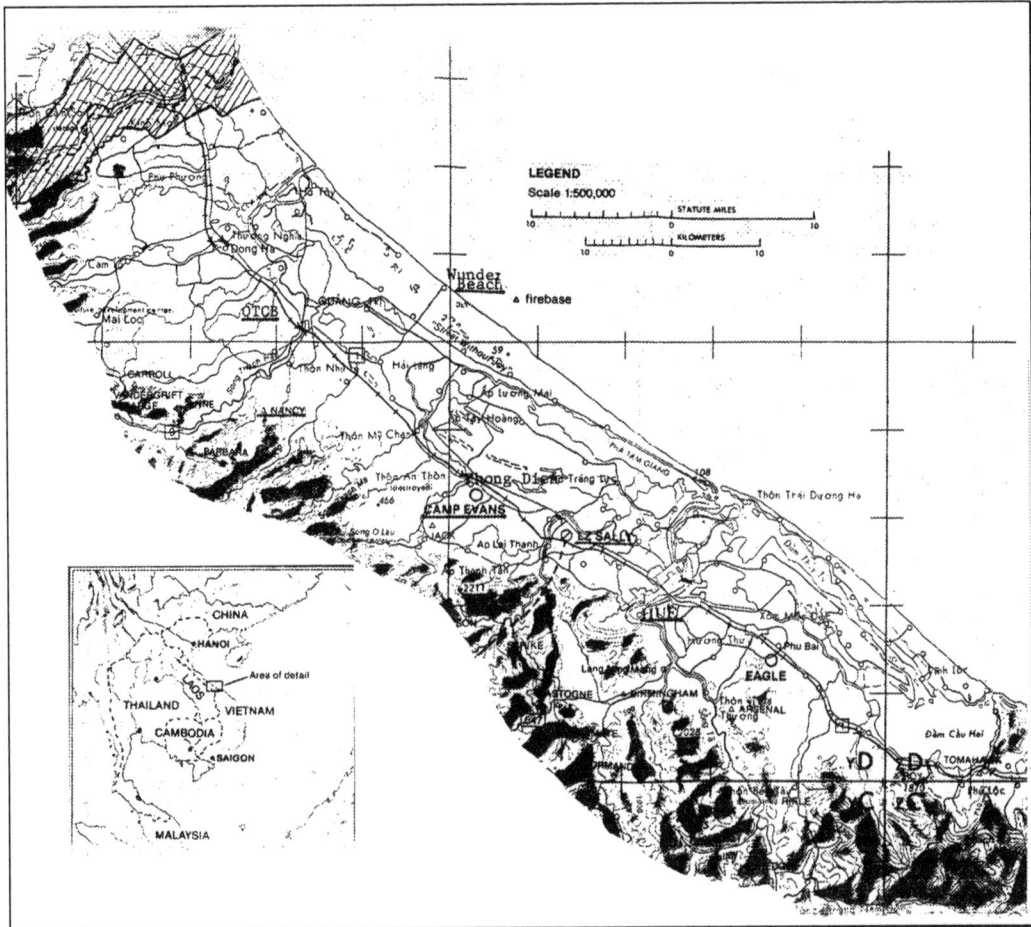

rockets hit, one in the river and one in the concertina wire. Lias has been standing next to the Jeep at the bridge apron. He dives under the Jeep.

It was over. Three rockets, no damage. Just memories of a very close call and a ringing in my ears.

They Need a Mechanic at Evans

About three weeks later, Virginia Ridge was winding down and we were going to be pulled off the bridge. We went to morning formation as usual. The CO said, "They need a mechanic at Evans." He had heard of Scummy Wrench, and would I like to go to Camp Evans?

I had heard that the platoon at Camp Evans were misfits. If you caused trouble at QTCB, you got sent to Evans. There were fourteen men there. They covered the road from Hue north to CP 42. There were just enough men to cover both three-man patrols, reliefs, their assigned bunker rats, an armorer, a lieutenant, and sergeant. The Company area consisted of five hooches and a small motor pool. They had four Jeeps.

Because the company was so small, every man was assigned two jobs. There were six regular patrol officers and three reliefs, each man working six sixteen-hour shifts out of seven. The reliefs also worked as bunker guards on the camp's perimeter, along with the armorer and radio operators. The armorer was also the clerk. The day radio operator also handled trash and shit burning details. The evening radio man got water for the showers and ice for the coolers. I was assigned to maintain the Jeeps, relief patrol, and relief bunker rat.

The men were not what you would expect of a bunch of misfits. Perhaps it was more that they responded badly to supervision at QTCB. There was Gerencer, the armorer, R.J. Schmidt, Ahrens, and Lambert, the radio men; Pappalardo, Rivera, Letourneau, Moses, Wilson, Curtis, patrol officers; Westerman and Lias, bunker rats; Lt. Mosley and SSgt. Bahm. We were everything from Michigan farm boy to Washington State laborer. There was a closeness that I have never felt before and many never experience again. Everyone gave 100% to the job.

They were a colorful bunch: Letourneau was famous for hoarding the Hershey bars from C-rations, not eating them, just hoarding them—until the rats would chase us out of bed trying to get to them... Pappalardo and Rivera could argue for hours about who was the most 'Italian', or 'New York', or who was the messiest or neatest or who would end up an Army lifer... but you knew there was really a deep respect between them.

The days were spent on patrols, usually from 6:30 AM to 4:30 PM. We would break for lunch at LZ Sally, LZ Nancy, or Camp Evans. After patrol, there was time to eat and relax at Evans. We cleaned our weapons, did maintenance on the Jeeps, read and wrote letters until about 8:00 PM. Then the bunker rats would go to the perimeter bunkers. I curiously observed the intensity and rapidity with which friendships were built. In high school, I had observed the cliques and felt the exclusions, but in Nam, there was immediate acceptance and because of the great need for sustenance and support, the disclosure and sharing came freely.

We supported each other well, and no man was alone in his responsibilities for a job. Voluntary help was always there, even for the worst jobs. This camaraderie was important to me then, and I missed it heartily later.

CP 38

CP 38 was an unprotected wooden bridge on QL-1, just a half-mile south of Evans. One night, while sitting on the bunker, Moses, Lias, and I saw an explosion from the area of the road. We radioed our base that we would be going to combat nets to listen in on the react teams.

The initial helicopters responding to the bridge were fired on by the enemy on the ground, who were retreating along the riverbed. We were treated to a display of the chopper war characteristic of Viet Nam.

The stage was illuminated by the artillery flares and searchlights of the choppers. There were two AH-1 Cobras and two Hueys in the air. The Cobras repeatedly sprayed the area with their twin miniguns, 1200 rounds per min-

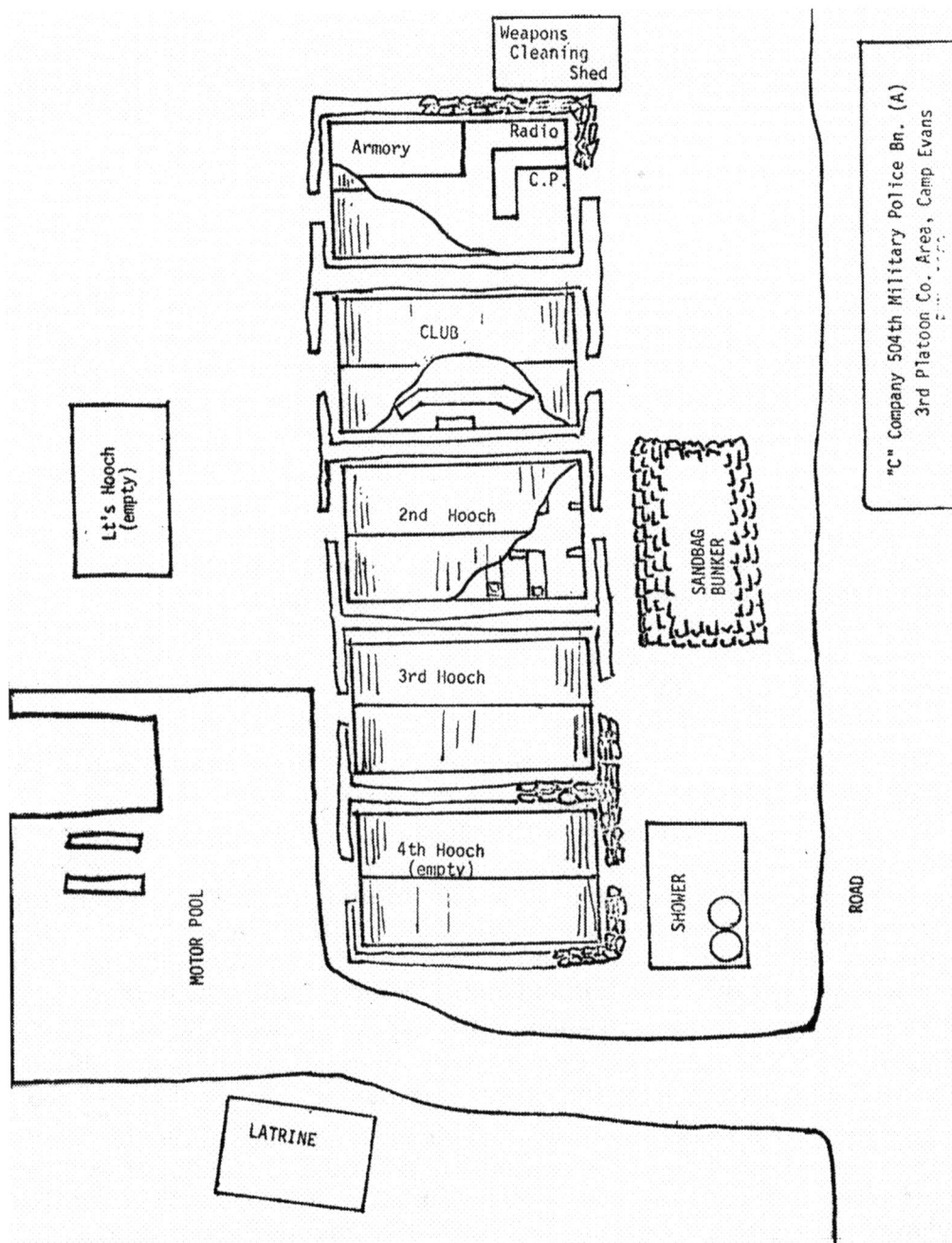

Camp Evans

ute—*awesome*. The Hueys were equipped with rocket launchers and fired about six pairs. And here we were on top of our bunker cheering them on with "Get some!"

As the pair of Cobras began their second pass at the riverbank, I began to feel concern or sorrow for the Viet Cong being fired upon, for the way they must have been completely overwhelmed by the modern American Army's mechanized firepower. After being rocketed by the VC and being harassed and fired upon by them, I could still see them as fragile human beings.

Au Shau Valley

Directly west of Camp Evans lies a foreboding mountain range that marks the border between Viet Nam and Laos. The NVA had built a re-supply route through a valley in those mountains into Viet Nam. The valley was known to the Vietnamese as "Au Shau" (or "Aushau"); it was known to the Third Marines and 101st Airborne as simply Hamburger Hill.

After CP 38 was rebuilt, our daily patrols were interrupted by door gunner duty. The 1st of the 502nd Infantry of the 101st Airborne was building up a force at the southern end of the valley in an effort to close the VC supply route. Every day, helicopters flew to the valley to drop troops in the LZs near the valley. Door gunners on those flights were MPs assigned to the Camp Evans platoon. The flights began with a call to patrols ordering us in from the road to report to the helipads. The flights west from Camp Evans to the LZs near the valley were a swarm of experiences and emotion. We waited at the metal helipad with the grunts about to ship out to the valley. They were casual, quiet, and pensive. Occasionally, they'd pass around a joint.

The choppers came in and landed, blowing sand in our faces. Each of the eight or ten choppers loaded eight men and two door gunners.

The choppers take off and fly single file like a line of dragonflies for 20 or 30 minutes to the valley. The sensation of flight in a Huey is at the same time calming and exciting. You feel the soft vibrations of flight caused by the rotors spinning overhead, you hear the whine of the turbine, you feel the coolness of the thinner air. You can look out and down from the door gunner's seat and get the sensation of height, looking at the tops of trees.

As you approach the LZ, your heart beats faster, breathing gets faster, the LZ is a flock of activities. Cobra attack choppers are finishing the job clearing the LZ with rockets and machine guns.

Two Hueys are stalled about ten feet above the ground, while the grunts jump off from both sides. The men on the ground are running ahead and taking cover. Canisters of green or yellow smoke send up clouds of color that is blown by the wash of the chopper blades. Two choppers empty and lift off, two more move into their places while the grunts disembark. Next, it's our turn to go in. I fire the machine gun into the brush as we approach the LZ at low altitude. The chopper hovers at ten feet and I cease fire as the grunts jump off, leaving the chopper to bob and sway as the load changes. The last grunt disembarks and it's time for our chopper to escape to the safety of the

Blue Vault, time for a sigh of relief. Time for a lonely ride back to camp, my job done—theirs just begun.

After arriving back at Evans, and the days patrols were done, we'd go out to the bunkers and watch the sun go down over the Au Shau, and watch the artillery flares come up.

The red cast of the artillery flares is etched permanently in my mind. The flares hang over the valley all night long, every night that I sat on that bunker. The action there was heavy and so were the casualties. I felt schizophrenic wanting to do something besides sit and watch and at the same time fearing the thought of going into the valley.

John W. Holle

On July 1st, 1969 Moses, Lias, and I were on the patrol in the north. We could hear broken radio transmissions from the south patrol. We were far enough from them that we couldn't communicate directly, but their transmissions still broke into our squelch and we could hear the base radio operator's responses...

"Blaze 6-2, this is Blaze, over." "Blaze 6-2, this is Blaze!"

(Unintelligible static)

"6-2, This is Blaze, say again."

(Static)

"You were hit?! 6-2, you say you were hit? This is Blaze."

(Static)

"6-2, what is your 10-4?"   (Location)

(Static)

"6-2, I copy. 1 Mike (mile) November (north) of Charley Papa (CP) 3-0, over."

(Static)

"6-2, we will be sending a dustoff (medevac helicopter). Be ready with smoke." (Smoke canister to signal pilot that it's OK to land).

(Static)

Our patrol was in the middle of confiscating some beer and marijuana from some Marines in a low-boy. We told the Marines to go on, then we got into our Jeep and headed south to meet the south patrol. We crumpled up the twenty or so joints from the Marines and scattered them along the road. We threw the beer at some ARVNs on one of the bridges along the way, then locked and loaded our weapons.

We had about 25 miles to drive. The radio operator, Schmidt, reported that the senior patrol partner was thought to be KIA (Killed In Action). The senior was Holle, the Junior was Reece. Reece had been in my class at MP school, had come into country when I did, and was sent to Evans shortly after I was. John W. Holle (03/06/1948 – 07/01/1969) was a 21-year old SP4 from New Caney, Texas. As he was not killed in live fire, his official record in the CACF lists him as "Non-Hostile. Died-Other". Holle had been in Nam six or seven months. He was married and his wife had delivered a daughter just a month or so before. He was excited and had shown the pictures all around. Every one of us grieved for Holle, but it was especially hard on Schmidt. Schmidt didn't deal well with the Nam and would always be getting high in his spare time.

When we got to patrol 6-2, the medevac had already left. Reece had been taken to the MACV compound at Hue by the Hue patrol. He was shaken up and would be examined there.

It was a mine in the road, apparently remotely detonated. The Jeep was totaled. When Reece got back to Evans, we talked. He couldn't believe it. He was a black guy, cocksure and smooth-talking. Now he looked small, harrowed, and worried. He went back to QTCB that day.

A Chaplain was sent that night to hold a service after dinner. He'd never even met Holle. He was trying to comfort us, but all he did was foul things up. We felt outrage. We could do a better job of comforting each other, and we did.

The night before, Holle had given me a pin for my bush hat. I still have it.

JOHN W HOLLE

As July Steams Into August Then September...

The days flew; innumerable, indistinguishable and turbid. The following are memories of incidents during those days. Days filled with road patrols, door gunner duty, water details, Jeep repairs and... Fourth of July. A party, hurriedly planned and executed. Canned roast beef, sliced thick and cooked over an open fire, plenty of beer (Black Label and Falstaff—brewed in Fort Wayne!), but no girls and no fireworks (*thank god*). Observation—the more you try to make it feel like home, the further from home you feel.

On another note, I remember... A day off; Sunday spent at Wunder Beach. The beach was cleared by Seabees some time ago. It is about 1/8th mile long, and deep in white sand. When you're at the beach in the Nam, you carry your M16 and grenade launcher, steel pot, flack vest, and swim suit. The beach is protected by a line of sandbag bunkers around the inland edge. Plan on spending half of your time sunning yourself on a bunker, while the others swim. The swim in the warm, salty Tonkin is relaxing and cleansing, but it is a guarded relaxation, and I certainly could have enjoyed my first dips in the Pacific more.

On the *Mercy*

Later, I spent two days floating in the Pacific. I was scheduled to go to the US Navy Hospital Ship *Mercy* for some blood tests and an exam for hepatitis. I reported to the hospital at Quang Tri CB and was medevaced out to the ship.

I climbed into a Huey with red crosses on the sides. Also loaded on was a man completely naked, with red bloody splotches covering his body. He had been in a road mine explosion earlier that morning, as the minesweeper team opened the road.

The chopper flew much higher than the troop transports I was used to and there was no door gunner. We flew east out over the coastline a couple of miles then dropped down onto the chopper pad on the ship's deck.

A hospital ship is like a city in itself. My tests were scheduled for the next day and I was assigned to a bunk in the hold, but that afternoon and evening, the time was mine. I ate lunch at a table with a tablecloth and real silverware. That afternoon, I explored the ship. I found an ice cream shop, a store, and a theater. I had brought some money with me just in case, but was disappointed to find that the store was for crew only, and that my MPC (military currency) was worthless there. An understanding, pipe-smoking sailor bought me two tins of Flying Dutchman and a Mars bar.

At dinner that night, I stole the silverware given to me. Compared to the disposable gear I had been issued, it seemed like it was gold-plated. After dinner, I went up onto deck with the sailor who had given me the tobacco. I sat and watched the sun set in the west, behind the mountains of the Laotian border. And I watched the arty flares come up, but from a much greater distance than usual. The cool breeze and the sound of the water were so relaxing that I intended to stay on deck all night, but an officer with a black armband made me go below around 10 PM.

Reluctantly, I went to the bunk, a rack made of iron bars and wire-hinged to the wall. I didn't try to sleep. I just lay there, feeling the peace. There was no danger of incoming tonight, no bunker duty, just safety.

The next afternoon, I was ready to leave the ship. That morning I had waited in the labs and examining rooms with the casualties of war, in wheelchairs and on gurneys. Quiet young men, deep in thought or deep in pain, whole men only a few hours or days ago, now were wondering how much their lives had suddenly changed.

Later that summer on one hot bright day, I was following a three wheel Lambretta bus down the highway. The four by six foot cabin was crowded with people and there was a motorcycle strapped to its top. The little bus hit some rough spots in the road and rolled over. One elderly Vietnamese woman was killed and several other passengers were bleeding. The bus driver ran around yelling, until he and some of the passengers got the bus upright and back on the road, then he went on his way. They left the young man with his motorcycle, the old woman, and her daughter to wait for an ambulance. Apparently, the Vietnamese don't worry about liability or insurance, or another human being. After all, what's another death in the middle of all this? The bus driver was satisfied to blame the young man for wanting to put his motorcycle on the top of the bus.

In some ways, the Vietnamese seemed to value the lives of their water buffalos and dogs more than that of a human being. Maybe they've just had to accept death as a way of life.

Everyday Hassles

The last thing you want after a long day is a hassle, but if you expect any different from the Army, you don't know the Army. We had been out on patrol, been called in for door gunner duty, and on this particular day after going back out on the road, had come across a broken down CB supply truck that needed a tow. We called for a "hook", and then waited with the truck to protect the supplies. The hook was slow getting there and so we were late getting in from patrol, so we went straight to our perimeter bunker. As we passed the command tower for our sector, we noticed a formation of twenty or so grunts next to the trail. We continued to drive on past, but a Second Lieutenant called after us. He claimed he was "conducting a guard mount here." *"Fall In!"*

Moses, Westerman, and I backed up, parked, and then piled out of the Jeep with our machine guns, rifles, and grenade launchers, which we'd carried with us all day on the road. Westerman was German born, husky, blue-eyed blond. I would catch him holding my tin of pipe tobacco up as in a TV ad and saying in his heavy German accent, "Flying Dutchman—a legendary mixture..."

The Lieutenant had fresh green fatigues and polished gold bars. His stateside jump boots shone. He barked us to attention then grabbed the grenade launcher from Moses for an inspection. He glared at Moses and told him that there was dirt in the barrel. Moses started to tell him we had just come off the road, but was told to *"Shut Up."* Next, he grabbed the machine gun from me. He looked at the mechanism and asked me if I couldn't see the dirt there.

Moe said, "Aw shit, what is this? We don't need it, let's go." Then the three of us walked to our Jeep and drove to the bunker.

A little later the rest of the men were going to their bunkers and some of them stopped and talked to us. We explained that we had worked since 6 AM, hadn't eaten, hadn't had a chance to clean our weapons and what was this FNG doing holding a guard mount anyway?

They said he was new in country which was obvious. Right out of OCS, a real "Shake and Bake." We asked them to spread the word that our bunker was "wired" (booby trapped for anything approaching from any direction). Then we called R.J. for supper, and cleaned our weapons. That Lieutenant never bothered us, never approached our bunker, never said another word to any of us.

Gooks

What can you say about these people? It was easy to feel sorry for them because they were childlike. Some behaviors were not so endearing.

An ARVN walks up to you and asks for a cigarette. You say you don't smoke. He proceeds to pat your pockets to see if you're lying.

I've seen the National Police beat confessions out of people. This included breaking both legs with a 10" rubber truncheon. This was in the case of some cartons of meat stolen from a Marine base.

In a small village between CP 42 and LZ Nancy, a child ran out into the road in front of an Army Jeep pulling a trailer full of supplies. The Jeep flipped and the contents of the trailer spilled. While the GI lay in the road with a broken ankle and a badly lacerated arm, the people of the village made off with the cargo. The same thing happened in the same village a few weeks later.

For a while, we had a Vietnamese interpreter working with us. He was a volunteer and worked only for the four or five cartons of Salem cigarettes we gave him every couple of days. Ho Tam lived in Hue, and the south patrol would pick him up each morning and he would ride with the patrols all day, changing to the north patrol at noon.

He was hoping that his association with us would get him a paying job with the US Government, which would keep him out of the ARVN. Ho didn't hesitate to ask us to pull strings for him. However, he didn't want his neighbors to know he was working for us, so we picked him up and dropped him off several blocks from his house. He did not want his association with the Americans to appear too strong in case things went the other way. In the end, the way things went makes me wonder how Ho did fare and whether he is even alive today.

Nights

We always said that we were free to go wherever we wanted in the day, but at night the country belonged to "Victor Charlie". Before the Nam, there was just day and night. In the Nam, there was day and many qualities of night. Night had texture, variety, and characteristics that alerted you to a certain level of caution. We followed the phases of the Moon as the ancients must have. Movement, mood, and talk were different in the day. Sometimes the whole Viet Nam experience seems like one long night, many, many long hours sitting alone with my thoughts.

Sitting a bunker is a necessary job. Every night, men had to sit on a perimeter to protect what was ours. Paranoia ran deep among these men. Frightened they had seen something move, afraid to look too closely.

I sat for hours looking out over my fields of fire. Sometimes I couldn't see the rifle in my lap. Those were the nights we were most likely to be attacked. Not that you could feel safe on nights with a full moon either. [Ed. Note: Although some Starlight night vision scopes were deployed in Viet Nam as early as 1964, they were not widely available to all ground troops.]

What goes through your mind during four hours of watch at around 3 AM in Viet Nam? Mostly it's just waiting, you know. We were targets. Once you were fired upon—return fire—buckle for dust. But it's unlikely that you will know where they are before they see you. The waiting can be anguish.

Like knowing that a terminally ill man will die, you know the waiting will be over and you will be trying to pick out targets by watching tracer rounds or muzzle flashes.

It is more difficult to think about the present here, so boredom was divided between dreams of the future and remembrances of the past. Out of my past were movies of water skiing at Lake Wawasee, drag racing with Dawsons, playing hockey, walks to school with my friend Dave Lyons, and Susie, who always occupied a corner of my mind, sometimes all of it. I felt sorrow, I remembered happiness, I shed tears. I asked why she had to die. I feared returning home and trying to make my way through life without her. I thought about my family: Debbie had grown up while I was in training and had interests in dating, Dave had graduated college and was teaching, Dennie was getting married.

Mom and Dad, those people who had tried to teach me a worthwhile set of values. These values, for the most part, do not apply here. In 1968, it was considered a type of failure to be drafted. I've always felt that I let them down when that draft notice came. I felt that there were other ways in which I let them down—my interest in cars was never understood, my performance in school was not the best and less than I was capable of, and I'm sure they never approved of Sue. I hoped that my being here was not causing them too much worry. It's rough writing them letters. I write about the country, the people, and the positive things I do, but I don't say much about the duty.

I remembered holidays past and tried to imagine what the rest of the world was doing. Those weeks of anticipation and preparation before Christmas were missing. When we observed Christmas at Quang Tri, it was very late Christmas Day back home. The last Christmas at home seemed like much more than a year ago.

As for the future, the immediate future never seemed certain. Riding patrol on the roads was dangerous due to mines and snipers, doorgunners were in an exposed position, bunker rats were sitting targets. So the future began the day you stepped off that freedom bird back in the world. Our plans for back in the world were expressions of celebrating life. Plans to make up for lost time. Parties back on the block, driving, drag racing, dating, and even the joy of working only eight hours a day.

Nights were spent remembering, planning, making commo checks, listening to someone else's war being fought in the valley, and occasionally smoking a joint.

"NG"

NG stands for National Guard. If an NG missed some training meetings or got into trouble with his Guard Commander, he could be activated—sent to active duty. This was the case with Ed. I don't remember his last name and he wasn't with us very long, but we called him 'NG'. He had been placed on active duty by his Guard Commander in Kentucky because NG kept getting drunk on Friday nights and missing his Saturday Guard meetings. NG was no better in the Nam. NG seemed to be drunk most of the time, and if he wasn't drunk he was so hungover that he was barely operational.

I remember a patrol with NG. We drove out of Camp Evans heading north. I was driving and NG was hunched over in the passenger seat, holding his head. At the north end of the first ville, Phong Dien, we came upon an ARVN Jeep lying on its side in the road. The Jeep had hit a road mine and flipped. The driver had a bad head injury and was unconscious. I stopped our Jeep, got out, wrapped the ARVN's head with a field dressing and called on the radio for a medevac chopper. NG was still sitting in the Jeep holding his head. In the next few minutes, I had to stop traffic far enough back to allow the chopper a place to land on the road, coordinate with Blaze for its arrival and landing, and get the ARVN loaded into the chopper.

NG sat in the Jeep with his head in his hands. Once he got on the radio and was telling Blaze that the Jeep was heading south and totally confusing them, because that was not what they had asked. After the medevac lifted off, I turned the Jeep around and went directly back to Evans and told SSgt. Bahm never to assign me patrol with NG again.

A short time later, NG fell and cut his neck while drunk. We took him to the hospital and while getting him admitted, we told the doctors he needed drying out. We never saw NG again. Hopefully, he was sent south to get the treatment he needed so he would never present a threat to himself or a patrol partner again.

Painted Red

One of the grossest, most nerve-fraying things I've ever seen happened at the chopper pad next to our company area at Evans. The pad was used by the 101st Airborne choppers that were covering for the grunts working in the Au Shau valley area. They would fly a LOCH (small helicopter) at a low level to draw out snipers into the open. The LOCH was followed by a Combat Huey that would then attack the sniper position. On this day just before noon, a sniper had poked his head out to fire a burst of rounds from his AK-47 at the LOCH. A Currahee Major sitting in the back of the chopper took a round through the back of the thigh, severing a major artery there.

The wound bled freely and the Major tried to stop the bleeding with the pressure of his hand, but the blood must have just spurted between his fingers. The LOCH pilot knew they had been hit, so he turned back for Evans. As the chopper flew, the Major's lifeblood ran out along the side of the chopper, was picked up by the propwash and subsequently blown back along the side of the craft's fuselage. The chopper landed amongst waiting medics who went to work immediately. I arrived on the scene as the medics were giving up their futile fight for the Major's life. In the aftermath, small pools of blood were collecting in the dust under the tail of the chopper. The tail of the LOCH had been turned from green to red by the pints of the Major's blood, and it appeared that the chopper itself was bleeding from the wound of the now lifeless Major.

The next day as we were returning to Evans from patrol at about 6 PM, seven choppers from the 101st flew in formation over the Camp. The right-front position was empty in tribute to the Major.

That Small Moment

Many times I've been asked, "How many VC did you kill?" It's not a question that I like, but I answer honestly. I don't know if I ever killed any or if I even came close. The firefights I was involved in were at night and the targets were AK-47 tracer rounds or rocket/mortar muzzle blasts.

It happened a couple of times at Evans and Quang Tri that while sitting in a bunker we would see tracer rounds or muzzle flashes within our range, within our fields of fire and very quickly, someone else's war became ours.

The very quick reaction is to raise the barrel of the M16 and begin to squeeze off bursts of rounds, using tracer rounds to determine windage. As your finger touches the trigger, the thought passes through your mind that the series of explosions from your own muzzle would awaken a response from the enemy that could easily overwhelm you.

In that small moment of reaction when flesh contacted metal, a commitment was made to buckle to the death if necessary, to prepare to become someone else's target. It was a commitment that you could not choose and it was not reversible.

The World

Viet Nam seemed so far removed from *The World* that there were two spheres for us *Viet Nam* and *The World*. Reality was a problem. The Nam was reality but it seemed like a bad dream, and our fantasy, The World, seemed like the only reality. When Holle died, that reached across the reality gap, reached his family, his wife and baby and their lives were never to change back. If there was a large offensive or battle, the evening news would reach into the lives of those back home and most would ignore it, or some would get angry on our behalf, but our world was as unreal to them as theirs was to us. This gap has never been closed because of the many things about Viet Nam that people have found distasteful. People were to discover what any Viet Nam grunt already knew, that there was no point to this war, there was no way to win. Vietnamization, the systematic turning over of US Army bases and equipment to the ARVN, like *Operation Phoenix* and *Hearts and Minds* before it, was not successful. The bases were overrun by VC and NVA shortly after the last American left. The fall of Saigon was expected by every Vet that served after the TET offensive in 1968. The American public was being mis-led by politicians who could not publicly admit that Viet Nam was our worst mistake, into believing that we could win there. The steady chain of bodies from the Rock Pile and increased enemy activity around Quang Tri, Evans, and Hue told us differently.

Freedom Bird

Well it's happened, I worked and sweated and counted the days and prayed; *then suddenly* the day arrived. *I* could get on that Freedom Bird and put Viet Nam behind me.

If I hadn't the time to pay attention to details or be aware of what was going on around me for the last few months, I didn't want to miss a moment of this: the packing, signing forms, traveling to the Freedom Bird. One day I'm in Hue, I spend that night in Quang Tri to process out of "C" Company; late the next afternoon, I fly to Cam Ranh Bay. Two days at Cam Ranh and I fly to Seattle via Tokyo.

Cam Ranh was so crowded with people on their way home that the two nights I was there, I slept on the beach. During the day, I stood in long lines to have my ID checked, shot record, luggage, orders, etc. checked. *Finally,* I was given an airplane boarding pass. The next day, I was taken to the airport. I stood anxiously with 140 other men in a corrugated metal post building called simply "TERMINAL". It was so hot, around 115 degrees, that men in the building were passing out. My palms were sweaty and my shouts of joy were barely concealed beneath the surface.

Finally, a large jet landed and talk in the building became very excited. The plane taxied around until it stopped in front of us. We waited quietly after it stopped, the ramp was moved to its side, then as the door opened those sweet screams of joy were unveiled and the building shook with the roar—until the first FNG in his fresh new fatigues stepped out of the door. We then watched about 140 men come off the plane and line up in formation. A few of us called out things like "I feel sorry for *you,* you sweet thing" and "I hope you don't go to An Khe (Phu Bai, An Hoa, etc.). But seeing them did dampen our spirits and caused each of us to reflect on the day we arrived, such a long time ago.

They were marched off, our replacements, and our attention returned to the plane. An airport truck had rolled out to the plane, loaded with long silver boxes. There would be more Vets going home in that plane than just those of us standing in this shed. They began to load the caskets into the plane. On the trip home, part of my mind would be on the stainless steel boxes with the blown-apart Vets inside.

We landed in Seattle in the afternoon of April 6th, 1970. I stood in the last Army lines of my life that night and the next day. I ate my last mess hall meals on April 8th, and on April 9th before sunrise I was discharged and taken to the Seattle airport.

Underdogs

I suppose I could be accused of living in the past, but the heroic efforts of the grunts in the Nam are etched on my mind like the hearts with initials etched in the bark of young trees, still legible many years later. Those initials carved there become a shrine to something that once was, just as my memories from Nam have become a symbol and shrine for those underdog heroes.

Two Leathernecks of the 26th Marine Regiment take a break, rain and all, during Operation Bold Mariner. January 1969. (Source: Nat'l Archives)

By 1970, the grunts had become the predicted losers, the victims of injustice and persecution—the underdogs. Caught between a policy of command seemingly gone mad and an enemy as devious and deadly as any ever encountered; forced to take, then retake obviously worthless villes, hills and paddies over and over again. I never lost my wonder at how we could do what we did so well.

After sitting in the blistering heat for days on end or sleeping wrapped in a poncho liner in the rain in a seemingly suicide position, when it came time to buckle for dust, we reacted, deployed, and defended with such tactical precision that I can only describe my feelings as amazement. It did not end there, along with efficient reaction goes the ability to identify the caliber, type and location of an enemy rifle by the crack of a round, the ability to treat wounds and to talk a medevac into our position.

These things are done repeatedly, and the miseries and terrors are so frightening that all emotion becomes protective numbness. Fear is always there, like our collective skeletons in the closet, always present, but never discussed. Death is not discussed among us, nor does anyone look too closely at our chances of getting out of here alive and in one piece. You live

Company E, 2nd Battalion, 9th Marines, while under heavy firefight with NVAs within the DMZ on Operation Hickory III, are carrying one of their fellow Marines to the H-34., 07/29/1967 (Source: Nat'l Archives)

superstitiously one day at a time. You keep track of the days and you don't scratch one off until you are sure it is over.

Who appreciates our misery? Long before I was able to return to the World, where sanity was supposed to reign, I learned that I was subject to being spat-upon for wearing my uniform in public, or maybe my property or car would be spray-painted "FACIST PIG" just because I came here, willingly or not. My Lai had had its effect. Because I could be labeled "Baby killer" it became harder to talk about the Nam.

Now my life feels like a deck of cards, the one we used in the Army hospital, old, faded, used up. I feel worn out from waking up in the Nam morning after morning, tired and sore from sleeping in the back of a jeep, on a bunker or on the ground. Irritable from too little nutrition, too much diarrhea and from constantly fighting the weather and insects. The year was a constant battle against the little Anopheles dive bombers. We were armed with Mosquito netting, jungle fatigues designed to protect against them, "jungle juice" repellant and Premaquine tablets. Within three months I surrendered, having already become infected with malaria and become ill.

Worst of all, I just feel used. The way in which I was used leaves me feeling angry, confused and with a rotten self-image that I have to deal with every day. I was naive, I didn't know what to expect from the Army or Viet Nam. I was afraid of Nam but nearly neutral on the issue of our involvement there. In Basic Training I was indoctrinated that our victory in Viet Nam would be a noble experience and that I should want to go, that combat was my birthright as a man.

> "I want to live a life of danger,
> I want to be an Airborne Ranger,
> I want to go to Viet Nam,
> I want to kill some Viet Cong"

This was my war, my chance to become a man and a hero. I knew before I boarded that Trans-Pacific flight that, come heaven or hell, I would be a different man on the other end of this experience. When I landed in the Nam, this was confirmed in the faces of those on their way home—those incredibly aged faces of men maybe as much as a year older than myself.

While in the Nam, a change began to occur that would continue for years afterward. I began to see how I'd been lied to, how the indoctrination had been a veiled attempt to charge us up to do the impossible for the ungrateful. The Lie was too big to cover and I began to see through it the way you see through fabric stretched too tight. The message angered and frustrated me. It read, "They are all dying for nothing." Young men who should have been learning about life and love in the back seat of the old man's Ford were learning about death and hate in this blistering heat. That anger began to resound in my head like the Doors' music, dark, angry, death-preoccupied and insane. Everything John Wayne stands for is a lie.

There have been times that the Doors' music has been so loud in my head that I've worried that people passing on the street could hear it too. I've made attempts to forget about the Nam and be a normal regular guy, but I feel silly and inappropriate. I lack the experience of not having been to Nam. And the music is still there, my secret insanity.

My deck of cards is faded, a few have been chewed by the dog and you can tell the ten of spades and the three of hearts because each has a corner missing. War is hell on anyone who recognizes humanity. I've come a long way since then and I'm probably as humane as ever, but I've got a long way to go. Now, when I think about the Nam, I see a desert wasteland haunted by the ghosts of the thousands of Grunts who had suffered and died needlessly there.

A friend recently said, "Wouldn't it be nice if we didn't ever have to think about Viet Nam again... just forget about it all?" Yeah, wouldn't that be just great!

In Memory of Charley Knepple

(07/06/1948 – 04/28/1997)

By John Knight, Captain USMC (ret.)

I did not serve with Charley in the military sense, but I did work side-by-side with him for four years. We were Work Release Correctional Counselors together in Indiana. We shared stories of events that happened during work and he shared stories of his military time as an MP. I did not understand the depth of his caring and insight until I spent 12 years active in the Marine Corps. Charlie was compassionate and remembered his wife and family often in conversation. He was dedicated to what he was doing and to the people he was helping

He took his skills out of Correction and into Probation work, only to have his life ended by a probationer who went berserk. It's not right that the Charleys of this world are taken from wife, family, and friends in such a manner as this. He fought for God and Country and for his survival in a time that was not popular to serve, but he did serve anyway. Charley and I lost contact with each other over the years and when I heard he was gone, I cried and felt a void in me that could not be filled.

I thank you Charley for the time we had, for the compassion you dispensed, and for the spirit you instilled in others. I am a better man for knowing you and I know your sacrifice will never be forgotten.

4   Poems (ii)

NUMBER 7

I was a
Good Humor Man
I lost my job
I got drafted

I can never
go back again
I lost my
Good Humor

I lost $80.00 a week
I can never
have it again

You gain
Goodwill
being a Good Humor Man.
You establish a route You make
friends
I lost them all.

My bike my cart
my bell
are all gone now
My smile too.
All my friends
    cried
on the Last Day.

On the Last Day
I gave all my
ice cream away
    Free
to all my friends
They still cried.
I did too
I came Home with
an Empty Cart
and my Boss said
    "Good
        All Sold."
I said
                  "No, All Free."
And cried.

He didn't cry
He said
         "You owe me $16.00"

I think his brother
works at my Draft Board

DOUG RAWLINGS

FOR LACK OF A NAME

THE BODY COUNTS CONTINUE
53,000 MORE EMPLOYED
CAUSE FOR CELEBRATION
LESS THAN 110,000
LAST YEAR'S UNEMPLOYED

TEN YEARS AGO
48,000
DEAD IN A LAND UNKNOWN
DEATH FOR A REASON
UNDEFINED

SO ADD 10,000 MORE
WE'LL SHOW THEM
DEATHS NOT IN VAIN

STATISTICIANS
COUNTING SOULS
ONE DAY THE COMPUTERHEADS
WILL LEARN TO COUNT
THEY'LL USE REAL NUMBERS

FAMILIES TORN
MISERY INCREASED
A BOWL OF WHEATIES
FOR TWO OR THREE WEEKS

THE GNP EDGES UP
DEFICITS ABOUND
WHILE THIS MORNING
A MAN WILL DIE
FOR LACK OF FOOD
TO GO AROUND

WE ADD
WE SUBTRACT
NUMBERS OF LIFE
WE DO IT SO OFTEN
WE FORGET
THE SPIRIT OF MAN
AMOUNTS TO MORE THAN
THE NUMBER ONE.

PAUL WAPPENSTEIN

BACK HOME

How small is the town where I was born.
How little the people have grown
Bob Green hasn't changed that red checkered
shirt in all the years I've been away and
Reverend Brady still chalks his sermons on
the church door.

It has hardly altered, not the houses,
the billboards, the people or the beech-lined avenues.
Only the size is different; everything is
suddenly smaller and I am a giant
striding through my kingdom, looking down
on places I once owned, people I once knew.

Who can say if I would be down there, among
the miniatures had I not enlisted?
Who can know if I would not have blended with
the vistas, roared by motorcycle down Main
at two A.M., fell in love, married, bought a house
and entered the urban establishment.

It is too late to speculate; I am infected with Asia
and can never live with the dwarfs
of my hometown in quiet middle-age.
There have been too many new sensations,
provocations to thoughts I might never have
had, too many agitated tauntings of loves and
fears I never knew existed.

I am not the same pink-faced boy
who left the town to fight for his county.
The town gave me my roots,
but I flowered in Asia.

AUTHOR UNKNOWN

MEMORY BOMB

I expect to remember other things.
But it is always the color that comes first.
The incredible greens, almost sinister
in their growing. The flowers, red or yellow,
silk-like, sick-sweet and potent. And with
their shells of fine art, the insects
dancing insanely in the gross heat.

I should recall
faces edged with fear.
The foolish, brave talk of young men.
The lies told as bedtime stories. The panic
The panic spreading like fog,
whenever the incomings cut the dark
with red, hot light. And Death
always there, always waiting,
the lecher on the nude beach.

Those I can hardly see, barely conjure.
Yet they are in me.
A sleeping seed Waiting to grow.
A piece of metal itching to travel.
A book of pictures dying to be seen.
And someday they will move on me
like murderers in the dark.
The bomb of memory will explode
into a red, hot thing.
And no screams of pain, pleas for mercy,
or barring of inner doors will
be able to keep out the fire.

R. JOSEPH ELLIS, Viet Nam, 1966-67

LORINE

i've been at war in my brothers' mind

face down in a puddle of rice

i've seen the needle in my brothers' arm

crashed out OD'd on the bathroom floor

               i can't take no more

i've seen my life with a bottle of wine

in a stench that wasn't my own

i've known the disease of a crippled mind

pasted on the labels of a sick head

               i ain't gonna take my life

               no, i ain't never gonna take my life

where do i find the time

i've got to take the time

i got to learn to find

my time to learn to care.

LARRY McFADDEN
October 1977

SSN-587[1]

i have never known a woman quite like
i knew the mistress of the sea
quite like the calm and stillness
while everything raged about me
quite like the peace and gentle touch
through the very darkest of lonely nights
quite like the silence and vision in each
whispered word of need
i have never known a woman with the
undying love for me like the possibility
of death at sea
if the metaphor of the wise is to be perched
upon mountain tops then what belly of a woman
has birthed with a sigh how a boy becomes
a man at the bottom of the sea
today my bunk is still empty in the nights of
greatest need till in the nakedness of my dreams
i taste the salt air and find myself in the cradle
of her arms as the oceans rock me still
and some mornings i awake and again i swear like
a sailor when i find in my shoes the sands
of distant shores

LARRY McFADDEN

---

[1] SSN-587 the *USS Halibut* was commissioned in 1960, served 16 years, and was eventually recycled in 1994.

UNTITLED

Ask me not what
    I really don't know

Of knowledge I'm empty
    Please let me go

There's nothing to say
    No answer I see

By coming to ask
    Life questions of me

So leave me alone
    It's time you waste

In doubt you came
    Depart in haste

What you came seeking
    Is not found here

For instead of life
    There is only fear

T.K.

• • • •

With blazing speed the darkness came
Silent, quick without a name

Across a land already dying
Broken bodies, dry eyes crying

No one asked, but many chosen
Immortalized forever, in actions frozen

Life's delights; so fleetingly gone
Sleep forever; E-ter-nal Dawn.

T.K.

<table>
<tr><td>5</td><td># "Yes Sir, Yes Sir, Three Bags Full"
By Don Bodey</td></tr>
</table>

[Ed. Note: This chapter is an excerpt from Bodey's novel *F.N.G.* and follows the exploits of one Gabriel Sauers through his tour of travails. This novel, formerly out of print for 20 years, will be available through the *Reflections of History* series by Modern History Press.]

Prologue

This is a piece taken from my novel, and is loosely based on an experience of mine in Viet Nam, 37 years ago. Our LZ was overrun and we killed three NVA sappers. Instead of burying the bodies, we were ordered to hang them from the concertina wire that surrounded our position, and they hung there until they stunk. I'll never be able to forget that, but I have rarely talked about it. Sometimes it makes me cry, and I am 60 years old. So that's part of what the war did to me.

You have to understand how solitary Viet Nam was for almost everyone who was there. GIs got orders to report for a troop movement, and, after having trained for about four months with pretty much the same guys–which was your salvation, if there was one–the guys you shipped with came from all over the country, from a plethora of training units, except for elite units, like Special Forces. So it was starting all over again. You made friends as best you could: in shipment, in staging areas, and finally in the unit to which you were assigned. Realize, though, that everybody you met in your unit had been there longer than you. Not until someone rotated and a replacement came did you have any sense of belonging.

The tour of duty was a year. You've never known what a year is before, but once you were in Nam you knew. You counted the days. You didn't lose track of a week and then go back to count. You never forgot. If you were still alive after a year you went home. Simple. Because every guy counted his days there was no mistaking who was "short," that is, who would leave soonest, who would be still counting when you left. It's a weird way to exist. Time is very, very important.

When I hit my unit my squad leader was a little guy. He was three years younger than I but that didn't figure into the scheme of things. He had been in Viet Nam eight months, and was omniscient, as far as I was concerned. The character 'Pops' in this piece is meant to be like him.

Your life literally depended on other men and the 'I' in "Yes, Sir, Yes, Sir, Three Bags Full" has been in country about 4 months and am thoroughly depended on Pops, and Prophet because they are experienced. My kid brother was drafted while I was overseas and made into an MP once he got there. Some of his responsibility was centered on controlling, or reacting to, racial tension at the big bases around the Delta. This is inconceivable to me because there was no such thing in the "bush." In this story, 'Callmeblack' is merely a black soldier. When I was writing, I could visualize him because I had black men to draw from. We were all one. 'I' and he sleep in the same trench, lean on each other during guard, and count their days together because they are due to rotate at the same time. If anybody, Callmeblack is modeled from a black friend I trained with, who was killed his first day in Viet Nam.

All my novel's characters come from somewhere back there, and back then, but the truths that show up come from a distance from all that. That there is horror to my war, maturation to my bewilderment, longevity to my intense fear, and confusion to my experience becomes my legacy as a writer. My debts are to the dead and to the survivors, and I wish to acknowledge that. And so we begin...

• • • • •

The squad goes out in file, and as we go the guys who are digging nod and give us mock salutes. It's brotherhood, not manhood. The brush thickens and ten minutes outside the wire, it's a different world. Prophet is walking point with his steel pot on and his ruck rides high up on his back. Peacock is next with the Sixty over his shoulder, its belt of ammo coming out the side like miniature ears of corn. I follow him and Lt. Williams is behind me, then Callmeblack and Pops. I can't look behind me, but I can envision Callme carrying that grenade launcher like a toy.

We go downhill for awhile and my legs soon ache from the strain. We're on a trail that is pretty clear, but a little slippery. I lock my eyes on our left side. Our pace is fairly gradual until we come to where two trails branch, then the walking gets harder. Once in awhile I hear somebody slip or grunt but usually I can only hear my own steps, squishing sounds. After forty-five minutes, we get to the bottom of the hill, where Prophet stops and Callme and Peacock go out on security.

"Higher-higher said there oughta' be a bunch of dead dinks out here," Eltee says, looking at his map. From where we stopped we can see the tops of two nearby hills. We are in the saddle between them.

"I'm for going out as far as we can get. We don't want to be somewhere between the LZ and Charlie's mortars tonight."

"Dig it."

Pops has his map spread out too. He and Eltee are so completely opposite looking it makes me think of a comic book drawing. The lieutenant is tall, black, and thin. His face is smooth and handsome. Pops is thick, ruddy, ragged, and his face is rough and square. His eyebrows have grown together.

"This is just about where Artillery will be wanting to drop rounds tonight."

"And Charlie knows that LZ is almost as fucked up as it was last night, so if we're close to one of his big supply routes or the main hospital around here, he's gonna keep fucking with us."

"Prophet, you see anything that looks like he was this close last night?"

"Not really. Hard to tell. It rained too much."

He is on one knee, breaking chunks of mud between his hands. His deepest blue eyes move slowly from Eltee to Pops.

"Want somebody else to take a turn on Point?"

"Nah."

It seems to come all at once, a fog that makes everything look like a fading photograph. Like there's a sheet of thin plastic on my eyes. What didn't stand out before now seems like all there is: the vines and leaves are erased by this fog and the tree trunks are straight and dark; it makes me think of the charcoal after a fire has died. Besides, I hear something. We all hear it at the same time. Walking.

It is two dinks carrying something and everybody is so surprised that the dinks see us just when we see them. There's not even time to react before they take off running. Nobody gets a shot off, it all happens so quickly.

Eltee is up and runs in their direction, but that's all that occurs.

"Goddamn, that was quick. They came right between our security."

They were carrying a body. It lies there limp now, no bigger than a ten-year-old American boy. The top half is face down and it is lying on one leg that's been shattered; there's only a day-old stump of the other one. Its only clothes are a pair of black, bloody, shorts.

"Why would they be carrying this body? So we wouldn't find it?"

"I've got a hunch," Eltee says. He pokes the barrel of his rifle into the shorts and I can't believe he is going to blow the guy's nuts off, but there aren't any nuts. His rifle barrel spreads the shorts apart just enough to show the pubic hair and the woman's cunt.

"I'll be damned."

"One of those guy's wife, or what?"

"I'd about bet on it."

"Jesus Fucking Christ."

"Call higher-higher, tell 'em we found one. Don't tell 'em it got delivered to us."

"What about those guys?"

"They won't fuck with us. We're too many. Maybe they'll hide for a couple hours and sneak back for this, who knows?"

We make radio contact and report one enemy KIA.

"Let's move."

I feel like this fog is inside me, easing around my mind like it eases around the tree trunks in front of us, and easing around something foreign in my gut that lies there like this tiny woman we leave behind, dead in the foggy jungle.

The new trail is narrow, slippery, and steep. Prophet manages to keep pretty good footage, but I have a hard time. I go down to one knee a couple times and my rifle jabs into the mud once, so I am walking and trying to pick the mud out of the barrel at the same time. Eventually, we get far enough from the stream that the fog thins out a little, but there is still too much canopy overhead to let the sun through. Besides the dim light, the trail gets fainter. I see that Peacock is stopped a few meters in front of me, so I stop too, in an awkward position but glad to catch my breath. Peacock looks back and flips me the bird, then disappears again around some vines that entangle so perfectly they look braided.

My legs and feet are hurting; and I experiment with walking splay-footed, then pigeon-toed, then I try taking smaller steps. But nothing eases the pain much. I am concentrating too much on getting rid of the pain because I dumbly walk up on Peacock who is facing me. For an instant I panic, and my confusion must show because he chuckles and holds out his hand. Then I realize I am pointing my rifle right at him.

"You'd be so fuckin dead now..."

"Man, my ass is dragging, ain't you?"

Eltee Williams comes up. The fatigue shows on his face. He goes by us to Point to talk with Prophet. We are in a small glen that has a cup-like shape and will be full of water during the heavy monsoons. Callmeblack comes, panting, and bums a cigarette. His face is the color of dirty oil and spotted by sweat. His ODs are soaked and he stinks. He drops his ruck and sits on it.

We've been humping for probably three hours total. The glen we're in doesn't allow view of anything beyond a hundred feet. I wonder how far from the LZ we are, directly. Peacock is lying on the ground with his feet resting on low vines; the rest of us are in a rough circle, facing out. The fog is sparse now, but the light isn't very bright either. It's late afternoon. There are birds in the canopy. Once, when my eyes are beginning to close on their own accord, I think I see a big snake hanging from a tree, but it's a vine. Callme is humming very softly.

"Let's ride. It's getting dark."

"Somebody take a turn on the Sixty, my neck hurts."

I take the Sixty. I haven't fired one for six months, and I look it over to remember what I know. It feels about four times as heavy as a rifle. There's a carrying handle mounted on top, but it isn't balanced correctly when there's a belt of ammunition in. There are two legs that swing down from the perforated forestock. I inject a round and it tightens the belt up. The ammo belts are about four feet long, and I loop it over my left shoulder. Switching from an M16 to this is like changing paint brushes for bigger work; it takes some getting used to. Since this is longer than my rifle, the butt plate keeps getting snagged on my rucksack strap at first. Finally I give up trying to carry it in a ready position and flop it onto my shoulder, the way I'd seen Peacock carry it.

The trail evens out and gets a little bit more worn. It isn't as muddy but there are soft spots. The hardest part is stepping over the vines, which seem to be extra big here. We are about three-quarters up a mountain and walking around a kind of horseshoe plateau that looks down into the thick cul-de-sac we've been coming through. We are going down as often as up for the first half hour, then it's a steady but gradual climb. We are headed west and the sun is low enough that the streaks it cuts through the fog are almost horizontal.

The M-60 works to my advantage, too. It is just enough heavier that, going uphill, I can use it to help stagger. I keep watching my side of the trail, but it's hard to concentrate and instead I recall my neighborhood, the playground with its always broken merry-go-round. Certain glimpses through the fog trigger flash memories of particular spots in particular woods. *Homesick.*

Prophet stops at a place where the trail curves around a rock face of the mountainside. Pops begins calculating where we are; Pea takes the M-60 and goes out for security. The rest of us begin setting up. Callme and I dig a shallow trench trying to be as quiet as we can. Prophet and Lt. Williams set up claymores against the rock wall and aim them in opposite directions along the trail. There is trouble making radio contact so Pops takes it up onto a ledge of the rock face, then calls in our position. When we're set up it is too dark to see more than five feet. Pops reminds me and Callmeblack not to leave the trench unless we tell somebody. I make sure I can lay my hands on my frags and I lean the rifle against my ruck with one bandolier of full ammo clips over the barrel. I open the first can I feel in my ruck; it turns out to be beef and potatoes. I'm glad it's too dark to see the grease that is always at the top of the can, but I can feel it make my lips slippery. I can't find my water so I borrow Callme's. It tastes like he put an extra purification tablet in it.

We'll pull middle guard and there is not jack-shit to do in the meantime and I'm not tired. Our trench is nearest the trail and one of the claymore detonators is wrapped around a small root at the top of our trench. If we detonated it, there would be a blast powerful enough to ruin a concrete wall two feet thick, six feet away. I think about that a couple minutes while I'm trying to get comfortable, in my poncho liner. We've got our ponchos stretched over the trench to shed the water and as soon as I'm comfortable it begins to rain, but softly, so instead of claymore blasts, I'm thinking of laying underneath a tin roof. It works: I'm almost dozed off when Callme accidentally kicks me.

I give him a little more room and now the water runs down the poncho and right on me.

Fuck.

Callmeblack begins snoring. Plenty loud, I think. I lay there for another hour I reckon, trying to keep from laying on my hard on. Then I begin thinking about the whore in Cam Ranh and about the little Vietnamese girls at the convoy point who were eating lice out of each other's hair, then about the dead woman today. Then I'm not hard anymore. Even though I deliberately try not to, I begin figuring how much longer I'll be here. Over 250 more days, 250 more nights. Peacock rolls over in the trench next to us and makes some kind of pained grunt.

It is raining harder now and I try to guess what Eltee and Prophet are doing on guard to keep dry.

From our position, the LZ is over the mountain on the other side of the gulley. They are calling in Artillery illumination around the Z to set up Night Fire positions. The illumination rounds come down on their parachutes, to plot Heavy Explosive rounds. Dinks can mark where they land and could plan routes around them.

It's sure different to be out here, so much easier to understand how a few men can invade a complex Army outpost and get away with it: the jungle and nighttime are allies. The illumination rounds cast eerie patterns through the canopy. Shapes and shadows dance around. The rain is sometimes plain to see. It is still soft and steady. Other than the soft *pffts* it makes, the only sound I hear is the distant thuds of artillery, and Callme's gentle snoring.

It seems so fucking unreal. Once, when I must be on the verge of sleep, I feel like I am seeing it all. Like I am part of a painting? Floating between wakefulness and sleep, my mind roams like there's no difference between what is real and what is imaginary. It's pleasant, but I can't quite relax.

I'd like to get up and walk but that is impossible. I'd like to get that red-headed Lifer into a gunny sack and beat it open with a tire iron. I'd like to call ten or twelve rounds in on the Peace Talks in Paris. I'd like to go home and paint a house. I'd like to be nine years old and playing hide-and-seek along the railroad tracks instead of hiding in the jungle somewhere in Asia. I'd...

A rifle burst, an AK. Not very distinct and for a minute I'm not sure if I'm awake or dreaming, then there are explosions in pairs, and machine gun fire, more explosions. I know the LZ is getting hit, I roll over on my stomach not quite sure what to do other than waking somebody up, but everybody is awake.

I hear Peacock jamming home the machinegun bolt. Prophet comes down the trail repeating "New York Yankees" over and over.

"O.K., they're getting hit again. Everybody know which way the trail is from here?"

"Which Claymore is which?"

"That one is the one looking up the trail."

"Come with me, Gabe. You guys stay here, we're going down the trail a ways. Don't panic. I'll take the radio with us. Stay cool, it'll be Chevy Supersport if I come back. If you hear anybody going by and they ain't namin cars, blow the mines."

The action seems far, far away. I think of the first night we got hit, the RPGs everywhere, the impact of the explosions, the smells. We're going uphill, climbing around on the ledge of rock where the radio reception was good; Pops is using a flashlight, but very carefully. I try to be quiet but Pops is mostly in a hurry instead of worrying about noise. When we get to our position, he sets the radio up and dials it to the emergency push. The LZ is calling in guns and before the voice is done transmitting there is an explosion. The push goes dead.

From up here on the ledge, we can see a little of the LZ. There are all colors of explosions. Red and yellow and blue, white. It is awesome, from this distance. There are handheld flares up everywhere and plenty of M16 fire putting tracer rounds in every direction, but most of it towards us.

"Muthafucker, they're getting hit hard."

"Listen," he says, "the dinks are probably working in waves. They'll send a squad in and then another one to cover their ass, then maybe another one to keep the confusion going. Unless there's a shitload of 'em, they'll hit hard and fast, then they'll scatter in every direction. I'd say there's a damn good chance they could come this way, and if it happens to be the first wave who come this direction, it could happen soon. So don't be fuckin halfstepping."

"Chevy. Supersport."

It's Lt. Williams' voice, below us. "Whatsa matter, Eltee?"

"I'm coming up. Nothing wrong. Not yet."

Pops shines the light once just as Williams is climbing over the last small cliff. Somebody is with him, but I can't tell who. This all seems rehearsed but dangerous. A script would call for somebody to stumble and fall, but instead it's all so smooth. This is a safe place to be, as far as ambushes go, backed up against a stone wall and higher than the trail.

"What's up, Eltee?"

"I was looking at the map, Pops, and it shows a trail that must be right on the other side of this." He knocks the end of his rifle against the rock. He brought Peacock with him and he is setting up a Claymore.

"So, what're you saying?"

"We oughta cover it."

"C'mon, Eltee, we can't cover it. Unless we climb over this sonofabitchin rock right now and get all set up an--" "Yeah, let's go. You and—"

"You're crazy, man!"

"Pops, I noticed, when we were coming up, that this trail was going up faster than the slope. We were cutting us at a sharp angle. And on the map there's a little trail meeting a big one right up above us. I thought we were on the big one, but I think we're on the little one and the big one is right up there."

"Fuck, we can't climb up there now."

"The Claymores down there will cover that little trail, no matter what. Even if some shit hits, we're still right above it."

"Right above our own guys, and it's night."

"The dinks aren't gonna stop and fight; they're just interested in getting the fuck out of here."

"What if we're smackfuckindab in the middle of their staging area or something? We're fuckin sitting ducks when it gets light."

"So all the more reason to cover the other trail. They'll sure as hell be using the speedtrail."

"Unless they know we're up here. Those guys this afternoon with the woman... maybe there ARE a bunch of 'em around here. So we can play it cool, just sneak the fuck back out of here tomorrow."

"We don't know anything, Pops. We must play the odds." "We don't even know if they're coming this way."

"Damnit, I've thought of all that, and we're going up there."

"This is stupid, man. Stupid. This is my squad."

"Pops, don't make me order you. I respect you to the utmost, I just feel I'm right."

"All right, fuckit. What about the Sixty?"

"Peacock is set up so he can see down the little trail and if that other one comes up right at the top of the ridge, he's within range of that side, too."

The top of the ledge is closer than I thought and we're there in five minutes. Since we're even higher now, the Base Camp is more visible, but there's no time to watch right away.

We scout the section out with flashlights and rig up two Claymores. There isn't enough space to set them both up in opposite directions and still compensate for the backblast, so we set them in tandem about ten feet apart. We're shielded from the backblast by a rock the size of a coffin. Callme and I get set up on one end of the rock and Pops sets up with Eltee on the other side and down the trail a little. It's necessary that we know where each other is, as much as we can.

There are illumination rounds hanging all around the LZ. It looks like a distant sports arena, seen from the blimp. All the sound from the Z is mixed together. Artillery is coming in in groups now, awfully close to the Z. Those flashes are red and yellow. Evidently, there are two different batteries firing and their patterns crisscross, then work around the Z. Most of the defensive fire is directed towards our side of the Z so apparently the attack came from this side. I hope the dinks run the other way. The action has been going on for more than half an hour now. The illumination rounds have come from artillery, mortars, and handheld flares. There are probably fifty rounds in the air now, hanging at different heights. The only thing it illuminates from here is the smoke and fog. As we watch, heavy explosive rounds land in purple flashes. The flashes are walking away from the Z, beginning to comb the surrounding ridges, so maybe the offensive is over for tonight.

Callmeblack is huddled beside me, his poncho wrapped around him with the hood up. He is shivering and his M-79 is rapping against a rock. The sound annoys me. I am so soaked through that the rain doesn't seem to stop at my clothes; it's like I can feel individual drops hit me on the shoulders.

Gunships are coming. At first their sound is steady and soft, a medium-range and constant sound. They come in twos, two pair. Blinking lights: Red and green. They strafe all around the base of the mountain the Z is on, and there's no way to describe the sight. Rockets and miniguns and, even though only every seventh round is a tracer, the air and ground is lined like a neon screendoor. One Cobra gunship can cover a football field with a round in each square inch; there are four Cobras circling and firing. It is such a visual show I have to hold my breath. I'd like to know the number of rounds, and what the rounds are hitting. The pattern of the artillery has moved into a wider circle now and some are coming closer and closer to us, walking our way in giant purple steps. Pops comes over to our side.

"They're throwing everything we've got at Charlie. If anything happens, be damn sure you don't forget where we are. Callme, use that launcher carefully, hear? Gabe, fire short bursts if you fire. We'll all wait on Eltee. If this is really a speedtrail, then they could be getting here soon, might even be riding motorbikes. If they come down the trail Prophet and Peacock are covering, you guys come around this way, behind us, but don't fire down there unless there's all kinds of shit coming our way."

"Muthafucker, I ain't ready for a goddamn ambush," Callme says, his voice as deep and black as the jungle. The gunships are still working out and Artillery is firing illumination rounds again.

My nerves are hammering my insides and the rain is drilling me in the face now. My muscles are all hard. I think of hiding underneath a car and hearing the cops run by five years ago. I can feel myself sweating. My legs ache but I can't move. I can smell Callmeblack's B.O., like goat piss.

The Cobras quit firing and are only motor sounds now, above the clouds or smoke. The smell from the illumination rounds has drifted to us. Rhythmically, illuminations pop above the smoke and drift into the canopy and make the whole sky somehow look like a petticoat, just before I see the flashlights.

Coming up the hill like dirt bikes coming across a pasture: lights, then voices. The voices aren't clear. I'm in a daze. I feel Callme move beside me. I hear the voices like I am listening to a television from a different room. I flash on opening the kitchen door to a Chinese restaurant I used to have on my garbage route: quick, chatty, sounds. They are even with us, twenty feet away. They are half-running. Eltee opens up. The Sixty chatters. Callme launches one. I fire a quick clip. The Claymores.

The Claymores start something on fire for a minute and I can see spastic movement like a chicken with its head gone. Then it is dark again. There's a thrashing sound, then nothing but quiet. Dead silence.

I hear either Pops or Eltee puke. I can smell Callmeblack's goat-piss BO, gunpowder. The rain sounds too perfect.

There's a rock behind me to lean on. Callmeblack is lying down, I think. There is not much sound from anybody: some rustling around, once a stifled sneeze. I am wide awake. Every sense is acute, although it's so dark now without the illumination rounds drifting it is hard to see anything. Still, my eyes won't stay shut. The scene that stays with me is that last bit of scrambling after the claymores went off. It was brief, instantaneous, but I'm positive I saw flailing. No screaming, at least none that I heard. Fifty, maybe seventy-five feet, away are some dead gooks, caught in our ambush. *Why don't I feel more than I do?* I get my bootlaces untied. My feet stink. I'd like to have a cigarette. I run my tongue around the inside of my teeth until the tip is sore. Light can't be more than a couple hours away.

What does it look like down there? When I imagine it, I think of a painting from a history book. I think the picture I keep seeing is from the civil war: soldiers in the foreground and bodies behind them. Clean, old-fashioned battle death. A claymore has something like 150 pellets in it. The pellets are a little smaller than rabbit turds. We blew two claymores so there's not going to be anything clean about these guys. They'll be full of holes.

The canopy creaks in a wind and it starts raining harder. I've been wet for a week. The way I'm sitting catches water in my lap. Nothing matters, so I piss in my pants. The piss is warm and feels thick. I suppose piss is thicker than rainwater. Goddamn, to be sitting on a toilet right now, only hearing my piss instead of feeling it.

The rain is so steady I can imagine every single leaf getting a drip at the same time. I want to count something. I try to count every drop that hits me. Then I try counting the drops I can hear land on my steel pot. Then I try to quit counting but my mind keeps on trying on its own to count something, just measure time, measure these slowest minutes of my life. I feel like beating off. *There are 3600 seconds in an hour. Light must be 5000 seconds away. One thousand one, one thousand two, one thousand three. Shit.*

I wonder if mom still shuts the bathroom door now that nobody's there.

Movement. From where Eltee and Pops are, comes a sliding, dragging sound. The rain is constant. The movement is careful and very slow. It can't be more than twenty-five feet away, but if I didn't know where they are I couldn't have estimated the distance from the sound. It is going away from us, towards Peacock. He must be crawling. I try turning my head different ways to find the angle I can hear it best. While he's moving across the underbrush, the sound is more muffled than when he hits rock.

Only once does his equipment make noise, a metallic noise, and it enables me to get a better fix on his position. The movement stops and there is whispering, then the movement again.

No, more than one movement. One set of sounds goes back towards the other position and the other sound comes towards us. I strain every bit of my eyes to see, but nothing. There must be no moon whatsoever. Whoever is coming is walking instead of crawling. He is sliding his feet along the ground. He isn't very far away when he bumps something and moves to my right. I don't know whether or not to say anything. His sliding steps stop.

"Ford Mustang," it's Peacock.

"We're here, to your left."

Our voices aren't any louder than the rain, but the rain doesn't do anything to cover them up either. His steps begin again. I guess he is twenty feet away. I try to figure out if he is coming at the proper angle. I count his steps. At twelve, I whisper again and his direction changes towards me. Twelve more steps, but he doesn't seem much closer. I wonder if there are rocks that fool us.

"Hey, dude," Callmeblack whispers.

"I'm fuckin dizzy from trying to see," he says. It sounds like he may be facing away from us.

Callme taps something against his rifle four or five times, then Peacock's slow steps start again. He kicks a loose rock and it rolls a few feet and stops with a sploosh. He is close now, honing in on Callmeblack's steady clicking. Seven more steps.

"Who's making the noise?" "

I am," Callme says.

"Where are you, Gabe?"

"Here"

"Okay, I'm between you."

So now, we three are the highest up. The ambush sight is downhill in one direction and Pops and Eltee are downhill in the other, our left. Prophet is further below them. Peacock is setting up the Sixty. I wonder which way he faces it. I hear the bipod snap into place. I have to rest my eyes even though I haven't been able to see anything.

I think of Chickenfeed crying a month ago; and, I can see his pewter thigh bone tied to his other leg. I wonder if he is in a hospital in Japan and if they had to cut the leg off. I purposely keep my eyes shut until I count to one hundred, rushing the nineties. I hope to see a trace of light when I open them. I try again to foresee the scene downtrail.

The rain sounds like a giant wadding paper.

"Pea, what's the plan?"

"Wait'll it gets light and take it from there. Eltee sent me up here to you guys in case there's dinks up above us. The Sixty is good for covering our ass."

"Think there's much chance of more dinks?"

"Hard to say."

"Sure as hell a lot of medevacs going to the Z."

"Charlie poured shit onto that hill for a good twenty minutes before they got any support, and Charlie makes a lot more rounds count than we do."

"Especially when there's no sandbags on the hootches."

"We'd better shut up."

So it's back to waiting for light and listening to the rain: *dif-da-datta-dif*. There's still the drone of distant helicopters. They could be Cobras standing by, probably above the rain clouds, or there could still be medevacs and re-suppliers going into the Z. From the other direction comes barely audible thumps of artillery rounds walking guard over other mountains. My saliva glands are working hard to keep off my wish for nicotine. The small of my back is sore and periodically I catch myself gripping the stock of my rifle so tightly that my fingers go numb. I've been sitting crooked so long my lungs feel like there would be a crease in them.

The very first light that shows resembles wax paper. The canopy, even though we're partway up the mountain, is still very thick and the light seems to seep through it slowly at first so that straight above me looks like a black roof with very light frost on it— just the minutest change of color. When I first see it I expect to be able to see around me, but ground level is just as black as it's been all night. I suppose my eyes are playing tricks until I look up again and it is still there, changing. It must have something to do with the cup of land we're in. There is nothing ambient about the light. I swear this stuff that was frost-color, then movie-screen color, is now as dull as chalk above us but only finally reaching the ground. I see Pea and the Sixty in silhouette, then Callme beyond him.

Gradually, I can see further. The jungle comes in jigsaw pieces that are edged by the dark trees and vines. Everybody lies completely still and looks around, weapons ready. I can't see over the cliff, but I hear somebody mov-ing down there. As it gets lighter Peacock adjusts the machine gun so he can swivel it almost 360 degrees. I don't know where to look, or what exactly to look for. The spot where the dinks are is over a ridge from us so we can't see it. I look mostly into the trees, for movement, I guess.

Suddenly a huge bird flies over us low and we can hear it beat wings to a stop, then a throaty caw-caw that sounds like an enormous crow comes back from where the dinks are. It is the weirdest, coldest sound I have ever heard. It sends chills down my already-cold backbone. I am aware, too, of the sound of other birds in the trees.

Another vulture comes from the other direction and the two birds begin talking to each other. I look at Peacock, and he makes a face full of disgust.

"Goddamn, that's gross, man."

"Fuckit, it's only dinks. I don't want to look at the sonofabitches anyway. Let the buzzards eat 'em up."

I hope, almost pray, that there aren't any dinks still alive but wounded so bad they can't move. Watching a bird eat your buddy when you know there is somebody watching you would be the utmost punishment. I'll never be that hard, never think of anything that awful without remorse, or... *shit! Quit thinking Gabe.*

The other three guys begin coming towards us. First, Prophet, his boonie hat low onto his forehead and his rifle held high in one hand so he can claw up the cliff with his other. He is mean-looking, soaked through by the rain. His shirt is half undone and the beads around his neck swing silently as he takes giant steps up the trail now. Behind him is Eltee, still good-looking de-spite the red streak of mud covering the front of his ODs, from crawling. He is carrying the radio, but its weight doesn't keep him from walking unbelievably erect. Pops comes last, dumpy and rugged. On the way, he picks up a clod of dirt and heaves it, and the vultures take off together.

When I was very young, Grandaddy used to make me cry because he said the buzzards would be back for me someday, that I was left on a buzzard stump: *"Lookin for mushrooms one day and scared a big ol' buzzard outa the creek bed, said to m'self, 'What would a buzzard be eatin on down there?' and when I went on down in the creek, I see a ol' sycamore stump there and whattaya know? Gabe, you was laying there suckin your thumb, naked as a buzzard baby. Them buzzards'll be back to get you someday unless you get strong enough to fight em off."*

Am I strong enough to fight the buzzards off now? These real ones?

"What do you think the dinks are worried about around here, Eltee?"

"Probably a hospital."

"How close are we to Cambodia?"

"Close."

It is light enough now to feel a little confident. We can see a hundred feet in every direction. We're at a kind of summit. This is the first time to see the big trail. It doesn't look that much different than the trail we followed up, but most of it is rock instead of mud. There are two sets of boulders between us and the ambush point instead of one set. The rocks are the color of old telephone poles and they're mostly smooth. The mosquitoes get bad all at once. Big fuckers.

"What did higher-higher say to do when it gets light?" "Said get a count and call 'em."

"It's light enough to count."

"No, it ain't," Pops says, "if them fuckers were boobytrapped we don't wanna be fuckin around in this much light."

"How could they be booby-trapped?" Callme asks.

"When they go on these raids, a lot of times they boobytrap themselves, so if they get wasted and some dumbass G.I. rolls him over, boom, they're even."

"Or, if we didn't get 'em all, the other guys might have fixed 'em up last night."

"Shit, we woulda heard 'em."

"Bullshit, you know how good Charlie is, man? Those little fuckers have been ambushing here for twenty years, and their old man before them, fuckin etcetera and ad infinitum," Pea says. He has that professor look.

Even though we're all subdued, Prophet seems especially so. He very often sits a little apart from everybody else like he is now, but he has a kind of nervous energy that usually keeps him doing something. Not this time. He is sullen-looking. His face is colorless and his gaze wanders from the circle we're sitting in to the jungle without any change of expression. There is something so charismatic about him that he is a kind of spiritual leader of the squad; even though Eltee and Pops outrank him, he's the one we trust.

So, since he is so quiet everybody seems dumbfounded. As if to underscore what I'm thinking, he bums a cigarette from Pea by hand signals and sits smoking it without ever taking it out of his mouth.

The rain has slowed way down, but it is chilly. I am debating whether or not to unroll my poncho; it seems like a tardy thing to do since I'm already so wet. There are a lot of bird noises now, mostly high in the canopy. The light is still uncommonly dull, as though there should be fog, but if there is, it's so evenly distributed that I can't see it. Maybe my eyes are just that tired.

Callmeblack and Peacock are huddled together under one poncho, the grenade launcher sticking out one end and the machine gun out the other. Pops is curled up at my feet. He has his poncho on, too, snapped all the way up with the hood tied tight and his hat on top of the hood. It's a classic hat: the brim is shaped like a dried-up leaf. He has all the LZs he has been to written on the hat, probably thirty or more. There's also a calendar that I can't make any sense of, though it's apparent from all the ink that he's been here a long time.

"How long you been here, Pops?"

"Jesus Christ, what a thing to ask me. I don't wanna remember because it'll just make me nervous to think about it. You asshole. Twenty days."

I didn't expect him to jump my shit and it hurts my feelings, but I had it coming; it was a dumb thing to ask at a time like this. Still, it seems unbelievable to me that he has less than three weeks to go. It seems to me like he would have refused to go out on this hump—the bust couldn't be *THAT* bad. All of a sudden I realize time has gone pretty fast. I'm down below three hundred days. Big fuckin' deal. A guy is always conscious of his own days left, but I hadn't realized Pops will be gone so soon. It's hard to think what it'll be like after he's gone.

It is harder to think of what it will be like when I have 20 days left. Deep inside of me—no, maybe not so deep—I don't believe I'll make it. Even when I first got orders for Nam, I never thought I'd make it if I ever got here in the first place. All along, I thought something would happen and somehow I'd get out of it.

"Pops, man, I'm sorry. I'm scared, man. I'm an asshole."

"Hey, fuckit. Just because you're scared doesn't mean you're an asshole."

"Shut up you two," Prophet says. There's no insistence in his voice.

"Let's see what we got there," Peacock says. "The sooner we get it done, the sooner we can get back to building our hole."

"I am not ready for this," Eltee says.

"Man, you're the boss. If you ain't ready, what about us?"

"What's the difference?"

"Hey, you're an officer, that's what."

"Back off, Prophet. I'm just a man. I make more money than you do and I've had different training than you guys, and I guess I'm a little older, but I'm mutha-fuckin queasy. I grew up in a neighborhood that might make you guys tremble to walk through at night. I've seen bad street fights. My friends have beaten up cops and been beaten up and shot at… I should be one bad ass fucker. But, listen: I escaped, Y'hear? I made it out of the ghetto, I went to college, the whole fuckin success story but all that has not a goddamn thing to do with right now. I'm worthless. For two hours I've been trying to keep from screaming. I don't know for sure what I'm afraid of but, dig it, I am fuckin scared of something, and… well, fuckit."

"Sounds like a regular guy, don't he?"

"The way I see it, all we gotta do is get a count and get the fuck outa here so we can get totally fucked up and forget it when we get back to the Z, so the sooner it's over the sooner we can pretend it didn't happen."

"You guys are counting chickens we don't even know are hatched."

"Peacock, what does that mean?"

"Fuck if I know."

Blood.

Like cottage-red paint shot from a fire hydrant, blood everywhere: sprayed all over the leaves and rocks and running in the rainwater that trickles off the rocks. *Jesusfuckinchrist.*

"Oh, muthafucker, they're dead."

"We musta got em all."

"Let's go. We're lucky this didn't draw a tiger last night."

As we came up, some rodents scampered away and as we are standing there I look away and meet two little eyes looking at us from under a rock. I feel like I hate the goddamn rodent. I hate everything. There are four dinks. Two of them were cut in half by our Claymore. How goddamn much blood is there in a person? I might faint. It seems like everything should be still, but there are flies by the hundreds and the birds in the canopy are squawking. There must be an animal in the matted grass behind the bodies because there is noise there, too. At first I can't identify the other sound I hear, then I realize it is the static of the radio.

I have been breathing fast and I'm sweating, but I can't turn away. The rain is drizzle now. It seems like the rain would have washed more blood away. I smell something besides wet jungle, but it doesn't smell dead. *Does blood have a smell of its own? Is that what the vultures smell?*… Faint again: like my mind is swinging up there in the canopy, like I'm a vulture seeing us look at the bodies. *I see Pops break the silence.*

"Four of 'em. That's all we want to know. Let's go back to the top and call it in. I don't want to stand around here. Pick up the rifles." *And I can see me pick up a gun.* When I feel it my mind comes back to earth. We go back to where our rucks are.

The rifle is an AK-47. I can't forget the sound after the night Chickenfeed got hit. The rifle is beat to pieces. It only has half the original stock; the back half is a piece of wood with twig marks on it still, carved on the end to fit a shoulder. *Which of the four did it come from?*

"Greenleaf, this is Titbird. How's your copy?"

Pops has the radio up on a rock and the way he is standing there talking makes me flash on a cop, *downtown Cincinnati,* calling in from a beat box. I feel fuckin drugged. Okay, *this is war, man. This ain't Cincinnati you're part of this, Gabriel.* Everybody looks the same, empty. Muthafucker, can this be? I smell the rifle to see if it was fired last night, but there isn't any smell but metal. This ain't the fuckin movies; you ain't John Wayne. I wonder if it had shot any GI's. It's heavier than my rifle. The ammo clip is curved. The more I stare at the gun the more it looks unreal, toy-like. No, it actually looks more real than my plastic M16 but there is something childish about it. *The fucking thing looks homemade. That carved buttpiece, the way it's wired together. Homemade.*

Pops is scooting the radio up the rock now. It occurs to me that I haven't been watchful. I should be watching the bush. Eltee gets up and goes to help Pops. He seems to have regained his composure but his face is tight-looking. Peacock is picking his nose with one hand and toothbrushing the feed mechanism of the Sixty with his other.

"We got four rabbits out here. Coming back to your position. Over."

"Titbird, Greenleaf."

"Go."

"Standby."

"Them dinks caught our Claymores letters-high," Pea says, to nobody in particular.

"Think of how much damage they musta done to the Z."

"Titbird, how's your copy? Over."

"Good copy. Go ahead, damnit."

"Titbird, Higher says cut a chimney, they'll be out. Over." Prophet angrily slams his hat on his thigh and Pops bangs the microphone with his free hand.

"No way," Pops says to Eltee. "Fuck those Lifers. You tell 'em, we can't cut a chimney through that canopy."

"All they want to do is make sure we counted right, and I ain't fuckin doing it."

I can't imagine how we could cut a hole, big enough to let a Loach down, and I can't imagine why.

Pops reads my mind.

"They wanna bring a Chieu Hoi out here and see if he can tell what unit the dinks are from."

"There isn't enough left of the four dinks to tell anybody jack shit."

"Eltee, tell the fuckers to walk out here. We did," Prophet says.

Lt. Williams is standing up with his arms folded across the radio. He is rocking back and forth on his heels and toes. He never looks our way. The radio is low-volume static. If I can read Eltee's mind, I know he is torn, tortured, confused. He's going to be caught in the middle.

"Well, do something, for Christ sakes. We can't cut 'em a hole, and we sure as fuck don't want to stay here much longer. Charlie is gonna be looking for these guys."

"Greenleaf, Titbird. Code name William."

"Go, Titbird."

"Greenleaf, too much canopy, too high. We'll bring captured weapons to your papa. These rabbits are in parts. Repeat, in parts. Not enough left for I.D. Copy?"

"Code name William, code name Beaver. Wait one." Pops flips through the code book.

"It's that short, red-haired fucker, Billingham."

I didn't know his name, but I figured that's who it was. He's a kissass, a commando whose uniform always seems clean and pressed. He's some kind of aid to the Colonel and he carries a CAR-15. A few days ago I saw his radioman taking his picture. He had a flak jacket and helmet on then, and the asshole probably hasn't ever been to the bush. This is beginning to get real shitty. I'm becoming afraid again. We blew these guys away and their pals must be around here somewhere. If we don't get going, we'll be sitting ducks. I feel my anger and fear mount together. I have a quick fantasy of taking a swing at that fat little fucker.

"Titbird, Greenleaf."

Even the radio seems alive and against us. It must be my fear that makes me think that way all of a sudden. *Unfuckin' fair to be out here in the middle of nowhere and scared, talking long-distance and visualizing that goddamn captain sitting in a sandbagged Conex telling us to do something we already told him we can't fuckin do.*

"Titbird, it is essential that you provide us a way of identifying your rabbits. Many lives may depend on it."

"Bullshit! Our lives are the only ones relevant to them dead dinks, where does he get off giving us a lecture like we're still in The World? This ain't practice. There ain't enough of them dinks left to tell anything. Make the fucker understand they're using us for bait."

Peacock is standing beside Lt. Williams now, struggling to keep his voice under control. Eltee looks at him blankly, puts a hand on his back, then pushes his own helmet back on his head. Eltee looks five years older than he did yesterday, and he looks confounded.

"Oh, fucker..." Callme moans.

Prophet has been sitting with his elbows on his knees, looking away from us. Now he looks up at the canopy and shakes his head.

"Greenleaf, code name William, over." "Go."

"I repeat. No can do."

"Titbird, that's affirm. Transport your rabbits to checkpoint Bravo. Out."

No. BULLSHIT. I'm dreaming. Or is this a movie? Peacock slumps down into the mud and begins stabbing at it with his knife. He is soon using both hands to stab with. He's nuts. I feel crazy, too. Everybody else looks crazy. Eltee lets the microphone drop against the rock and stands staring at us. He looks like he's trying to get his mind to work.

"Okay... " he starts.

"Okay, so let's go to Bravo and they can fuckin' walk back up here without us. We'll tell 'em right where the ambush is."

"Listen up," Eltee says, "this is some real bullshit, but there's no alternative."

"No alternative? Let's just fuckin refuse to do it."

"Pops, you're a shorttimer. If we don't do it, we're all guilty of disobeying a direct order and we're all going to get court-martialed. You know that. Not just me. They'd bust us, send us all to jail, then send us back out here and that jail time is bad time. You won't rotate out of here until next February. Think about it."

Pops' face is stretched round with red anger. He looks like he's ready to explode. I expect an outburst, but instead he slumps down to his knees and turns his face upward to let the silent rain hit him. He sighs.

"Eltee is right," Peacock says.

"If we're gonna do it, let's do it. We'll get even with them fuckin Higher-highers," Prophet says.

Lt. Williams looks at him and opens his mouth but doesn't say anything.

"You never heard me say that, Eltee, for your own good.

We like you and I know what you're thinking, but just forget it. You're one of us, for now.

Jesus, this is complicated. I don't know for sure what Prophet is saying, but his tone is severe, and he isn't about ready to back down from anything the Eltee can offer.

"I won't hump no dead guy," Callme says.

"Dinks don't weigh much," Pea says.

Callmeblack makes his big black hand into a big black fist and drives it into his wadded-up poncho. Then he half buries his face in the poncho and either sobs or sighs.

Dear Dad: You won't believe this. Dear Brother Bob: Go to Canada. Dear President Johnson: Could you do this? Dear God: For my mother's sake, numb me. (FUCKING JAIL!... And everybody knows the horror stories about military prisons, especially in Nam). There's nothing fair about some Army officer three kilometers away telling us to obey this insane order or go to jail. But why should I expect fairness, I'm in the Army and the Army is in a war. It's simple. I don't have any choice. So I'm the first one to move. I stand up and unroll my poncho. I'm conscious of the rest of them watching me, but I don't look at them.

"Are we supposed to call 'em when we get there?"

"Yeah," Prophet says, "call 'em and say send the taxi after we dragged the muthafuckin corpses all the way through this damn jungle while they meanwhile sit back there getting dug in, then fly out to meet us."

He stands and is talking loud but not yelling.

"Then, goddamnit! Then, they'll turn that helicopter around and we'll goddamn have to walk back, too!"

"Those hardcore Shake-and-Bake officers don't even think about us killing these poor bastards, let alone having to haul around what's left. They probably CAN'T think of it, just have wetdreams about being a hero when they get home."

We're psyching ourselves up. Everybody but Peacock is getting ready now. Eltee already has his ruck on. He goes over to Callme and squats alongside him. They don't even say anything but I can see Callme's courage... or whatever it is... coming back. I feel a little jealous of Eltee right now. I'm ready. My ruck doesn't feel so heavy, and I'm not as tired as I was before it got light.

"Pray for luck," Peacock says. "If Charlie is around here close and sees this mess, you know he ain't gonna goddamn worry about big guns out here. He's gonna have our shit on a stick. He'll be hawking my goddamn watch in Hanoi if he knows what we're carrying and just happens to see us clodhoppin American boys here in his jungle. Them Lifers think about the wrong things, that's all. They call the war by numbers. They're gonna say them four dinks only had one arm anyway, so we really blew eight away."

"Peacock," Pops says, "I never heard you be so right."

"Man, I'm just talking to keep from seeing because seeing is believing."

"That's more like your old self, you asshole. That doesn't make any sense."

Jesus the flies.

We have two sets of our ponchos snapped into pairs and are going to gather the bodies onto the ponchos, then split the weight up so four guys can carry the two slings. Even then, two guys will have to hump the radio, the machine gun, and the extra weapons, we really we'll be fuckin-A useless if anything happens. Prophet goes to look for the best way, by himself! We want to keep him as light as we can because he will be walking Point. When he leaves the rest of us to go back to the sight together.

The flies are so loud I hear them from behind the first set of rocks, ten meters away.

We spread the ponchos out. Nobody talks. At first, we all stand still. Then Callmeblack begins humming "Swing Low Sweet Chariot" and Pops drags most of a body onto one of the ponchos. The guts drag along between the body's legs. The flies swarm in one extra-loud sound and land again when the body is on the poncho. Pops goes off from us a bit.

Right at my feet is an arm. It's short but looks like what is there is almost all of what there ever was, like it came off at the shoulder. There are green flies around its bloody end. Callme is still humming and has tossed a couple pieces onto the poncho.

I pick the arm up by the unbloody hand, and it is like shaking hands with a snake. I'm careful not to touch the fingers. I fling the arm onto the pile that must be most of two guys now. Or women. Pops is back, white and old-looking.

Callmeblack sits down and spits a lot, but doesn't puke, between his boots. The head that had been hanging onto Pops' body by a thread of skin is between Callmeblack and me, and we both see it at the same time. It is most of the face, but half of it is turned into the muddy trail so it looks like a mask except for the files. Callmeblack and I both look at it and then at each other, and he looks back between his boots and half spits, half retches. I kick the head and it is a good kick; the face sails a foot off the ground and lands at the top of the pile, then rolls over the top. I'm glad it doesn't end up looking at me.

Eltee and Pops are about to fold the poncho over their pile and tie it shut.

"Let's be damn sure they're about the same weight."

"I pretended I was splitting a hundred pounds of Cambodian Red weed, man. I eyeballed it like I didn't know which half was mine, I---"

"Ok, Ok, Ok. Shut up."

Peacock look hurt. His tattoo is showing. I don't think it's raining. I think what is coming down is dripping off the canopy. Peacock's face is eggshell color. In fact the light is all like that, the color of a dirty white dog.

I take as much air into my lungs as I can. I walk second, behind Prophet who is carrying one of the captured rifles. Peacock has the other end of the poncho; then Pops and Callmeblack carrying the other sling, and Eltee is walking last. We first tried slinging the weight on vines, in hopes that it would be easier carrying, but that didn't work because the trail is so sharp in places that the vines are too long to turn without the lead guy having to stop and turn around. So, I twist the corners of the poncho together and use both hands to shoulder my end. Prophet helped me sling my rifle with shoelaces so it at least hangs in front of me and will be possible to get at, if it comes to that.

Eltee stays quite a ways back from the rest of us. Incredibly, he has the radio, the Sixty, and an extra rifle, and he has to pull rear security. I am so uptight I can't breathe normally--it's more like taking a gulp of air in and walking until it's used up, then gasping again, like I've swum too far away from shore. The going is slow and seems noisy. For a while we walk on a fairly level trail and our footing is solid. The weight gets to us though and we have to rest. When we set the poncho down, the flies all seem to catch up and swirl into the holes between the snaps on the ponchos. The blood still isn't dried so when I pick up the knot that makes my handle, the blood squeezes out and some runs down my arms.

After fifteen minutes my back begins to throb. Trying to walk mostly downhill now and still trying to keep the poncho fairly level to make it easier on Peacock strains my muscles and makes me aware of the spots I slept on last night. I'm constantly gasping for breath and the bag keeps swinging so I have to struggle to keep my balance. I come to the utmost edge of my endurance. I want to cuss and throw something. I want to destroy. Finally, the slippery knot comes out of my grasp and the sling falls. Without looking back, because I am so goddamn out of touch, I keep walking, dragging the poncho behind me. It slides easily enough through the mud and makes a small sound like a brake rubbing against a bicycle tire. We don't go on like that very long before Prophet stops us and points at a swale below: Checkpoint Bravo.

I simply fall down, gasping so hard I wonder if it is possible to catch up on the air I'm missing. I lie there with my eyes closed, listening to the others catching their breath, and the buzzing of the flies.

It is almost as though I am asleep, momentarily, because the sound of the flies begins to sound like song. Honest to God: song. I hear snatches of nursery rhymes, and church choirs and classical music, and the ditty that is the commercial for life insurance... when my breathing gets closer to normal the smell of reality fights its way back, and once again the predominant sound is the bloodthirsty flies swarming. I could puke in my own lap and it wouldn't make any difference right now.

From a sitting position, I can see cleanly through the foliage.

Checkpoint Bravo is a small, almost round, swale. It looks marshy. Instead of jungle, it looks like tall grass. I wonder how deep the water is. My breath has come back now. I see that one of the arms has worked its way partly out from the bundled poncho. I'll be damned if I'm going to touch it again to shove it back in. I don't care if it gets lost.

Eltee is making radio contact. Otherwise there isn't any sound except for the goddamn flies. It takes skill to use an Army PRC-25 radio so that it isn't like hearing a supermarket speaker, and Williams is good enough that I can barely hear the transmissions from fifteen feet away. I semi want to smoke a cigarette, but my hands smell like the blood that is drying black now. I try to think of what it resembles, having squeezed out of the poncho, but it doesn't look like anything but what it is. Thinking about carrying these pieces of dinks to a helicopter landing in a small clearing makes the fear come hard, but who is there to tell I'm scared, and what good would it do?

"Wait till we hear the birds coming," Eltee says. "Pass it on."

We whisper it ahead and Prophet nods. His face is rock hard and dirty. The way the light is hitting his face I can see the rivulets of sweat running over the wax we use to camouflage our faces. He must have used mostly the stick of green. I used mostly brown. The camo sticks are precious; it is one more thing the Army never has enough of. Prophet sits quietly looking around all 360 degrees, spitting silently between his teeth. I'm glad the rain has quit, at least for now; nonetheless, I'm still cold, or shivering from fear. It isn't long before we hear the helicopters coming. We don't want to give our position away any sooner than we absolutely have to, so we don't move until the birds are in sight. As high up as they stay, their sound is no louder than the noise of the flies. Everybody chambers a round ready to pick up the ponchos for the last time.

"Pray, baby," Peacock whispers. I nod. I do. I breathe as deeply as I can.

The clearing is a shade different in color than everything else around, darker green. From this distance, it looks like briars, but I've never seen briars over here. I can tell the grass is too tall for a bird to come down in, that we'll have to hack some of it away. My question is what we're going to do with these fucking bodies, meanwhile.

Eltee is working his way up the line, whispering to everybody as he goes by. It strikes me as absurd, although not stupid, for him to be whispering. I don't know, maybe they aren't whispering: it's as though all I can hear are the goddamn flies, like a radio station off the air for the night—a low *hmmmzaat*. As Williams moves up, he walks hunchback to carry the weight of the radio and his ruck. My ruck straps cut into me all the way down the trail, but I didn't notice the ache much until now. Fuckit. All we have to do is get these slings another thirty meters, cut a hole, and catch the ride back to the LZ.

Before I know it, Eltee is at my side.

"We're about ready to move," he says. His face is like a clock, so exact is the intensity of his expression. I notice his nose looks wider on one side than the other. J listen to what he says, and it seems to repeat through my mind even after he's gone.

We'll be up and move fast. We're dropping the ponchos on signal. Three of us go out for security and the other three hack a hole in the weeds, good enough for a bird to come down long enough to pick up the pieces; when that bird is gone, another one will come in to get us. I'm going to be one who cuts.

My mouth feels like I've been sucking on a rubber band. The nylon pads in my shoulder straps look freshly painted, so I feel conscious of every one of the 500 more seconds we sit there.

Eltee is still up front with Prophet. I can see them both through a hole in the trees. Eltee is talking on the radio some of the time. Like watching T.V., first one of their faces shows in the hole, then the other.

We're up. I get the signal from Prophet and pass it on to Peacock who passes it on. Now we pick up the sling. Heavy. This time I'm very conscious of my rifle swinging in front of me. I've gotten used to having it in my hand when I want it and right now I want it.

We hustle. It hurts. Everything—my back, my head where the steel pot has bounced, my arms from having the sling behind me, my feet, my chafing asshole, even my goddamn eyes from sleeplessness. I hurt inside, too. I feel like a piece of shit, like nobody. But, on we go. In five minutes we're into the swamp. The water is quickly up to my shins, finally up to my balls. It doesn't feel warm nor cold nor thick nor clean, just wet and one more thing to fight against. We drop the poncho and it half sinks. The flies are there, like they're pissed off. They swirl in a wave like paint flung off a roller. I hate them. Air escapes from the poncho and comes to the surface, and the water turns color from the mud we stir up and the blood. It becomes the color of aged leather.

By pure luck, we stumble upon a hard bottom. So, we can stand up and hack away at the bushes exactly at water level. It's me, Prophet, and Peacock. We don't speak. We give it hell, our machetes swirling. The bushes are mostly easy to cut. It doesn't take long to cut a 10-foot by 10-foot hole down to the water line and it isn't long after that that the bird arrives.

It comes over the tree line like a hotrod cresting some country hill, then settles over us with the motion that only helicopters have, a gliding sort of motion, with its tail swerving from side to side. The machine gunners give us a long peace sign. We half carry, half float the ponchos over. It takes four of us to get them out of the water and into the bird. As we're loading the second one, trying to keep the chopped up grass and water out of our eyes and struggling to keep our footing, rounds begin pelting the windshield of the helicopter and either the pilot or copilot gets hit. I dive into the water and weeds and futilely try to keep my rifle up.

Rounds begin to ricochet all over hell. The gunners open up, firing directly over our heads into the woodline. The shell casings come off the gun in a perfect arc and some of them land on the grass we have cut that floats on the water now. I'm disoriented and afraid to fire because I don't know where anybody else is, but I get my safety off and try to be careful to keep the barrel pointed up while I work my way, staying oh so low, away from where the bird is. I glance quickly at it, and I can see the gunner taking the vibration of his gun with exact concentration. There is scurrying behind him and either the other gunner or a crew chief is leaned into the cockpit, probably aiding the pilot. I catch sight of Peacock who has his Sixty at shoulder height. He is pouring rounds out towards the treeline.

The helicopter gets up and hovers for only an instant before it banks slightly and takes off away from the treeline we're facing. It circles though, and comes back over, stirring up the water and cut weeds. It passes over the treeline and both gunners fire continually. Then it comes back again and keeps a steady stream of rounds slashing into the treelines.

Eltee is yelling and signaling to make a circle. He has the radio mike in his hand. His rifle is slung downward and the AK is strapped to the radio. Prophet and Callme come out of the weeds behind him and run as best they can through the water until they reach the edge of our cut. Pops and I begin making it toward the cleared spot from opposite sides. Pops' face is covered with blood. I can't tell if he has been hit or not. Just as I get to where I intend to stop, there is an explosion a few meters on the other side of Peacock. Then, another one; then two more. Mortars. The bursts hit the swamp in tandems now. First, two beyond us; then two in front of us. Peacock is trying to move back to our position, but he has to get down every time a mortar lands. They have the range on those tubes now, so I expect the next rounds to come right on top of us. The helicopter is still hanging above the treeline, firing.

Four more mortars. The first two are off target, but the second ones land almost right on top of Lt. Williams, maybe sixty feet away from me on the other side of the clearing. He screams. The wave of water from the mortar's concussion passes by me and there is still shit in the air. Pops slips out of his ruck and begins to work his way towards Eltee. Everybody else begins to pump rounds into the treeline. I fire about where the helicopter is working out because I thought I saw a muzzle flash come from somewhere near there. As I am looking I' see one for sure, a few feet off the ground. I squeeze three or four careful rounds off at where I saw it, then have to change magazines and when I look up again, the spot is being torn apart by fire from the bird's Sixties. I cheer to myself. Kill the fuckers. I expect more mortars any time.

Pops is coming back towards us. He has the radio in one hand and is dragging Eltee behind him in a sort of backwards walking fireman's carry. Eltee is no longer screaming. A second helicopter comes over the opposite treeline. Eltee is dead.

The first helicopter continues working on the treeline and the second one comes at us rapidly. We all make a break for it. I go to Pops to help him. Together, we manage to get to the bird with our gear and the body. He didn't live past the scream. More than half of that handsome black face has been ripped back towards his skull. As long as the body was in the water, the blood didn't show much, but when we are loaded and drag the body in after us, a pool of blood the color of fire spreads across the floor. We're all in, we're up, we head away from the treeline, high above which the bird with the ponchos full of bodies now hovers. Exhaustion hits and my body feels like a wet paper bag.

Jesus, there's no way to describe the ride. We got up fast, over a set of mountains, then up again. Riding along on the vibration of the bird is like being wind-rocked in a hammock. The five of us are sitting towards the front. I am leaning against the aluminum wall that defines the cockpit. The machine gunner is between me and the open door; past him I can see a patchy sky and beyond that I can see mountains, mountains, mountains.

The sound of the rotor is steady.

Rump thump thump rump thump.

God, I stink. I've been sweating into these same clothes for at least ten days now. I've been wallowing around in swamp water.

My mind just roams around like my eyes. The door gunner on my side is dark-complexioned and stocky. His mustache is trimmed and just a dab of black hair shows below the headset helmet. The back of his helmet has something painted on it, but I can't read it. Across from me, against the wall on the other side of the doorway to the cockpit, Pops is slumped into a heap. He's filthy. There is a line of mud that runs from the top of his head, over his face and through his mustache, through the hair on his belly, down to his pants. His shirt is unbuttoned and his flak jacket isn't hooked. Just a trace of a paunch hangs over the belt loops. He looks thinner now than he did just a month ago.

The others are leaning against whatever there is to lean against, and towards the back is Eltee's body. I stare at it and it doesn't seem like he could be dead. I can't see his head that is half mincemeat now, and I can't really believe he will never move again. Dead. Goddamn dead. It could've been anybody. He got a mortar; the dinks weren't going for the radio and they weren't going for him because he was an officer. They were just going for anybody, and trying to disable the helicopters. I wonder who will have to write a report up on this mission, and I wonder what Lt. Williams' family will find out.

Thump rump kathump kathump kathump. We are descending. I have to sit up straight to see the Z below us and I feel so tired. As we come down we scoot towards the door. It isn't easy because the bird isn't level and the ruck seems to weigh more than ever. I'm so tired. I just want to lie down. It seems like there should be more waiting for us than this goddamn hill full of holes. This, my man, is home for now. The lieutenant doesn't even have this. He's dead. There is his body.

Fifty feet up, then thirty. It's like working on a high, high ladder. The guys on the ground all move away from the pad and cover their eyes. Parts of C-ration cartons whirl up as high as we are and dive through the crazy air currents like bats going after insects in a porch light. All the dudes on the ground are wearing flak jackets and a lot of them have helmets on. The landing pad is built out of sandbags and from a few feet up it reminds me of a caned chairseat. We settle between two big slings of ammunition. After the bird shuts down to a low speed, guys start again at unloading the slings and carrying the ammo away. Most of it is for our mortars and artillery. The rounds come in wooden boxes about two feet long.

Over by the big guns are stacks of the ammo crates and guys are carrying these empties away to fill full of sand and build hootches.

The C.O. comes over to the bird with his face down. He is a stern-looking guy, maybe thirty years old. His expression isn't mean-looking but it sure as hell isn't happy-looking. He reaches up and helps us off the bird, just puts his hand under our rucks. When he helps me off, he is already looking at whoever is behind me.

"There's coffee over there," he says to all of us. "I want to see the whole squad in a few minutes."

We all drop our rucks as soon as we're far enough away from the pad. Getting the ruck off is like taking a good shit. It's cloudy and there's dust in the air from something. Since we've been out, there have probably been a couple thousand sandbags filled. Some are laid into flat parapet walls and some of the hootches are getting to be deep enough for roofs. Ammo crates and full sandbags make squat, solid, walls.

Most of three companies are on the Z now and it has spread out like a carnival parking lot. When we started to dig in, we were on the outside of the perimeter, but now the perimeter has moved out in all directions.

There are two guys sitting near the coffee pot smoking and waiting for us. They have been humping ammo from the pad.

"Hey, what it is?"

"It is a muthafucker," Pops says. It seems like a long time since I have heard his voice.

"You guys the squad that got some dinks last night?"

"Yeah, four. How bad was it here?"

"Bad, man. Mostly incoming, but they almost broke through on the other side of the hill. Over there." The guy points to our right.

"Charlie put some shit in here last night," the other guys says.

He emphasizes "put" by pounding his rifle's butt plate against the ammo crate he has his feet resting on.

"82's?"

"Mostly."

"He was keying on that side of the hill. We were over there, the other side, and everything went over us, wounded one guy out on L.P. Alpha Company got it the worst. I heard six K.I.A.'s and twenty wounded."

"Our Eltee ate an 82 round."

"Dead?"

"Fuckin-A dead."

"Anybody else get hit?"

"Nope. Freaky. We were loading those goddamn dinks and Charlie walked about a dozen round in."

"Bravo Company is going to move out that direction."

"You guys from Bravo?"

"Yeah. We aren't even digging in, but they keep trying to stick us on Ammo Detail."

"Well, man, Charlie's out there. Even though it musta been bad here last night, I'd rather be .here tonight."

"Dig it, but at least our whole company's going out."

I'm surprised the coffee tastes good. C-ration coffee sucks.

This came from a big urn shaped like a fire hydrant. There are some shit-green food cans lined up behind the coffee, but it looks like the food must have come in sometime yesterday because some of these cans have shrapnel in them. After I get my coffee, I sit down on a pile of sandbags that have been filled but not tied off yet. I can see the bad side of the Z, where there must be twenty shallow craters. The thing I didn't expect to see is the shrapnel holes everywhere and even a few small pieces of shrap. There's none nearby, but I can see it glint in the sun in a few paths.

Big guns sound somewhere. I wonder what time it is. The sun is still a little above the west ridge of mountains. I'd guess it will be dark in four hours. I wonder if these guys from Bravo are going to try to get dug in tonight. I look at them and try to see the fear that I know IS somewhere in their faces.

One guy is Italian-looking. He is sitting on one of the melomite cans, sipping coffee from his canteen cup.

"Eltee didn't have a shot at it," Callme says.

I don't feel like saying anything. I helped float his body through the water. I flash on the body over there in the bird in a pool of blood. The C.O. is just starting back from the pad. Even though there isn't any dust flying now, he still walks with his face down. Somebody is leaning into the helicopter. Slowly, the rotor starts to turn and when the C.O. gets to us, the bird is starting off. We all have to shield ourselves from the shit that flies around. When I look up, the C.O. is looking at Peacock, who's still looking down. So the C.O. looks right at me.

"What's your name, soldier."

"Gabriel Sauers, sir."

"Tell me about it."

"About the patrol?"

"Yeah, from the time you made contact."

"Well," I don't know what to say. Talking to an officer always bothers me. Eltee was an officer though, too. "Well," I say again, "it all happened awful fast. We were set up on a trail and me and Callme were pretty close together and the rest of them were spread out. Peacock was ahead of us with the Sixty. We heard them coming and somebody blew the Claymores. I could see the explosion and some action. I emptied a clip and reloaded. That's all I know."

"Did you hear anything afterwards?"

"Nothing, sir."

"Who's the squad leader?"

"I am," Pops says. He doesn't add, "sir."

"What's your name, sergeant?"

"Pops," he says. He has undone his pants and is standing there talking to the C.O. with his dick out, rubbing one finger all around the jungle rot on his balls. I notice the C.O. has rot, too, on his neck.

"You have anything to add, Pops?"

"I don't think Eltee Williams should be dead."

"What are you saying, soldier?"

"I think somebody fucked up back here. Those dinks were in pieces no bigger than these damn sandbags and there was no reason to bring 'em back here, but we hadda goddamn carry 'em down the fuckin' hill and into that clearing. ANYfuckin' body woulda known the dinks were gonna drop some shit in there, but if we coulda' got right in and right out of the edge of it, then Eltee wouldn't have gotten fuckin killed. They walked 'em right in on us."

"Sergeant, your squad killed four enemies who might be responsible for killing ten GIs. That's what you have to think of. And," he puts his hand on Pops' hand which is still on his nuts, and looks around at all of us, "I understand how you feel. There's nothing I can do about it. Echo Company didn't make the decision, you know that. Listen, I know how you feel."

The way he says it, the way he looks around at all of us with a tiny little smile, the way he gives Pops' ball-handling wrist an additional shank... something makes me think he does know how Pops feels, and probably how I feel even if I don't. I feel a lump, or something, in my throat. Prophet spits, Callme spits, Peacock spits. The C.O. turns to leave and spits.

DON BODEY

6 Poems (iii)

G.I. MAN IN VIET NAM

Dear G.I. Man in Viet Nam who in the jungles lie
And you who came back home to find the world had passed you by:
The weapon that has always won, you used without complaint—
Yourself you gave so generously and duty with restraint.

Between the steely bullets that seemed to have no power—
With all the little people, you spent a friendly hour,
The children gathered 'round you, the little ones you fed;
Your honest love they understood, if not all that you said.

And now in days of crises when pushed into the sea,
These little people suddenly grow to brave maturity;
The fires of memory burn bright: on earth where shall they go?
Where else but to the freedom land from which your love did flow!

And so they strive against all odds in peril day and night
plant their feet where once you walked-to gain the same delight.
Insight to work, to pray, to love—in shadow of the free—
With freedom's soul gained for themselves and their posterity.

Hear then, both living and the dead---away from freedom's shore,
five thousand miles away, you did not lose one war:
That war, hear me, you won, though death sealed deep regret,
The world was witness to your love, and this it can't forget:

Great is that nation under God that by His grace did find
The only battle that is won is that of heart and mind;
Your optimum of sacrifice to death or life of pain,
We pledge to you, kind G.I Man, will never be in vain!

SARAH BESS GEIBEL

RICE WILL GROW AGAIN

We were walking
On the dikes
Like damn fools -
Steppin' over dud rounds.
>Mitch was steppin' light
>When he saw the farmer.
>The farmer
>With black shirt
>And shorts.
>Up to his knees
>In the muck
>Rice shoots in one hand,
>The other darting
>Under the water
>And into the muck
>To plant new life.

Mitch saw the farmer's hand
Going down again
With another
>Shoot
>>But the hand
>>Never came up
>>Again -

After Mitch
Ripped the farmer up the middle
With a burst of sixteen

We passed the farmer
As we walked
Along the dike, and
I saw rice shoots
Still clutched in one hand.
He bubbled strange words
Through the blood
In his mouth.
Bong, the scout,
Told us the farmer
Said:
>"Damn you
>The rice will
>Grow again!"

Sometimes,
On dark nights In Indiana
The farmer comes to
>Mitch's bed,
And plants rice shoots
>all around.

FRANK A. CROSS, JR.

UNTITLED

Hush, hush
    Quiet time is near
    Sound
    so alive and vibrant today
Has fled
    Leaving the field to one
    you will not hear
    Without noise
    It has come
Already it's leaving
    Silent journey
    Passing
    through time
Eternal
    Sparing
    Not
    one.

                                        T.K.

FORGOTTEN WARRIORS

Nobody seems to give a damn
for those who fought in Viet Nam
And what about the men still there
in mind or body, don't you care?

After all wars, scars remain
but can't you help to ease the pain?
Apathy is a trend today
for those who fought and have to pay
the price of being proud to serve
all those who didn't have the nerve.

It was a war we should have won
but we shame those who held a gun.
They followed orders and were proud.
They would have won, but weren't allowed.

So why should they take all the blame
when they already share the pain?

Of all our vets, we were once proud.
We praised and cheered them very loud.
But now we all look down on them
when most of them would fight again.

Some still wake in sweat and fear
and no one's helped in all these years.

Unite and fight to recognize
the men who gave and risked their lives.
It's not too late to help them now
Come join our brothers
We'll show you how.

LONNA KIMMEL

HUNG IN DESPAIR

I look at the floor—avoiding...
the contact I have so desperately needed
the floor being my escape from...
my piercing pain—the same pain that
has left no scars or scratches for the unwary
eye—that naive and purposefully ignorant
eye that the American society has fostered and
nurtured
prying—my eyes bury themselves in
the seams and patterns of the unending floor
my mind aghast—alone here am I but
for my brother whose pain I must bear with mine
I know there are those who care but...
it is pain after all these years being alone
I know nothing else—with my head finally
hung in despair

He told me he loved me for the prodding and poking
that had been administered in brotherly love
it was too little and it was too late
too much additional pain had been heaped on by
a people and a country caught up in the heavy denial
of its own terminal diseases
for Rudy it was and is too late to live life as we know it
but the Rudys are around and about us and
if we are receptive to what they can show us—all of us
it won't be to late for us
I love you Rudy and all the Rudy's

Written in memory of a warm and beautiful human being - Rudy Meier

RICK RITTER

7

The Viet Nam File

By Paul Richard Wappenstein, Jr.

A funny thing happened on the way to work the other day. I began remembering. There was clarity of thought in Viet Nam. I imagine it's always been that way in wars. Morality is reduced to right and wrong. Right is reduced to survival. Whatever it takes. Spend a few years thinking that way and you'd be surprised how fast you can lose friends when you come back home.

It might not surprise you how hard it is to make new friends... except with those who understand. You take a lifetime learning to separate good and bad, and that much of life falls in between. You become part of a group of people who spend a lot of time and money teaching you that's not the way you should act. Throwaway morality. Grab them by the balls... twist and yank down. A man will be dead before he hits the ground. Another way is to stick your finger into the side of a man's throat... once all the way through, hook your finger and yank. There's no grey in death. Just dark. A decision that's been made with no way to go back. A decision that's made by someone else. Funny thing about being dead. It's only messy to those who aren't. The ones who are part of the decision. When you make enough decisions, you begin to see things differently. Clearly. Like looking at a man who has a giant hole blown in the top of his head, his brains spilling out slowly on the ground. There's a strange warmth that oozes out of a human being, no matter how hot it is outside. Flies don't gather right away, either, no matter what others tell you. They take awhile. The rest of him twisted in some strange fashion. I never knew that the human body could bend that way. There's something good about clean decisions. Like a weight off your back. Afterwards you just want to relax. Smoke a doobie, listen to some music. Maybe drink some Ba Muoui Ba, a local beer. Listen to some music.

Ever since *Apocalypse Now*, most people associate the Doors with the war. Bet you never knew that Frank Sinatra was pretty popular there. And a lot of good Hank Williams. He was great to drink beer to. Some nights, we'd be real shitfaced, a trip flare would go off, we'd run down to the perimeter and play shoot 'em up. Didn't matter what was there... or who. Like the time we decided to kill all the dogs because of a fear of rabies. There was this little puppy. Somebody put him on the ground and took a shot at him. He didn't die. That little sucker took off through the wires. Everybody opened up on him. Thought for sure we had killed him. The little bastard tried coming back through the wires about 15 minutes later. We opened up on him again. Scared the shit out of us. We thought the dog was gonna live no matter what. That would have really screwed us up. When something is supposed to die and it doesn't... kind of scary. Fortunately... he died. When I was a kid, I really loved dogs. I wonder what happened. I guess you have to give up your sense of guilt. If you don't, you'll end up blowing your brains out. Sometimes you think about that. It's like there's no real purpose. And maybe that's right. Sometimes it's a real struggle to hold on to my sanity. Other times I know that it's the world that's nuts. Like we're a giant mental institution for the rest of the universe. They stop by once in awhile... check us out and see if we're still around. That's why we've never discovered life anywhere else. They don't want any contact with us. They're not nuts.

That's what it was like coming back home. Nobody wanted any contact with us. Imagine... a nut being treated like a nut by a group of nuts. Talk about nutty. I knew how people with M.S. felt. You can see and understand what everyone else is doing. You just can't do it yourself. Other people think they'll get what you have if they touch you. You want to tell them it's not contagious... but what the hell... they'd never believe you. So you quit dealing with them. Then a new kind of insanity starts. You lose your self. No more identity. It stays that way for a long time until you've put it all away... when enough dust builds up that it seems to have disappeared. Finally, it seems like you can begin dealing with the outside world. You fake it... get through... pretty soon you really do forget. You forget what you've done to yourself. You forget you ever gave the bastards the power to do what they did. You go through the motions, believing your own lie. Until the winds begin. Something comes along to stir up the dust.

There's something new with the memories. An anger. This time it's clearer. You look around and realize all the sentiment and talk you hear now... wasn't there 10 years ago. When you needed the help, they weren't there. Now they want to talk about Viet Nam. Now it's OK. Well, you sons of bitches, you've done everything but kill us over the last 15 to 20 years. You've pissed on our souls, and scorched our memories with your silence. And now you want to talk about Viet Nam. Well, I don't want to talk about Viet Nam. I want to talk about those people you owe. Whether their names are on a wall or not. Men who died and men who live. You've let the bastards poison us in the name of corporate profit. You've locked us up because we never quite made it all the way home. You've defamed us and made us monsters to our children. No more. You've exploited us for the last time. It's time to pay the bill. Treatment for victims of Agent Orange. Treatment for post traumatic stress disorder. Discharges upgraded for men who were no more than victims of your inability to deal with Viet Nam. A veteran's administration that is responsive to the needs of Viet Nam era veterans. Educational benefits that are comparable to all other veterans. More outreach centers. More funding. Non-interference by government agencies in our programs. And one more note... leave our wall alone. If it makes you feel a sense of shame, then it did what it was supposed to. The way you treated us was a fucking disgrace.

Sometimes all this remembering can twist you up inside. Little drops of pain splashing around in your guts. There's a fancy name for it... post traumatic stress disorder... PTSD... they didn't have that name when I first came down with it. Most people thought it was bullshit. Another veteran lookin' for a fucking excuse. The V.A. Hospital in Indianapolis was really great for that. The Viet Nam Drug Rehabilitation Clinic. Another fancy name. This one as useless as tits on a bull. A priest for a psychologist... nurses right out of *One*

Flew Over The Cuckoo's Nest... and two ex-junkie counselors who'd never been any closer to Viet Nam than a travel poster. They said drugs were a cover up... a cop out... a symptom, not the real problem. They were right. There was only one problem. They didn't think Viet Nam had a whole hell of a lot to do with it either. I never was quite sure of what they thought the problem really was. I don't think they were too sure themselves. They were more concerned about getting you back out on the streets. Talk about a cover up. We kept trying to talk about the Nam. Thought of all the places in the world we could do that in safety... a Viet Nam Rehabilitation Program ought to be the place, right? What a crock of shit.

I'll tell you what I learned there. How to play their game. How not to talk about the Nam. They'd brainwashed me again! Don't tell me my mother never raised any stupid children. Christ, measure stupidity in terms of susceptibility to bullshit and I'd of won the fucking prize. I got out of there and thought I'd been born again. Of course I had to get out of there. Seems the law was after me. My ex-wife wanted child support... or my ass in jail. The hospital was going to turn me over to the sheriff. I said, "wait a minute, you can't do that. I'm a patient." They said, "Watch this." So they set it up for my discharge later that day. From a ward to a jail. Nice life.

Well, one of the nurses wasn't having any part of that crap. She told me to get my stuff together and get the hell out of there before the cops came. I said, "Yes, Ma'm", and split. If you think I'm a real asshole for not paying child support, you might be right. But think about this. I hadn't known where my children were for the past two years. My ex was busy telling everybody who would listen that I was crazy... a fucking crazed Viet Nam vet. Later in life when I finally saw my kids, I found out what she told them. Seems I had died in Viet Nam. I wonder if she ever knew how close to the truth she was?

The counselors at the hospital were right in a way. It wasn't Viet Nam that screwed me up so much. It was the coming home. When you come home to divorce papers, something snaps. I'd spent all that time in Nam with one thought keepin' me going. The thought of my kids. And the time we'd have together. That dream kept me goin'. Then I got a chance to watch somebody smash that dream. I went crazy. The insanity didn't end until my oldest daughter came to live with me eight years later. Only then did my life begin to straighten out. It's amazing how much a child can teach you about life. The care and love they help you find in yourself. But the years in between...

The divorce was only the first of my welcome back. That happened during my last six months in the corps. I'd spent over 7 years in the Marines. I was on my way to becoming a lifer, but Nam changed that attitude. I remember a First Sergeant of mine. We'd been lob bombed the night before. Flame tanks were sent out the next morning to burn the local village to the ground. All the people were told to get out. Funny thing about some people, they just don't want to leave their homes... places they'd lived all their lives. Liquid fire, black smoke and human screams. First Sergeant Jones and I just stood

M-67 "Zippo" Flame Tank

there and watched from the hill. Tears were rolling down his face. His words "This isn't what it's about." That was the first time I realized I wasn't alone in my feelings. We talked about it a year later over a beer. The day the village burned was the day he decided it was time to get out. So had I.

I'd forgotten the sound of those screams... until today. We were part of an artillery battery attached to the 7th Marines. One of their companies used to carry hatchets. They'd cut off an ear of dead V.C. and string 'em... like you do with fish. They only did it for a little while. Something about deteriorating flesh. I never ran into anyone who called me a baby killer when I came home. Might have felt better if I had. Somebody to strike out at for daring to tell the truth. I tried going to college. That lasted for about 5 months. Indiana University. Listed in the *Underground College Guide* as one of the party schools of the Mid-West. Also a center for anti-war activities. I was 25, just out of the Marine Corps, going through a divorce, trying to study... and surrounded by a group of teenagers who didn't have the slightest idea what the Nam was about. How could they. None of us who had been there had any idea what it was about. We just knew what it wasn't about. They said the war was wrong. Well, this is 1983 and I wonder how 6 million Cambodians feel about our pulling out. Those kids didn't feel the war was wrong. They just didn't want to put their asses on the line. What was wrong about the war was the way the politicians and the generals wanted to fight it... and didn't want to fight it. In *"The Betrayal"*, Bill Corson said that a lot of privates and PFCs were earning the colonels' and the generals' pay for them. He was right. There's no such thing as moderation in war. If you're going to fight the son-of-a-bitch, then fight it completely. If you're not committed to that level, then get the fuck out.

Colonels' decisions to burn down villages were stupid. If somebody shoots at you, shoot back. But don't go burn down his neighbor's house and kill his nieces and nephews. If you can't find the guy who shot at you, then count your losses and wait for the next time. What's so complicated about that? Oh, I know that doesn't take into consideration all the political aspects of Viet Nam. But what the hell. How many of us have ever stopped to realize the full political implications of Viet Nam to begin with? Our problem with Viet Nam was not that we never should have gotten involved in it. Just the opposite. We should have gotten involved in it the first time we were asked... 1942. That's when Ho Chi Minh asked Roosevelt to help keep the French out after WWII ended. Roosevelt was inclined to do just that. Unfortunately, for the Vietnamese, F.D.R. died too soon. His replacement in the White House, Harry "The Buck Stops Here" Truman, couldn't make up his fucking mind about Viet Nam, or Indo-China, as it was known then. So the French came back in. We all know what happened at Diên Biên Phu. The French got their asses kicked. You hear all that shit about them trying to fight a conventional war against a non-conventional army. They were fighting against a people who wanted their God damned country back. That's all. They were determined. Remember the thing called the Right of Self Determination? Do you think they could have done that shit without a lot of belief in themselves? An interesting thing happened when we got involved. It ought to show you how politicians use words to distort reality.

Up until this time, the fighting forces of Ho Chi Minh and the guerrillas of the southern portion were known as Viet Minh. Literally translated, that means Vietnamese Nationalist. Suddenly they were being called Viet Cong. That means Vietnamese communist.

We couldn't fight Nationalist forces. Christ, we'd just been involved in World War II where we spent a lot of time supporting Nationalist forces. Like the French. But this was the early fifties. Hating communism was a national pastime. And now we had some more communists to hate. And we could do it in the name of democracy... and capitalism. Here's how capitalism worked a la Viet Nam. In 1967, we gave a rice shucking machine to a local villager. We couldn't give it to the whole village. That would have been socialistic. Well, the villager we gave it to decided to charge his neighbors so much money... they couldn't afford to use it. So he rented it out to some other villages. Needless to say, he got wealthy... courtesy of the United States Government. But we didn't help that village. And they remembered. Villagers throughout the countryside remembered something else, also. We were nothing more than another Frenchman getting rich off of them. Another Frenchman killing their families. Another Frenchman trying to tell them what to do. And they wanted us out. There was another difference now. Democracy didn't look so good anymore. We'd made an enemy out of a friend. It had taken us a score or so of years to do it, but we had managed. Now we were going to really have a fight.

McNamara's answer to fighting was to draw a line across the border of Nnorth and South Viet Nam. Put a fence on the line and put troops along the fence. This idiot was trying to fight the Korean War in the Nam. Before you could put a fence across the country, you had to get rid of the vegetation.

Welcome Dow Chemical. Fuck the troops. Kill the trees. The Pentagon and Dow did both. Fucked us and killed the vegetation. Now we're finding out that Dow knew more than it was saying. What the hell. Seven dollars a barrel for all those barrels was a lot of money. It was a strange war. We could spend all kinds of money on fences and chemicals and bombs. But we couldn't let the grunt fight. Don't shoot at Vietnamese carrying lanterns at night. They're friendlies. The Russians don't have anything to fear from this country. Our generals will always figure out some way to fuck things up. So will our politicians. That's why we ended up "losing the war". Politicians trying to be slick and generals trying to be politicians. And us paying the price. We're still paying.

After the war, a lot of people saw us as the first military people to ever lose a war. There weren't any welcome flags hanging out. The VFW. and the American Legion said stay away. We don't want you. Oh, they'll tell you that's not true. Bullshit. Lately they've had to take us in. They're dying off. They need new blood. Some Viet vets are joining. But many of us are staying away. Who wants to belong to a group of people who spent years denying anything like Post Viet Nam Syndrome? Who wants to spend time around a group of people who sit around the bar getting drunk, telling war stories until they fall off the bar stool? Those assholes don't have any idea what's happening to the Viet Nam era vet. They just need more money coming in

**Sweeping over the treetops, this C-123 Ranch Hand aircraft
sprays defoliant over the target area. 01/1967 (Source: Nat'l Archives)**

through membership dues. Talk to them about Agent Orange and they get kind of scared. We might end up taking all their space in V.A. hospitals. Talk to politicians about Agent Orange. They get scared too. They might have to start paying us... and our children. Talk to them about Post Traumatic Stress. The fear comes up again. Suddenly we might have to understand why so many Viet Nam Vets have been to jail. Cops might not get to break any more doors down and kill vets who are suffering flashbacks. Or beat up on vets who are going through rough times.

Some Viet Vet cops might begin understanding why they're so quick to pull a gun or beat up on somebody. Yeah, don't talk to these people they might begin to see who they are.

January, 1981... the Iranian hostages are returned to the United States. They are given a hero's welcome with ticker tape parades. Welcome back, folks. We cared and we're glad to see you back.

January, 1981... 34 year old Gary Cooper... (just like in the movies)... barricades himself in his apartment in Hammond, Indiana. Police surround the apartment. Cooper is holding his wife and 8 year old daughter. Police order him to come out and surrender. He refuses. He lets his wife and daughter go. Police unleash a barrage of small arms, shotgun and rifle fire into his apartment. The former Marine Viet Vet is found dead when police finally enter the apartment. He had a double-barreled shotgun. His body was behind a large plant in the corner. Cooper was used to bullets. He had two purple hearts from the Nam. Before he let his wife go, he told her, "They come to get me." His step-parents and his wife said he was re-living his Nam experiences. Welcome home, Gary. We're glad to see you back.

And so it goes.

August, 1983... Police in Pasco, Washington, say a man went on a rampage in a quiet neighborhood Saturday and killed two men with a kitchen knife. A third man was critically injured. The police believe the suspect... George Johnson, a veteran of Viet Nam... was having a flashback and thought he was fighting enemy troops. (AP 08-22-1983)

It strikes from anywhere. Life will be fine and then... bam!

All of the instincts are back. All of the aggressions. Survival is the name of the game. If that makes me crazy... well, what can I say. Whenever I feel this way, I tell myself it's just a way of gaining sympathy and attention. Then I force it all back down. Focus on something else. Anything else. Just get away. The words are fading now. I need to go. Someplace.

I look back on those years and compare them with the prior years and the ones that followed. The first few years in the Marine Corps were filled with a sense of confidence that bordered on arrogance. By the time I got out, there was nothing inside. Not even coldness. Leaves had more sense of direction than I did. A lot of wandering. Trying to be part of something anything. Always there was isolation. I could be at a party laughing and joking with everyone else and another part of me would be standing off to the side... just watching. I must have traveled all over this country during that time of my life. Odd jobs. Sometimes living off the land. That's a euphemism for being broke and ripping off anybody you had to just to survive. At least it is if you live in the cities. Work one job for a few months. Then move on.

That part of me has gotten a little better. But not much. It has nothing to do with other people. It's me. Something inside me. But I don't know what. And I don't know if I ever will. Sometimes it's frustrating. Now, though, I see it differently. I don't want to translate my feelings through my feet. I'm beginning to change. All those years I didn't have a chance to be like normal folks are going through me now. Only at a faster than normal pace. I guess I'm gettin' too tired to fight the changes in who I am. Maybe that's what It's all about. Don't fight the change. Fight the resistance to change. I'm beginning to think those of us who fought in Viet Nam are going to get called into another type of action soon. An action where we're going to serve as this nation's conscience.

I listened to a man talk last night. He said this was the first time in the history of this country when former soldiers were not chosen as leaders. He said he thought that was a major part of the problem in this country for the past 15 years. He also felt that was changing. He may be right. We know the pitfalls of non-commitment. Not only by the government's behavior during the war. Our own non-commitment. Our unwillingness to deal with problems that we faced as a group. We have been denying responsibility for our own lives. We have not yet learned to separate what we have done to our selves and what was done to us. Only by understanding the difference will we begin healing our wounds. I cannot help everyone. I can help myself and those who understand me. Now... if I only have the courage to.

The violence of Viet Nam is not the only violence of our lives. Nor is it the only factor we have in common. It is simply the tie that binds. We've been surrounded by violence since day one. The violence of words... the violence of actions... the violence of stereotypes and roles. Quietly enduring the pain of men-children. Viet Nam was simply the passage into manhood. Sometimes when I look at it, I see a four dimensional picture, including the irrelativeness of time, painted against a dark screen. The colors of life starting out in the distant background, increasing in size and intensity until they finally culminate in the Nam. It's there that all the learned violence of life came into play. Whether it was used or not is really unimportant. Viet Nam was the epitome of violence... an immersion in a way of life. The end of a natural road.

But, from day one until the end of our involvement in the war, there was a proportional progression. One step led to the next. Each step caused a growing knowledge. A growing awareness. More violence. My father beating my mother made sense in boot camp. Women were weak. And when men were weak, we called them women. And we beat them for not carrying their load or doing their job. They were less than men. They were male children gone soft. Tears and feelings other than anger or self-righteousness were for women. So was sharing. We isolated ourselves. The strong silent type. Like John Wayne or Vic Morrow. Men prisoners were treated differently than women. They had been initiated into the life of warriors. Not so with the women. They were sneaky bitches. We were dominant. We were right. We were fighting evil. Destroying wrong. In destroying wrong we were saving others. The killing of the enemy became justified. So were the deaths of our own. No greater gift hath one man than to lay down his life for another. And so... we were great. We could not understand how anyone could question our actions. After all, we were our country. As there is a general building toward violence, there is a general decreasing in violence... or at least a time for reflection. Not so with Viet Nam. The immersion in war was cut off for us like a giant machete had sliced through the picture of the Nam.

Out of it spilled a small trickle of life... a thread with which to begin all over again. The violence in us was still there. It had not been allowed to end in its own right. It had no place to go. People in this country did not understand that. They were part of our culture, yet, they had no understanding of it. Situations of violence presented themselves to many of us. When children smell strawberry incense, they think of strawberries and how good they taste. When people hear the sounds of carnivals, they remember the days of Ferris wheels and roller coasters. When we hear the sound of cars backfiring, we think of death. Is there really such a difference in death and strawberries? Both are memories. Both are real. Our acts of violence cause us to turn and look in our minds. All we see is Viet Nam. We forget what occurred before. If we had been given the time for reflection if we had been allowed the natural order of progression or decompression... we might be able to better understand ourselves.

Our anger is as natural as the growing of corn in spring. You have fertilized it with your spit and your garbage and it has grown. You left us alone, hoping the weeds would kill us. We just have not turned out to be quite the field you expected to harvest. We have grown taller and stronger than any field you have planted before. We will not become old and withered corn on the stalk, destroying our roots with alcohol. We have caught on to that game. The VFW.'s and the American Legions are not for us.

You call us radicals... ne'er do wells... cry babies. We're beginning to fight back. We will be silent no more. You have used us. You will not use our children, our brothers and sisters children for your wars again. Not without a fight.

When I joined the Marine Corps, my father told me I was becoming a part of the most right winged organization in the country. I thought I was becoming a part of the most patriotic.

I was also becoming a man... I was going to prove it. My father was right. America for Americans. White Anglo-Saxon and Protestant. This was no place for fish eaters or kikes or niggers. In boot camp, drill instructors made comments about how blacks couldn't seem to shoot as well as whites. About how stupid they were. What he didn't tell us was how well they could die. Just like the rest of us. Racism became a problem in the Nam. It should have. It was a racist war... amongst other things. Funny though... when Blacks banded together for protection or fought with Whites, they were the ones who were racist. When Whites picked on Blacks, it was self-defense. After all, you know how niggers are when they get together. A war within a war. An officer corps that would have made the Confederacy proud. The same with many staff-NCO's. It's difficult to get many Black Veterans to associate with Viet Nam Vet's groups. It's also easy to understand. Discrimination had followed them to Southeast Asia. Not even in war were they treated as equals. Sometimes, not even in death. When they came home, it was back to the ghettos. Try telling a man who has risked his life for what his country said was right to take his place at the back of the bus.

You're going to have a fight on your hands. And that's what happened. Look around you. The unemployment amongst black Veterans. The number of black Veterans in our maximum security prisons throughout the country. Racism at its best. Is it no wonder they want nothing to do with Viet Nam veterans' groups. Is it no wonder they try to shut the war from their memories. Those of us who are white, could clean up our acts. Shave our beards. Deny the war. Hide in Middle America. Not so with many Black American vets. If there has ever been an indignity done in the name of democracy... that's it. But then, maybe the attitude of Black vets makes sense. Perhaps they better understand the war as being only symptomatic of our culture. Instead of Blacks taking the cue from us, we ought to try a little role reversal. Discrimination was there before the war. They know that. Things did not change after the war. The war was only a reflection of our culture. Not only for Blacks. For the rest of us also.

Look at what else has happened. You've taken your T.V. programs and made us into crazies. God, did it sell commercials. Show the junkie vet with a gun in his hand. Put him on top of a tower and let him start dingin' people. Is it any wonder we started to bury the war deep inside? Why we didn't want to let anyone know we were there? Why we tried to fit back into your world where "men were men." I was watching a pro football game last night. The announcers were talking about a rookie linebacker. "He's a real hitter. They say if you even come near him, he'll hit you... just for fun." And I thought, "Does this guy have any idea how many of us are around who would kill this guy if he ever tried?" Macho begets macho. Another reinforcement of the real man's world.

Have you ever seen two men crying and holding each other? So frightened because they knew they were going to die? Or seen a man cradle another in his arms as life fades? Or try to scream life back into another man as his blood spills out on to your clothing? Do you know what happens... how angry, frightened and frustrated you feel? Where's the macho then?

It's not that I can't fit back into your society. I just don't want to anymore. There's a need for change. "Radical" has its origins in a Greek word meaning "Roots... one who goes to the root of the problem." I'm becoming a radical. I want change... for all of us. Not just the Viet Nam veteran. All of us. The cop on the beat. The school teacher. The garbage collector. The politician... the businessman. Most of all, change for the children. If somehow, there was a way of guaranteeing that the children could grow up free of the bullshit we keep putting on them then everything would be worth it. The Beatles said it well "Imagine all the people living for today... imagine no country. Nothing to kill or die for. Imagine all the people living life for peace."

No, my friends, we're not the crazies. It's you who kill in the name of God and Country. It's you who are insane. Our killing days are over. We want more for ourselves and our children. No more living life from paycheck to paycheck. I've said it was time to pay the bill. The real bill is not to be paid in money. It is to be paid in change. The money will automatically flow. The change must be earned. We have an anger... not against individuals but against circumstances. The same circumstances that have molded you. What you have done to us, what we have done to ourselves is not a guilt to be borne by anyone of us. It is a natural progression of errors.

Sometimes I get the feeling that we're involved in a giant monopoly game. The weapons are merely the way of protecting the hotels on Boardwalk. The people who stay in the hotels are the ones who can afford to. Some of those people are good people. Obviously, some aren't. They make their money on our backs. They need us like a rancher needs cattle. People to work their factories. People to sell their products to. What the product is, isn't important. What's important is that it be bought. What the product does isn't important either. Only that it be purchased and, preferably, re-purchased. Generally, they're made under the guise of benefiting society.

Classic examples are the pesticides and herbicides we use. They kill weeds and insects that harm crops. On the surface, that sounds good. In Allen County, Indiana, a county surveyor authorized the use of Sylvex on county ditches. The water from those ditches flows into their streams and then their rivers. Some of the water ends up in reservoirs for use as drinking water. The Sylvex holds down the weeds and, as a result, helps keep the water flowing. There are more than 200 miles of ditches in Allen County. Sylvex is dioxin based. A county has been poisoning its own water. It has been illegal to spray Sylvex for more than four years. The EPA has said it can be painted on things like tree stumps, but it can't be sprayed. The ditches in Allen County are next to pastures and agricultural fields. In 1978, a University of Wisconsin study proved that dioxin does work its way into the food chain. Not only has Allen County been poisoning its water, it's also been poisoning its food. When the state chemist's office was first contacted about the spraying of Sylvex, they responded by saying in effect, so what? It's not really harmful. Allen County, Indiana is not unique. Viet Nam veterans better understand the effects of Sylvex than anyone. That's because we understand dioxin... the stuff Sylvex contains. Some of us have the deformed children Some of us have cancer. We also understand how the government drags its feet... unless you live in Times Beach, Missouri.

Those of you who live in the Allen Counties of America are killing yourselves and letting others kill you. Your local officials will not tell you everything you need to know when it comes to the chemicals they're using. They can't. They have too much invested in keeping the truth from you.

We have created death in progress. They talk of the public and the private sector joining hands. Why bother? They've been copulating in this country for more than the past two hundred years. They're having an orgasm in Central America. You need look no further than local politics to understand how leaders of communities are picked. They are no more than figureheads for the powerful. Seldom do our elected leaders do other than what they think is right for the more powerful lobbies... the more powerful special interests. The problems in Nicaragua and El Salvador resemble those experienced in Viet Nam. We could have gotten involved years ago on a better footing. Instead, we decided to represent the special interests of a few. Is it any wonder democracy seems not to work elsewhere in the world? It doesn't even work here.

In this giant game of Monopoly, most of us are not the players. We are no more than little toys moved across the board. But we don't have to limit ourselves. We can effect change. That damned constitution keeps getting in the way of the players. They keep trying to stack the deck. There's no question of that. What do you think the fight about the Equal Rights Amendment was about? Those few words in the E.R.A. amounted to this... "You can't use loaded dice when you're playing the game, fellas." But how they played the game to defeat the E.R.A. was a real educational process. They lied. They still do. Unfortunately for the amendment, the proponents turned the amendment into a feminist issue. It was never that simple. It was and still is a humanist issue. Men need to be included in the movement... on an equal basis with women. Men need to be educated. How many men, for example, give up custody of their children without a fight, simply because they believe a woman can do a better job raising the children? How many men judges give custody to the mother for the same reason? How many men judges think the only reason a man seeks custody of his children is out of spite against the woman? Why can't a man ask for custody simply because he believes he can produce the best environment for the child? How many men involve themselves in the raising of their children to begin with? There's a need for that kind of involvement.

We're familiar with the horrors of war. What better way to bring peace than have those of us who know death teach the meaning of life. Before we can assume that responsibility, we need to become aware. We also need to break some of our bad habits. Granted... those habits are often the result of the acculturation process. But they're still bad habits. Habits such as looking down on women. Seeing the feminine side of our nature as a sign of weakness. Since when is it weak to feel love and gentleness? Those are the feelings I have for my child. Those are the feelings I have for my friends, male or female. Is that a sign of weakness? In my grief for others and myself, I cry. Is that a sign of weakness? Of course not. It is time to throw down roles that so limit us as humans. Not only men... but women. Not only women... but men. If we can't do it for ourselves... then, at least do it for the sake of the children.

We as Viet Nam veterans have seen first hand racism, sexism, the destruction of the environment through chemicals and the taking of human life. More than any other single group, we have an obligation to speak out: to help bring about change. The focus of that change certainly ought to extend beyond any nation's borders. The stresses and the pressures we live with are the same ones many people are forced to cope with. Is there any insanity that rivals that of a potential nuclear war? We have people throughout the world thinking that it's necessary to have enough nuclear weapons to kill each other ten times over. Why? No one should be so foolish as to believe that nations can begin trusting each other today. The incredible competition level will not allow for that. Still, we can say, "Let's go no further." Some world leaders would have you think we would buy peace with our freedom. Pure rhetoric. We're not talking about giving up our freedom... or anyone else's, for that matter. We are saying it's time to cease threatening each other.

The United States and Russian leaders are acting like two children, trying to find out who has the biggest stick. Of course, they're fairly safe from the results of the dispute. But they're arguing with our lives. I don't know about you, but I never gave either one of them permission to do that. I want my child to grow up in a good world. Or at least, I used to. Now, I just want her to be able to grow up. They're threatening her existence. We need to involve ourselves in the nuclear discussion as if our lives depended on it... because they do. We, as veterans, know the face of death. As Viet Nam Veterans, we know that our country will sell us down the drain. We also know how to fight back, even though the deck may be stacked. The degradation we have been submitted to has caused us to grow stronger. That strength, combined with sensitivity, can lead to change: not only for ourselves, but also for those around us.

8 Gulag and Kyrie:

A Personal Reflection on the War in Viet Nam
By Rev. Timothy Calhoun Sims

The dream goes something like this. My company is dug in for the night around a low hill, surrounded by rice paddies. The command group sets up in the shell of an old stucco building, and I strung up my poncho between some coconut trees beside a wall. Pat takes the first radio watch, so I doze off as the Gunny and Skipper eat C rations.

I wake up, and a nice breeze is blowing. The moon is up, big and white, and the coconut trees are black against it, their fronds glinting silver as the wind moves them.

But something is wrong. Dark shapes are moving in the rice against the way the wind is blowing the grain. NVA sappers! Everyone on the perimeter dies silently, their throats cut. I try to shout but no sound comes. I reach for my rifle, but my limbs won't cooperate. They're coming for me, and I'm straining for my weapon, straining to cry for help.

My wife is shaking me. "You're having another one."

My problems with Viet Nam began soon after I returned to the States. I had seen major fighting at Con Thien, survived the siege of Khe San during the '68 Tet Offensive, and participated in many search and destroy missions, running firefights and the like from Quang Tri to Laos to the DMZ, as numerous as they were anonymous and inconclusive. And then in the fall of '69, three weeks after I had been holding some obscure bridge in Northern I-Corps with a Marine Infantry Battalion, watching for snipers, listening for the "thoops" of incoming mortar rounds, I suddenly found myself walking the pleasantly ordered paths of a university campus.

The quiet of the library, the civilized discussion of the classroom, the long hours of reading philosophy and literature, struggling through a botany chapter or the conjugation of irregular verbs... even the strange routine of going to the bathroom to relieve myself... all this and more culminated in a culture shock which drove me inside myself. I was afraid of unstructured time, terrified of leisure, for I believed that if even for a moment I should be found with nothing to do, I would be discovered for the alien that I was.

As yet there were no nightmares, no sleepless nights, no sudden reactions to loud noises, or rage ready to explode. But I would sometimes look fearfully up from my studying, shocked that I could have let my mind wander from wary vigilance, only then to realize where I was and what I was doing. In cold December, physically and emotionally exhausted, a recurrence of malaria put me in the hospital. This experience became paradigmatic for me: like the tiny, unseen parasite lurking in my blood, the Viet Nam experience lay subsurface, waiting for the opportune time to strike.

That spring was the Kent State tragedy[1], the invasion of Cambodia, and the height of campus unrest over the war. The university, at the demand of both students and faculty, closed down early, suspended exams, and let everyone go to march. Everyone marched. My classmates marched and shouted slogans about the violence America was doing, while wrecking buildings on campus and denouncing students who didn't agree with them. Ministers marched and prayed that our fascist country would stop turning young people into murderers. I began to realize then what I really was to my peers, to the prophetic clergy, to the whole nation.

That summer a pastor friend who was sympathetic invited me to move to his town and work in his church. I had never worked in a church, wasn't sure I wanted to have anything to do with church, but he was a friend.

Things went well at first. Church, it turned out, was a place to find some form of acceptance if you could maintain the appearance of normalcy. Even the social Christianity of that large downtown, full of blue-blood-quality-white-folks church had some loyalty to those they perceived to be like themselves. I worked hard to appear normal, but I was lonely, and I worried about being crazy. I wanted to do (and at times did do) strange things like putting on my jungle fatigues and sleeping outside under a poncho, eating out of a can, stalking through the woods at night. I wanted to talk and talk and talk about the war to someone, anyone, but society's message was clear: that which leaped against my brain trying to come out of my mouth was off-limits. I knew that my acceptance was conditional on my conformity, and to be normal you did not speak about Viet Nam as I wanted to speak.

The coffeehouse I ran for the church was a constant source of irritation to some of the members who frowned on the "hippies" (normal teenagers of the time with long hair and bluejeans) who wandered in and out. But when the Black children started to come, that was it. This of course was never given as the reason, but the deacons urged, and the members voted, to tear down the coffeehouse and build a parking lot. I resigned.

Back at the university, everything hit the fan. I still don't know how I managed to graduate. Nightmares about Viet Nam woke me screaming several nights a week; alcohol cut that down to several times a month. I was paranoid about people and what they saw in me, what they were saying about me. I knew I was screwed up, didn't know what to do about it and was certain everyone could see plainly how disturbed I was. Once when I was walking out of the quiet library in the afternoon, a jackhammer started up at a nearby construction site, and I jumped behind a stone wall, books and papers flying like a flock of frightened birds.

Church was out of course. It was out as soon as I left my job as a youth worker. Thinking of church made me envision deacons shutting down the

---

[1] Ohio National Guard shot and killed 4 students, wounded 9 others on May 4th, 1970 during violent student protests of the American invasion of Cambodia.

coffee house because of fear for the "niggers," marching ministers who cried out against the injustice our militaristic country was visiting on the peace-loving North Vietnamese, and churches which advertised counseling centers for draft evaders and deserters, but not one for traumatized vets. I decided that church was the last refuge of the ridiculous.

Church was out, and I yelled at God for all the whoring of which his Bride was guilty, for I yearned for its ministry. I cursed God for my night-mares, for my rage, for my disturbed life, for being a stranger in my own land. I felt that the country was embarrassed by me, that the government had used and then flushed me, that my classmates condemned me, and that my family and few acquaintances were unable to understand why I didn't act "normal." Everyone, even my lovers, appeared to be the enemy. Everyone had protested the war, betrayed me, and encouraged the foe who killed my friends, wounded me, and caused war orphans to scrounge in garbage for food. Everyone had made the politicians changed military strategy so that, by the time I left Viet Nam, we were no longer fighting out in the bush guer-rilla-style (at which we were successful) but were made to stay in one place, "holding secured positions," while the North Vietnamese pounded us with heavy artillery .

So I tried to exorcise God from my life, but his presence would not leave me alone. His love was maddening. Never before had God been so really pre-sent as when, even in my rage, I could feel Love near me, arms around me, tears washing me.

I reflect at times on the impatience of some ministerial colleagues at anything which smacks of "me and Jesus" or "me and God" religion. I know what they don't like about it, and I don't like it either: the notion that faith in Christ is a private, personal affair, unconnected to others and a certain his-tory, something you can enjoy in the comfort of your den with your Sunday morning TV and coffee. Worse, "me and God" is often a wicked self-righteousness by which people deliberately avoid God and God's call to faith-fulness to the family of God and discipleship in the world.

But the thing some of my colleagues have difficulty understanding is that there are all kinds of Jesus-in-the-desert experiences, Jeremiah-in-despair experiences, and Paul-awaiting-trial experiences. And wherever, in the gu-lags of the world, there is a solitary man or woman who cries out in rage or fear or need, there is the "'me and God" experience.

Alexander Solzhenitsyn taught us what a gulag is. Gulags are Russian forced-labor camps. But there are other kinds of gulags besides the state-run institutions. Gulags can also be unspoken societal conspiracies to over-look, avoid, ignore. During college, I entered the gulag of the ignored Viet Nam vet.

"Me and God" was not pleasant it was agony, but it was all I had. My mystical experience of God's presence then is still more real than anything I have had since in the church. I suppose that is the gift of mystical encoun-ter: the desert is a place of clear contrasts. Dark and light. Cold and heat, hunger for the comfort of bread and hunger for deliverance from evil—these things tear away the accidents of time and place. And there is apotheosis, the "unveiling" of the mystery of God which God desires one to behold. My vision was of Heavenly Mother, crying and howling with me, seeking to hold me to her comforting breast; the vision was of Heavenly Father, grieved and wounded with me, holding me with aching arms.

God's mystic presence would not leave me alone, and so I decided to give his "dirty bride" another look. I had dropped out of grad school where I was studying for a degree in English. (Why continue with such apparent absurdities as exploring the anti-Catholic bias in the eighteenth-century English novel when I couldn't explore my own soul?) I worked a series of jobs: forklift operator, electrician's helper, short-order cook, secretary, even a singer in bars. It was during this period that I recalled a Lutheran chaplain who visited my unit near the end of the siege of Khe San. The mere fact that he came to us impressed me. I remembered him, preaching no sermon, simply going about among those of us who were left with bread saying, "...the body of Christ... the body of Christ..." We had not washed or shaved, changed clothes, eaten properly, or had sufficient medical attention for three months when he came. Yet with the smell of our dead buddies, stacked in empty bunkers still in our noses, he walked among us with another broken body.

This incarnational representation years later now bore fruit in me. I came to see that amidst the suffering and brokenness comes another suffering and broken One, not to condemn or judge the parties in conflict. but to save and heal. When I first attended a Lutheran church, it was only because someone who had cared had been a Lutheran.

Thinking back on my first experiences with the Lutheran church. I believe what hooked me was the Kyrie. It came to me that people had been praying for two thousand years, with little demonstrable change in the ills of the world, "Lord, have mercy!" Yet they continued to pray. I began to understand: no quick and easy answers, no techniques to make sure you get what you want from God, no claim of heavenly endorsement for earthly programs to bring in the Kingdom by some other way or some other means than the Cross. Here was only the gulag cry I had made so many times myself, even in fits of rage and swearing: "Lord, have mercy!"

Liturgical worship was strange to me, but something whispered there were deep roots here, and it calmed me. My rage subsided. Though some nightmares still came, now there was Kyrie. Somehow, a little suburban church of middleclass families, positively reeking of normality, captured me in the sharing of that ancient prayer. It was refuge, sanctuary, for no one who cried out, "Lord, have mercy!" could be a stranger where all cried out, "Lord, have mercy." It was officially codified right there in the worship book, so no matter how hedonistic or spiritually self-righteous one got (two states of soul very similar indeed), one could never forget what the truth is about the nature of life in this world! We are at every moment in need of salvation.

I reflect on this as I conduct Sunday worship now. There is a mystical quality about the ancient liturgy which ministers to the wounded soul. This strange conversation which God's people have Sunday after Sunday that we call "liturgy" so transcends the super programs, the hype to "get people involved, the giddiness of born-again and Spirit-baptized religion which reduces the Gospel to one-time experiences!

Active churches with super programs make me suspicious. Constant numerical growth, trumpeted as "success," gives me visions of old 666 of Revelation as the Census Beast. Too much fooling around 'with the liturgy, too much affected excitement and planned enthusiasm, too much pressure to be where the action is "prophetically," too much false advertising about what God will do for you from the official doctrines of most churches—all of this, I believe, springs from the evasion of personal emptiness. It is given by grace so that we may be still in that desert place and know (Hebrew *yada,* "participate in") God.

Worship to me is the most important thing the church does, no matter how irrelevant or anachronistic it may be perceived to be by the healthy who do not need a Physician. Any group of people can, and do, speak out and work for justice and peace, and that is good. Any band of caring people can minister to the material needs of the world, and that is also good. But it is only the church that cries out "Lord, have mercy!" on behalf of itself and the world in an intentional act of worship and intercession. The surrender implied in that cry is faith, not just anything called faith, especially not the self-generated willpower of modern-day enthusiasts nor the positive-mental-attitude hype of those who, by virtue of such wishful thinking, remain sadly myopic to history. Both of these non faiths are in. fact magical strategies to cajole from God or conjure out of life that which the adherent wants. But the surrender implied in "Lord, have mercy!" is the faith of the Hebrew *ani,* God's poor, the "poor in spirit" of the Sermon on the Mount, the ones who have nothing to offer, nothing to claim, no resources, and therefore can only call upon the mercy of God, neither able nor presumptuous enough to 'name in advance what it is they need.

My nightmares still come, though less often now. I sometimes suffer small fits of rage. There are days when I cannot eat meat or anything with tomato sauce or even anything at all. There are nights when I sit and ponder why it is that the societal conspiracy continues, why the prisoners are still held hostage in the gulag of the nation's disease: avoidance, and embarrassment over the Viet Nam War.

So many Americans confused the war with the warriors! Even when the country decided it did not want the war, did not want to win, the blame for the war was placed on some alleged warmongers in Washington and their legions, not on the society as a whole. No confession of sin was forthcoming from the country, either for the war or to the warriors, and no hint of recognition that it was, after all, the country who produced whatever warmongers were leading us. Not only was there no confession of sin, there was no facing of failure. We are poor losers. To ignore the war was not to have to face losing. To ignore the warriors was not to have to face the guilt of what this country had done to thousands of young lives during the war and after.

Two kinds of bad fruit spring from this ill-spawned seed. The first is that to serve in the military is no longer an honorable occupation, and those who do so anyway do not receive the spiritual nurture and support they need from their churches. There is an antimilitary bias now in many mainline denominations which, in part, is the continuing result of an emotional reaction to Viet Nam. Wherever a "prophetic" agenda, shaped by the times and topicality, is being acted on, wherever complex issues are reduced to emotionally satisfying slogans ("nuclear freeze" could be one), the danger of such a bias exists. One sad result of this automatic disdain of things military by the churches is that the people who serve in the military still are overlooked, only this time the confusion arises from the nuclear weapons issue and the size of the defense budget. The self-styled "prophetic" churches, pure in their anti-militaristic orthodoxy, are then irrelevant to a whole class of human beings. It makes one wonder what John the Baptizer was thinking when all he said to the Roman soldiers, those agents of oppressive militarism, was, "Don't complain about your wages, don't extort money, and don't falsely accuse." Apparently he did not know what it meant to be a prophet.

But the second bad fruit, and more important to me. is the unresolved issue between the society and the warriors which keeps the gulag operational. There is, you see, something very important which must happen to warriors when they return from war—especially if they have been nurtured on even the illusion of morality or religious principle. The warriors must receive the society's absolution for what they have done, for what the society sent them to do. Murder is a terrible crime, and people who are sent to fight society's wars must be absolved from blood guilt. The promise of receiving that absolution is implicit when society sends out its warriors to do battle.

In the case of Viet Nam, American society, including the churches, did not keep that promise. The warriors came home and found that they were considered murderers, people who had no permission to commit society's acts of violence. But having committed them nonetheless, they were now disowned, unaccepted, and unacceptable. And now many of us wander like mercenaries, deprived of citizenship, from failed job to failed relationship to failed attempts at normalcy. The bottom line, theologically, is that there is no forgiveness of sin, no reconciliation of the warrior and the society which cannot, no matter what it wills, deny its responsibility for them.

I know the church is half harlot, half Bride, and I grieve for our sins, for our affected worldly wiseness, for our sad and empty attempts to appear both prophetic and respectable at the same time. But somehow this dirty Bride still claims my loyalty, my labor, my tears, my dreams. Today I serve the men and women of the United States Navy as a chaplain. You might say I am repaying an old debt. In a way, I guess that's true, but it's not my debt alone.

I worry about my own denomination when it undermines the mission of the church so much in sociopolitical terms that its spiritual mission becomes subdued. Can it be, in the rush to get our prophetic credentials in order (something which perhaps needs attending to since, beginning with Luther's invectives against peasants and Jews, justice has not historically been an item high on our agenda), we are committing a kind of selective works righteousness, as if it were possible to wash our hands of guilt in this world of complex interconnections? We talk of divestment of stock in corporations who do business in South Africa, while ignoring the same issue in respect not only to other repressive regimes, such as South Korea, the Philippines, the governments of Eastern Europe, and the Soviet Union, but also the deeply ambiguous policies of our own government which is the world's chief arms merchant. Perhaps we don't want to think such things through too thoroughly, for if we do, we shall discover that Qumran is no longer possible. Righteousness is by grace alone, and there can be no rational apologia for any kind of selective works-righteousness.

I have been accused of fatalism, but my countercharge is that selective works-righteousness is a form of pride which blinds us to the nature and scope of the evil with which we are dealing, our own implicit and explicit involvement in it, and our call to be blessed because we are poor, meek, and mourning. In the end what we have to offer those who cause it and ourselves who, in the world's way of doing things, have become both oppressor and oppressed is a Word from God, a shared Meal, and a Kyrie prayed in hope. Nothing more. But with this God can cleanse and save us all, those who fought the country's wars and those who did not, those who are in some gulag and those who stand outside, any place and any time in our fallen world. Only God's final answer to the plea, "Lord, have mercy!" will do.

I am thirty-four now, Viet Nam is fourteen years ago for me chronologically[2], but right here and now on any given day. Right here and now when the rage comes up and a car backfires and my belly turns over, right here and now when I wake, yelling in the night. I even have flashback smells now and then: C rations, napalm, spent ammunition, body sweat after a ten-day hump in the hills—Hue, lovely Hue, before Tet—dead bodies. (It happened once as I conducted a funeral. I could smell the body.)

Most days, I'm OK. I've done all right. I have a good marriage and a good ministry. I have refused to let the traumatic neurosis (popularly called "delayed stress") from which I suffer beat me. Many others aren't so blessed. But sometime in the future, I tell myself, the churches and our society are going to have to get serious about dismantling the gulag once and for all. Until then, there is Kyrie.

On March 29, 1973, the last remaining U.S. military personnel were unceremoniously withdrawn from Viet Nam and the war turned over to the South Vietnamese. Two years and five thousand South Vietnamese deaths later (the number from the North is not Known), the Hanoi government took over the entire country.

After ten years Viet Nam continues to haunt us. For a while this country seemed to proceed as if the war had never happened. Now, however, scholars are beginning to probe its many puzzles and problems that the war presents-with some surprising, not to say disconcerting, results. (See "The New Viet Nam Scholarship" by Fox Butterfield in the New York Times Magazine, February 13, 1983.) The American public too seems to recognize that Viet Nam somehow represents unfinished business without being sure exactly what to do about it or how. Even the design and erection of a memorial to the more

---

[2] This article was written in 1983; Timothy Calhoun Sims served in 1969.

than fifty· seven thousand Americans Who died In Viet Nam was not accomplished without controversy.

About the Author

Timothy Calhoun Sims was an LCA pastor until his death in 2002. He is survived by wife Rebecca and three children. Following two tours of duty In Viet Nam as a Marine between 1966 and 1968, Timothy studied at the University of North Carolina and the Lutheran Theological Southern Seminary from which he graduated in 1978. His active duty as a Navy chaplain was preceded by service as associate pastor, Messiah Lutheran Church, Knoxville, Tennessee, and pastor, Trinity Lutheran Church (Rocky Mountain, NC). In 1981 he led the Bible study at the LCA Youth Gathering on the campus of Purdue University (West Lafayette, IN).

Timothy is a native of Gainesville, Florida. He is survived by his wife, the former Rebecca Lynne Banks.

<table>
<tr><td>9</td><td># America's Uriah:
The Viet Nam Combat Veteran
By Chaplain Cephas D. Williamson</td></tr>
</table>

America's Uriah:
The Viet Nam Combat Veteran
By Chaplain Cephas D. Williamson

Cephas D. Williamson is Chaplain at the Veterans Administration Medical Center in Fort Wayne, Indiana.

King David was the greatest Hebrew king ever to live. For two and a half thousand years, he has been revered for his military prowess, administrative achievements and religious sensitivity. He has been remembered as well for one scandalous sin and the despicable crime by which he attempted to cover it up. This story is as sordid as any corruption and coverup attempt in government in our time. King David had his own "Watergate" and it contributed to his eventual downfall.

King David's sin involved a beautiful woman named Bathsheba with whom he had a secret adulterous affair. Most people have heard of her. However, many people do not remember Bathsheba's husband and the crime committed against him in an effort to cover up the secret scandal. Bathsheba's husband was the truly tragic victim, and for that reason he should not be forgotten. His name was Uriah.

One must know what kind of man Uriah was in order to understand how great the crime was against him. Uriah was an officer in King David's army. He was not an ordinary officer, but a great military hero. In fact, he was one of thirty-seven military heroes who were known as "The Thirty". A soldier could achieve no higher distinction. More importantly, Uriah was a professional soldier who placed loyalty to his superiors and comrades-in-arms above every other obligation in his life, even above loyalty to his family. That such a worthy man should become the victim of corruption was, indeed, a tragedy.

This is how Uriah was victimized. While he was at the battle front, King David happened to see Uriah's beautiful wife, Bathsheba. Abusing the authority of the throne, King David had Bathsheba brought to him and they engaged in a secret adulterous affair. Unfortunately, Bathsheba became pregnant from the illicit relationship, so King David plotted to cover up his deed. He ordered Uriah home for rest and recuperation so that when the child was born, Uriah would assume that the child was his own.

Uriah reported first to King David to give account of the progress of battle, then was excused to go home to his wife. However, Uriah did not go to his house but stayed at the palace. He slept in the quarters of the palace guards, taking a simple cot as his only convenience.

The next day, King David was perplexed, and asked Uriah for an explanation. Uriah's answer was that as long as his troops lived under the hardships of battle, he could not allow himself the comforts of home. To Uriah, enjoying such privileges would be an act of disloyalty to his comrades.

King David next proceeded to get Uriah drunk, then sent him home again. Yet, even though he was drunk, Uriah still did not go home but slept among the palace guards a second night.

Becoming desperate in his efforts to cover up his sin, King David sent Uriah back to the battle field, with sealed orders to be delivered to field commander Joab. The sealed orders were quite expedient. Uriah was to be placed in the front lines where the fighting would be the heaviest and then units were to be withdrawn in such a manner as to leave Uriah isolated and surrounded by the enemy so that he would die in battle. Thus, King David expected to prevent a public scandal.

King David's orders were carried out and Uriah was killed in combat. The loyal, heroic Uriah had been betrayed by his Commander-in-Chief, his Field Commander, his fellow officers and his troops. Uriah should not be forgotten.

One can easily imagine what weighed on the minds of everyone involved in this tragedy, most of whom were innocent participants. Some felt the lonely despair of being abandoned. Others felt the shame and guilt of deserting their comrades. All pondered the senselessness of the tactic, the meaninglessness of the casualties, the folly of senior authority.

Most important of all, there was surely a gnawing feeling of betrayal throughout the ranks. They were crushed with guilt. They burned with anger. And a dark cloud of depression hung over them.

One has to wonder what would have happened if Uriah had survived this battle. How terrible it would have been for him to learn that he had been betrayed in the battle and that his home had been violated. Although he had always carried out his duties to the very best of his ability, he had been made the victim who must bear the consequences of problems and frustrations for which he was not responsible. For this reason, Uriah should not be forgotten.

Combat burdens every warrior with guilt, anger and fears. The Viet Nam combat veteran is burdened also with the guilt, anger and fears of America. Sometimes he has been charged with crimes. Other times he has simply been ignored as a symbol of embarrassment. Very seldom has he been welcomed, honored and embraced. A warrior so burdened can never escape the battlefield.

There are many Viet Nam combat veterans even today who, like Uriah, feel isolated and surrounded by hostile forces, the victim of our national problems and frustrations. It is long past time for us, the American people, to regroup our forces and rescue them. It is long past time for us to bring them home to compassion, understanding, dignity and peace. It is long past time for our combat veterans to study war no more and lay down their burdens. We gave them the burdens and only we can lift them.

Remember the Viet Nam combat veteran. He is America's Uriah—still fighting for his survival.

10 Masculinity and the Viet Nam Vet

Bringing War Home: Vets Who Batter

By Rick Ritter, MSW

"When he sees jets or hears planes he still ducks and tries to get away-he gets real paranoid. Then he'll start talking about dead bodies that he used to see... There are times when he loses control, but it is never with the children... I would rather let him take out his hate (the war) on me. ...He doesn't always know when he's hit me... I ask myself 'Why am I still hanging around for this?' ...Sometimes I confront him with God, and he just gets real quiet and stops—those are the times he is more aware. Our daughter is five and she tells him that he shouldn't hit mommy and then he feels guilty for awhile."

—Excerpt from a case history of a woman battered by a Viet Nam War veteran.

Battering is a problem for a large number of Viet Nam era veterans who come to Ft. Wayne Vet Center seeking assistance in dealing with the Viet Nam experience. The Nam vet is similar to other men in society in the sense that he has a very difficult time confronting the fact that he may have battered a significant other. This denial is accompanied by guilt and shame. One difference between the vet and the non-vet batterer is that the vet may also be dealing with guilt and shame from his combat experience in Nam. He is more likely to react to stress with the use of physical violence, and those veterans trained to be ground troops are even more prone to react this way.

Counseling vets at the Center focuses on "readjustment counseling," an umbrella term that includes counseling for delayed combat stress, physical and mental disabilities, bad paper, family problems, herbicide poisoning, employment problems, drug addictions, and anything else that is a "problem" for the Nam vets. The majority of the vets at the Center are also struggling with their definitions of what is male. Socially imposed machismo gets in the way of their being human and of relating effectively to the people they are close to. They want so badly to regain this portion of their identity that was lost in Nam and to be successful and productive human beings again—but not necessarily the way this society defines either success or productiveness. The problem of battering does not come to the forefront in some counseling sessions until the vet gains some insight into the healing process and also develops a trust in the counseling staff. The majority of vets are ashamed about what they have done. They believe that we will judge/reject them because of what they have done to a woman or a child. (Approximately 1/3rd of the 600 vets presently at the Center have been involved in battering women or children.) Though vets have come to the Center specifically to get better control of themselves so they will not continue as batterers, in some cases we deal with the victims of battering, because the vet may not come in.

It is tempting in beginning counseling to allow the vet to use tangential issues to legitimize his battering. However, I cannot, in all honesty, tell a vet that he batters because he was drinking, or because his wife or girlfriend deserves it, or any other false reason for having initiated abusive action against another human being. I can empathize about his being a batterer, but I cannot and will not condone it under any circumstances.

I prefer to focus primarily on the revivification of the military training and the vet's combat experience. This can be uncomfortable, and the counselor must be prepared to help the vet dig to the very bottom of the material that he has so effectively suppressed over the last ten years. There have been many instances of battering situations where the root of the problem has been a flashback/nightmare, yet it seems that in most cases the psychiatric community and the legal system have turned deaf ear to what has actually occurred. Instead of trying to listen and understand they have crucified these vets for flashbacks/nightmares that they have little or no control over. These occurrences cause the vet to perceive that he is back in combat and feels that his life is in danger, and he act out survival strategies. During a flashback/nightmare, he is not conscious of his actions or his surroundings. If the vet feels as though he is in any type of physical danger, real or imagined, then he will act out the survival mode of his previously learned behavior patterns (i.e. training).

This phenomenon is seemingly difficult for many women and women's counselors to accept. The reaction that I have gotten from many counselors is that this is a cop-out we are using to excuse the vets' behavior. Let me stress that we are not making excuses for Nam vets but rather encouraging people to understand a generally ignored problem. The existing literature in the field of delayed stress would seem to indicate that through the revivification of the Nam experience, a vet can begin, even if only rudimentarily, to more successfully process that experience and again be a whole person.

After these experiences have been relived, it is our job to see that those experiences are properly identified and correlated to the vet's behavior and attitudes as they exist today. This is crucial if the vet is going to have the basic tools to heal himself. Those vets in particular who were trained to be the ground troops in Nam were given the type of training that made them killers. They were taught to react to certain types of stimuli in a physically aggressive manner. What seems to unnerve the people of this land is that the same Nam vet is fully capable of using those same destructive skills against the general population. These dehumanized troops never had the opportunity to be deprogrammed from the aberrant methods of the war. They are simply sent home to deal with the Viet Nam experience in the best way that they can.

The Nam vet is a survivor because of his conformity to such destructive patterns of behavior. A vet has faced death experiences and has survived.

Because he has survived he will not deviate from those behavioral patterns that served him so well in the military setting. Most combat vets react to everyday stress situations in similar ways, no matter how seemingly insignificant the stimulus may be. The survivor syndrome is one that must be dealt with if a vet is to gain insight into his battering behavior. Once the vet begins to understand that it's OK to show emotion and to communicate those suppressed feelings about Nam, he can begin to understand what it is to be a male in the most complete sense. Once the vet begins to feel capable of caring for and nurturing other human beings, the attitude that "a woman should be beat daily whether she needs it or not" will not be acceptable any longer. This process also requires that the vet have role models other than John Wayne, Wyatt Earp, The Rifleman, George Patton or survival expert Lt. Colonel (Ret.) Anthony Herbert.

Many Nam vets feel they lost a portion of their humanness over there. Isn't it high time that they be allowed and assisted in regaining some of what they lost? Isn't it time that some gentle...men appear on the societal scene in much greater numbers.

An Average American

By T.B.

As I sit and wonder what will happen to me, my mind races like the second hand on the clock. The untold story still burns deep in my mind, the story of a Viet Nam vet. Looking back, I see the horror of so many tragic events. How could I have been a part of such a thing? I am still trying to sort out the good from bad and still finding it hopeless after ten years. Refusing to deal with myself by turning to drugs and booze, the feelings never leave. Feelings running wild like an animal in the night. Always with the same results—death and mutilation.

Being seventeen when I first went in the Army, I learned first-hand how to deal with the people of Viet Nam. It comes back... the training for such a place called Viet Nam.

> I want to be an Airborne Ranger
> I want to lead the life of danger
> I want to go to Viet Nam
> I want to kill a Viet Cong.

I recall the endless running to exhaustion as we yelled it over and over and over again. An average boy learns the best way to make war on people he never knew. Learning to hate before I ever learned to love. I was a teenager caught up in a rain of bullets and hell. A hell I am unable to live with now. I never thought this could happen to me. I wanted to do what was best for my country; little did I know my country did not know what was best for me or the people of Viet Nam. My heart is with the people of Viet Nam, a people who have suffered so much and have so little. I know we have wronged the Vietnamese people. I pray to God for our forgiveness. I ask God, "What kind of people are we?" A country so strong yet we fail to see the problems of others and of the Average Americans who "fought to keep what we have today."

After returning home I have died a little more inside each day finding my friends and country are now my enemies. I see in them the average person I once was. I ask myself, "Why does this happen to me?" I think about all the time I have spent in jail for drugs and trying to kill people here in Northern Indiana. The only answer I can come up with is the good training I got in the Army. It's hard to explain what happens. A situation with a breaking point, a crazy situation and you need a will to survive.

I can consider myself lucky, because I have not killed any of my family or friends. The situation is alive in all Americans that are Viet Nam vets. How many more people will die and pay the bill for this costly mistake? Most people say this can never happen to me. That is what I would have said ten years ago. Never would I have ever imagined it would have happened to me. Living from day to day in confusion, never knowing what tomorrow may bring. Nightmares of reality in the darkness of night or the bright sunlight of the day. No longer hiding from the Vietcong but from myself and perhaps the world.

Peace,

—T.B, A combat vet of the Viet Nam War
From Northern Indiana

Men's Voices

Edited by Rick Ritter and Bobbie Depew

A collection of quotes from veteran men in 1982 about the subject of Viet Nam.

...On Boot Camp

"The military prefers young men who are unsure of their individual identity. I remember basic training as one of the worst experiences I have ever been through. It involved the reshaping of men to fit the military mold."

• • • • •

"I don't remember that basic training had much impact on me. The weather was very hot at Ft. Polk, Louisiana. I thought it would be much more demanding than it was. It was mostly boring and dull. For me, basic was something I had to bear until I could start my training. I'd only flown once in a little plane for ten minutes.

• • • • •

"I can remember talking with guys who had gone through Navy boot complaining of how they only got to go to the commissary once a week. We didn't see a Coke or candy bar until we got out of boot. The Marine boot (which I never want to go through again) completely demoralizes you. They take away your identity and force you into physical shape whether you like it or not."

• • • • •

"I think what they do in boot during a 'warlike situation' is necessary. I wouldn't do it again, but it's necessary. By the time you get out you think you can whip the world."

• • • • •

"The whole purpose of "boot camp" (I don't know how they get "camp" out of it; they should call it redevelopment training) is to make you act on response—to do it without thinking. If you stop to think what you're doing, you will be dead. They have a limited amount of time to train you, to teach you how to fire a rifle accurately, how to take a position on top of a hill, basically how to stay alive."

• • • • •

...On Rape

"Throughout time, women have been subordinate to males. Not as good to be slaves or whores; the male plaything. After a hard day at the battle it was okay to go into town and brutalize a woman. If they had already won the land then it was okay to defile the defeated foes' women as a conqueror."

• • • • •

"Violating women appears throughout history as an effective tool in humiliating one's enemy. I think that we as American males fear that if we lose a war or are occupied by a foreign Army, then our women will be violated; and this issue, I feel, is what causes us to be warlike."

• • • • •

"I think that the people who use rape as an interrogation method think that even the idea of rape is so terrible that they will tell them what they want to know. A psychological method used to terrorize the women of the population. It was probably less than 10% effective, so they were using that as an excuse."

• • • • •

"Men, particularly in the service, must prove to themselves and to the woman they they're big, tough guys... while he beat her or holds a gun or knife on her so he can do what 'he' wants to her."

• • • • •

"Torture, rape, and murder.

"'Access and opportunity' are only two of the prerequisites.

"Anonymous masculine-feminine dynamic.

"How much at stake—officer present?

"Frustrating semicombat situation.

"There has been a lot of rape in wars. I keep thinking what it would have been like to be Vietnamese.

"They never sold their sister."

• • • • •

"Westmoreland sanctioned whorehouses. Just another instance of his ego trip—his sick idea of the Vietnamese people as weak, or children with no feelings. Good for the morale of the men probably, and a get-rich scheme for some."

...On Masculinity

"First of all, I can relate to the hero as a warrior because of all the movies I have watched. Between Clint Eastwood, Audie Murphy and John Wayne I had the view of war as a glorified event. The grossness of the war just amazes me. It seems so senseless to me, but when I put myself into their (the soldiers') place, I find that I would probably do the same."

• • • • •

"I hate war movies. The actors are mature adults. Nam was organized and run by adults who had kids fight it. Nearly all war movies are misrepresentations. When war and violence are stripped of romance and glorification, that still leaves us with the questions—what has war really been?"

• • • • •

"It's a lot easier to act tough when you don't have to be tough. How easy and attractive it would be to be hard and tough and manly. All I'd have to do would be turn off my feelings. It is more important to be human than it is to be a man, to some."

· · · · ·

"Where the hell would we be with no military? I don't think everyone should be made to serve, but if they want to—let them. If women want to be in combat—let them. They want to wear pants—let them. They can know what it's like to be shot at, to see their friends blown apart, let them see..."

· · · · ·

It would seem that America suffers from the negative trait of masculinity on a national level. Society is more afraid of loving, of making itself vulnerable, than it is of killing. There is an entire thought process here that needs to be turned around. Moral inversion.

"It is better that we do what we do and live the way we live because we love what is good, not because we hate what is bad. The spirit of our motives will permeate our lives.

"There are many rituals and customs that keep societies functioning smoothly and interacting with each other. We have a need to understand. There are times when what is important to a society is that they feed themselves.

"I could see the pain in Viet Nam, the pockmarks of the bombs, the blots of defoliated areas. I knew the people were human and just wanted to be left alone. Their country was so beautiful. I felt like we raped them. Nam was a war of our making and it was ugly. Viet Nam was and is their country and it is beautiful. They just wanted to be left alone. I felt like I was destroying something, like a piece of art.

"The Vietnamese love their land, feel deeply about the land where their ancestors are buried. They really are human beings. It's wrong to rob any person of their humanity. Nam was human suffering. Everybody who touched it suffered."

...On Service

"Men who went to Viet Nam were deceived and manipulated by those who made a career out of war. The political rationale for our involvement in Viet Nam never concerned me. All I cared about was my men, and I would do whatever was necessary to help them."

· · · · ·

"It takes guts to stand up against the entire Army, more guts than taking out a bunker. I know how hard it is to buck the system, and you never win. If they get it in for you they've got you. You've there to do a job, right or wrong. I would rather be shot by the other side than my own."

· · · · ·

"For years, men were exposed to a value system that emphasized loyalty, duty, and honor. We as a people had been socialized by our own patriotism and love of country to accept something as absurd as VIET NAM!"

• • • • •

"As a child and youth, into adulthood, I accepted what I was taught and told at face value. My great-great-grandfather and my great-grandfather were in the Civil War. My grandfather was in the Spanish-American War. My two uncles and my step-father were in WWII, and my step-father had been in Korea. My father had been 4-F during WWII. Nam was my war, my turn. There wasn't any reason why I couldn't go. I wanted to go."

• • • • •

"Before, I always related duty, honor, and country as the forces that pervaded our thinking and actions. The whole patriotic flap appears hollow when looked at from the masculinity angle."

• • • • •

...On the Insanity of War

"So many times while I was in Nam I'd say to myself, 'This is crazy. This is crazy.' It wasn't till I was on the plane home that I realized that each time I said 'This is crazy,' I had meant, 'This is Insane!' So I made a commitment to never participate in anything like that again. In a year of combat, I'd learnt the art of understatement.

"I feel like I returned from Nam with insights on war, all war, human behavior, and especially on violence; yet with the terrible frustration of not being able to articulate my perceptions so others could or would understand. I've been afraid that people would not understand that I've been through something real. It has been so difficult to explain what I've been through and why I feel the way I do. I wanted so much for my parents to understand. They didn't. They are both good people. They are both conservative, and my dad's a WWII vet. I knew they were good persons, and I knew I was correct. I knew I was correct even though I could not make them understand. Then I learned that I can't make anybody do anything."

• • • • •

"I wish to tell the truth to the American people so we can *all* go from the unreal to the real."

• • • • •

"As young men, most of us developed a value structure that we believed in and later found to be untrue in some respect. But doing a total 360 degree change in beliefs and values can cause an individual as many problems as trying to deal with the troubling issues and events—in this case Viet Nam. This resocialization process can be just as confusing and traumatizing as the war itself."

• • • • •

"I volunteered for flight school because I didn't want to walk. I was correct. When a person is 'on the other side of the bar' (rank) they are treated much better, like a person. This means that if you are on the low side of the bar you're treated like a child or a slave.

"Many times I've done something because I was more afraid of something else. I was afraid of jail so I went into the Army. I was afraid of being a 'tunnel rat' so I went to flight school. There was more to it than that, but these were fears that I allowed to limit my self-determination.

"Flying requires absolute self-control. No matter what's happening, the mind is in charge. The emotions may be screaming, yet the body is trained to only respond to the decisions of the mind. Emotions got in the way of clear, fast thought: like on a spacecraft when non-essential life support systems are turned off. Emotions were not necessary for my survival. In fact, they got in the way. (Turning them back on was the problem)."

• • • • •

"I'm against dehumanizing. This is an important point. Very important. To dehumanize others is to dehumanize oneself. The same applies to value. I believe that the military gives very little choice between rules, orders, and conscience.

"On the plane trip home from Nam, I spent the time deciding if I was going to kill God. There was never a doubt in my mind that I could.

"I was never afraid that I couldn't kill. I was afraid I wouldn't have the chance to kill them before they killed me. Killing is when you stop beating your head against the wall. Killing is when the toothache stops. Killing is a momentary relief. It felt so good to start shooting, to feel and hear and smell the M-60. Watch the brass fly. Rules of engagement: if it moves, kill it. If you can't shoot it, burn it. If you can't burn it, blow it up. We were very practical, very competent, and a little arrogant. Experience made us competent. It's a world of difference from training."

• • • • •

"One, or the, fundamental problem of the Viet Nam War was the misrepresentation by those who were in charge. Those people with decision-making authority, of whatever rank, fulfilled the roles of either commander or leader. Each decided what someone else was going to do.

"It seems that there were many times as a co-pilot that I looked at my aircraft commander and thought, 'This guy is going to get me killed!' Fighting over the controls of a helicopter was something I avoided doing. There are people with decision-making authority who, because of the stress of combat, felt compelled to do something immediately. In other words, when the stress of combat gets to their individual stress point, they stop thinking."

• • • • •

"Where we (troops) worked and how we worked, I always felt like we were playing King of the Mountain with the NVA. Like it wasn't real, just deadly. I felt like I had more in common with the NVA we fought than with those who were forcing us to fight. Like two fathers who force their little boys to fight each other when the boys don't want to.

"There is no medal high enough to show what it meant to get up and go out and work every day.

"We used to steal stuff that we all could use, like jeeps and trucks. We'd go down south to Da Nang and 'sling' them out. What were they (authorities) going to do? Send us to Nam? Send us to I-Corps? Send us to Quang Tri? Have us fly scouts? I mean, we were going to die, and the punishment had to be better than that. Yet I had a very strong desire to finish what I'd started."

• • • • •

"The day I came home from Nam, I told my family I was for amnesty and they didn't understand and I didn't understand why they didn't. They as society need to maintain their numbed guilt to protect their own "symbolizations around national virtue and military honor." I've had a large inner conflict for the last ten years, carrying around in my mind the knowledge of the insane that most people thought was good."

• • • • •

"I got out of Nam and into the Peace Movement in Japan. It's a great feeling to know I was right and all the other people were wrong. The idea of knowing now, after all this time, that I was right in what I did, that I did get the right knowledge from Nam. Enough to know that what we were doing was wrong: that we were hurting the people, not helping them. But that is to my own satisfaction. Too bad we all couldn't have realized it in 1969."

Common Problems Of Veterans
And Women Partners

Some women have described the following as problems of their Vietnam veteran partners. Their descriptions are consistent with the delayed stress symptoms commonly presented by the veterans themselves. Although it has not been possible to specify which or how many of these concerns affect any one woman, those which seemed to be most universally shared within our sample are indicated by (*)

1. He seems always to be in a crisis state although the identified reasons may vary from week to week.

*2. He is irresponsible in terms of holding a job and/or staying in school, and contributes little in child care or household chores.

*3. He exhibits erratic behavior without specific reasons such as rage reactions which alternate with remorse and reconciliation efforts (Jekyll/Hyde Syndrome).

4. There is heavy use of alcohol and drugs, as well as suicidal ideation.

5. He is extremely demanding; considering his needs only or that they are more important.

6. He isolates himself from his partner, family and others with a "leave me alone attitude".

7. He is unable to express or share his feelings or to be close to family members.

8. He is unable to handle frustrations or even to identify them.

9. He seems unable to handle it when things are going well, from a standpoint of not feeling worthy and may appear to be sabotaging.

*10. There is low self-esteem, great insecurity and feelings of worthlessness and helplessness.

11. There is jealously of the partner's relationship and activities.

Women partners describe the following as problems which they experience. Again, what seem to be central issues are indicated by (*).

1. She is overwhelmed by pressure and feelings of having assumed total responsibility; e.g. the strain of financial insecurity because of the man's job instability.

*2. She believes that she is somehow responsible for the man's rage reactions and feels guilty.

3. She experiences many self-doubts which are generated by emotional and job instability of the man; she is caught up in continual crisis-responding, losing sight of her own needs or overall patterns.

4. She is afraid to say anything to him and in not knowing how to respond, feels frustrated in her ability to help.

*5. She experiences confusion as to whether the problems are Vietnam-related or not and whether there will ever be any resolution of the man's conflict.

*6. She feels responsible for "making it all better", having to mother or nurture, hence, fostering greater resentment and irresponsibility on the part of the man.

7. Or she feels the converse—that it is all "his problem" and refuses to be involved, (seemingly, a defensive position or survival stance when all else has been tried and failed).

8. She feels that he has separated from her and their children with little sense of family and poor father-child relationships.

9. She feels that her support is not welcomed by the man; that she is being discounted.

10. She may be subject to emotional, verbal and physical abuse.

*11. She sees both partners building defensive barriers in the relationship and unable to be supportive of one another.

12. She feels dragged down by her partner's negative attitudes.

13. She is hurt by his extramarital affairs.

*14. She suffers from low self-esteem, is anxious, and feels a sense of hopelessness.

Adapted from Candia M. Williams, PsyD. "The Veteran System With a Focus on Women Partners" in T. Williams. PsyD. (Ed). *Post-Traumatic Stress Disorders of the Vietnam Veteran*, Cincinnati: Disabled American Veterans, 1980.0

So You're Not Sure...

By Terry Springer

I first came to the Vet Center a month after it opened. It took a lot for me to convince myself to walk through that front door, at least five trips around the block to find a parking spot. A lot of positive things have happened in my life since that first day. I'm back in school again, my life has settled down a lot. I credit the people here at the Vet Center with most of it. There were times I know they were the only people in my life to give me any support. They told me they cared, but most important of all they showed me that they cared. I was on the edge of self destruction several times, and they always made it a little easier for me to back away from that precipice. I'm sure they never knew how close I really was.

I've been accused of being "Gung Ho" about the Center. I think now you can understand why I feel the way I do. They don't hold all the answers any more than "Nam" is the source of all our problems. I come here now partly because I enjoy being around the "Brothers" once again, but also because I fell like I have a debt to pay to the brothers that have not arrived at the "Special Time" in their lives yet when they are ready to confront their problems and their memories of that country still so very near to us all, as well as that period of time in their life. I believe that everything has to run a cycle. Before you are ready to confront the problems, you have to be hurting. You have to have a lot of guts to walk through that front door.

It feels good to see the brothers pulling together to overcome all the obstacles placed in our path by the bureaucrats, only this time we are more prepared to handle it. We are even stronger than before, mainly because we are starting to band together. We are showing them that we can be winners if given half a chance.

I do have one question. Where are all the Vets who have no problems? Why can't they help their brothers and sisters (yes, I said "sisters", there were many service women in country) and they have their things to work out, just as we do. Where are all the Vets who have everything worked out and put in their proper perspective and are 'dealing with their everyday problems? Why can't they help us? Why can't they explain to us how they did it, how they put all that behind them? You know, it just might help another Vet open that first "important" door.

I have to admit that the problems I had when I first came in here have not all worked out like I wanted them to, but they have been worked out for the most part. They are starting to stay worked out. They are starting to stay where they belong behind me. I suppose one reason I wrote this was to let the people at the Vet Center know how I felt and that I appreciated how they have helped me. But the main reason I wrote this was to let my "Brothers" know that there is a safe place to go, to be with people you can trust. You can let your guard down, turn off that switch, it's like an oasis, and it's a safe place. They know where we are coming from and they really care. They've always got an open ear and hot coffee. What more could you ask for?

I hope because one Vet spoke up it will be easier for the next Vet to find the parking spot, easier than it was for me at least. Have you ever heard the old saying, "It won't hurt you half as much as you think it will," well its true, believe a brother Vet, who is at last on his way home.

<table>
<tr><td>

11

</td><td>

Wives, Children and Other Survivors

</td></tr>
</table>

A Message to Evergreens

By Everett McKeeman

[Ed. Note: Everett McKeeman is the son of a Viet Nam veteran]

I have lived the last several years of my life, if you could call it a life, as an evergreen tree, growing needles to keep others from getting too close, while keeping myself alive in my own cold, barren world. When I found myself unable to deal with the mental anguish caused by the many misfortunes that at times make life seem a punishment, I started living my life with very few emotions. As soon as I would start to feel an unwanted emotion, I would suppress it, and bury it deep in the back of my mind. This life robbed me of my spirit, leaving me with complete apathy toward everything, with no life goals or raison d'être. As such a life could never be any more than a pitiful existence, I discovered the need for a radical change and made it.

I made this discovery and change not on my own, but with the selfless aid of a girl I love, and the help of a good friend to whom I am eternally grateful and indebted. Both of them I let get too close to maintain my green façade. Thus, a wise folly on my part had uncovered the pit I so long ago fell into, and now I am saved. Now, unlike the evergreen tree that responds the same way under harsh or pleasant conditions—with stiff needles and uniform structure that reflects it monotonous, boring existence—I live as the broadleaf tree.

In the harsh winters of my life, I lose my leaves, the leaves that with beauty reflect the joyous sunlight they absorb. Then, when my winters are over and my summers approach, my leaves grow back, broader than before for having felt everything, both pleasant and unpleasant. My branches no longer grow uniformly like those of the evergreen that ignores the world around it and the wonders nature has to share. My branches twist, turn, and bend as they are led by nature's lessons, gifts, and demands. The evergreen grows only to live and then die. I grow as the broadleaf, to make myself special, an individual with branches that have a different shape than the branches of other trees, due to both joyful and sorrowful emotions. Emotions identical to those felt by others but different in their stimulus.

Who am I?

By D.M.

[Ed. Note: D.M. is the widow of a Viet Nam vet.]

If I saw someone crying, I would reach out and gently wipe away their tears ... but when I had to cry ... I would find somewhere to hide ... and cry alone. I didn't deserve the same gentle touch ... my tears fell to the ground.

If I saw someone hurting, I would hold them in my arms and offer comfort ... but when I was   hurting   I would go to my room ... curl up on the bed and cry ... blaming myself. I didn't deserve to   be held   to be comforted.

When others shared their joy with me, I laughed along with them ... but inside I was crying ... I didn't deserve to be happy.

I opened up the doorway of my heart to give love ... but I quickly closed it ... if anyone tried to enter. I didn't deserve to be loved.

When I started group, I told you I was here to deal with the loss of my husband. But it ended up being so much more than that.

What I didn't tell you ... is that he abused me physically and emotionally. He knew my fears ... my weaknesses ... and he used that knowledge to control me. He took away my innocence, my self-respect, and my self-worth. I buried all my pain deep inside and I put up a wall.

When he died ... he left me feeling empty and alone. I was lost. I didn't know who I was anymore. But, as I listened to each of you and what you've been through, my wall started crumbling, and my pain resurfaced. I kept trying to rebury it, but as hard as I tried, the pain kept pouring out. It overwhelmed me ... I was drowning.

It's very hard for me to open up and let anyone inside, but I know I need to deal with my past if I want to heal and get my life back. I need to break down the rest of this wall... let my pain go ... and allow myself to feel again. My life will never be the same ... but I can make it a good life.

I want to thank Rick Ritter for not giving up on me, and pushing me when I needed to be pushed. I think I resisted just about everything he threw at me, but in the end he was right ... he was always right.

And I especially want to thank everyone in group for sharing who you are and what you've been through. That's what chipped away at the wall I so carefully put up. That's what allowed my feelings to surface. Painful though they may be, they're a part of me, and in time ... with help from everyone here ... I can let go ... and heal.

Who am I?   I am somebody!

What Was It All For?

By Connie M–W

Dear Rick,

Thank you so much for sending me those materials so promptly. I've been slogging through them—there is so much that it's overwhelming—and I am feeling quite a gamut of responses. Initially, I felt such excitement that it was almost exhilarating; there were so many "moments of truth", seeing words in from of me that corroborate my suspicions and assumptions, that crystallize my thoughts. Also exciting was the feeling of discovery; learning new theories, new facts about an area of deep interest to you is always exciting. I think, even when there is little in those theories and fact to stir positive responses. And then there were the feelings of sorrow, anger and finally even moment of despair-from the sheer weight of the materials, grasping the scope of the problem, seeing so clearly the inter-relationships among *all* the kinds of violence this society not only accepts and tacitly condones but overtly encourages. And I wondered, for an uncountable number of times, what it was all for? This is, for those of us who fought against the war here, what happened to that energy, that dedication, but most of all, the *coalition* against the anti-human forces?

So, once again, I'm having the civilian war-protester flashback blues. And now we all have our mortgages and 2.7 kids and upwardly mobile jobs and station wagons and at least some of us, when we face it, our feelings of emptiness and meaninglessness, or at least of shoveling against a tide of shit in our own small areas of social commitment, without that shared vision that used to connect us. And we work hard, the anti-nuke people and the anti-violence people and the anti-poverty people and all the other shit-shovelers—and we wish each other well and I wonder how many of us feel as I often do that they're picking us off one by one, because while we're not divided among ourselves, neither are we together.

And people like me, in our "Very Good Suits for Conferences and other Important Occasions", meet vets like you, with the hair and the earring and the other symbols we abandoned a while back and POW! Culture shock. There's a feeling of humility almost to shame: the anti-war work we did *was* important, but we often got caught up in our own sense of danger and our own sense of importance and let slip our awareness of the individual suffering of the guys who were actually *there*. There were then often moments of great warmth—we were kin—and often now there are flashes of nostalgia for the good old days of our war-protesting youth. Sometimes when a bunch of us from the old days of youthful escapades, I hear from the 50's fraternity boys recounting their adventures with beer blast and panty raids and campus cops. And DAMN, there ought to be a difference. Because those guys we were out to save are still dying from the war while we nurse our Irish coffees over memories of fooling the feds.

My husband and I went to see *Coming Home* in Merrillville, IN, a sprawling suburb of Gary which is founded on white flight and is sucking Gary dry.

The audience was incredible—somewhat open to the subject but genuinely puzzled not only by the emotional intensity of the film but by its *content*. For all they brought to the film in the way of personal knowledge of what was going on then, it might as well have been about the War of 1812. When the FBI agents began shadowing Fonda and Voight, the people around us thought that they were burglars, setting up a robbery. But there was a guy in front of us who was hip. Latin, looking macho in his old field jacket, he knows the words to all the Richie Havens songs in the film and boogies in his seat to Hendrix. Until the scene when the hospital ship came in. Violating every rule of American society for male behavior in public, the Vet went to pieces. As he was sobbing aloud, in his woman's arms, my husband and I sat with tears flowing down our faces. I wanted to reach out and touch him and say, "I understand, it's alright. It's all right." Only I had seen the opening scene—actual vets, not actors, disabled, still in the hospitals and rehab centers, in a scene shot years after the war was "over". And I knew that I didn't understand, and that it would probably never, never be all right for him and for countless others.

And then Saturday, I was cleaning out a small storage area in the basement and I ran across a box *not* marked "Glass—Careful". In it was my ex-husbands Marine memorabilia. My God—when we were married in 1964 he was fresh out of the Marines and this stuff was so important to him—he didn't leave the Marines, in his head, until a few years before the close of our seven year marriage, which dwindled off not with a bang but a whimper. And I've been carting that stuff around, in that box, since 1970—carrying the youth of a man to whom I no longer am connected around from place to place for twelve years.

I looked through the albums, pictures carefully labeled in fading gold ink, looking at the uniform sneers on the faces of the eighteen-year-old world-fuckers, remembering what Eleanor Roosevelt said about the Marines being trained killers and rapists and wondering how it was that in all those nights in all those bars I had missed clean that look of contempt on his face, how I hated the Marine Corps language—not the filth. I went to college, we cultivated that, but the contempt for everything expressed in everyday word that always seemed to demean the ordinary thing they described; grunt (infantry/new guy); spuds (potatoes); grub (food); weed (cigarette); shit-kicker (western film); dog, pig cunt (woman); old lady (wife, mother, girlfriend). And the hostility between us as I grew to loathe more every day the supposed values he'd been taught in the Marine Corps training such as simulated POW camp experience—and the anger and frustration he felt, because I couldn't express *why* I hated the vet buddies he never brought home to look through his albums more than once, and he couldn't *tell* me that what he felt from me was not hatred of the Marine Corps and what it symbolized, but a personal putdown of him and what he was and what he held dear.

I remembered the shock with which I heard him say early in our marriage that women were too stupid to drive or vote... we hadn't talked about that in the bars and the alleys where we parked afterwards. And I remembered watching him move more and more left, until he was full-fledged radical war protester, but still with that underlying layer of contempt for women and the world outside whatever male experience he was having, as he went from Mr. Marine to Mr. More Radical Than Thou. He was always telling me, "YOU don't understand". And now I see that he was right—I didn't understand, I only blamed. And I remembered his brilliant mind, and his tenderness with small children and animals, and I wondered what he could have been if he hadn't gone off to that great male indoctrination experience fresh out of high school; and what I could have been in response to that, whether I could have grown together.

As I stacked the albums into a pile of things to drop off at his mother's the hair stood up on my arms. On the radio was a song, obviously by Charlie Daniels... "Still in Saigon".

Aren't we all?

Thanks for reading this—I needed to write it.

From the Daughter of a Vet

I was at a young age when my father received his orders from the military to be shipped overseas to Southeast Asia (Viet Nam). Since my father was a career man, if war broke out he would inevitability have to serve his time. At the time, I was really proud to have "My Dad" as a fighter pilot in Nam.

However, the year he spent overseas was tough for the rest of the family. My mom showed a great deal of strength, but I'm sure she was aware of the risks that were involved when my father was on his tour of duty.

When dad left, I was told very little about why and what he was going to be doing. I knew that war was bad, men died in it, and that dad was in the service. I understood somehow that had to do what was right because it was part of being in the military. I did sense sadness and fear when dad left us in the airport with tears in his eyes, and there was something scary about this particular departure.

I cried terribly when he left, and emptiness and fear flooded my body and mind. The family held up well while dad was gone. We received news from him time to time and he sounded real good, just like I remember him. I excluded the possibility of my father getting killed or wounded in Nam, either because his was death inconceivable or perhaps I just wouldn't accept the possibility of it.

My father came home earlier than expected from his scheduled year-long tour of duty with a hearing impairment that happened during a training mission. His resentment today towards his deafness (I think) is still eating him up inside, because it has gradually gotten worse over the years.

His attitude and behavior had changed a great deal on his arrival home. He now had nightmares and would dive into the bushes at the slightest provocation from an instinctive learned fear acquired during the war His drinking had progressed quite a bit, along with his anger. Violence entered our house for the first time roughly a year after his return from Nam. He physically abused me and the rest of the family. Verbal abuse was almost inevitable too. I never ever knew what to expect after my father had a couple of belts before dinner. His unpredictability aroused a tremendous amount of paranoia in my daily living in the house.

It seemed like he had his own war he was fighting inside himself. With added affect of alcohol, he couldn't control his unbelievable rage that would explode in front of everyone.

My resentment toward my mother grew also. I felt she didn't care for us kids or else she would protect us from this insane man. I saw terrible, horrid fear in her eyes and face when my dad would lash out and attack us as if we were the enemy.

For quite a few years, I could feel only bitterness, hatred, anger, and resentment but never pity. During this period, I felt I was trapped in a vicious circle of fear with neither a way out nor anybody to understand me and talk with. I held myself responsible for my father's behavior, because I felt I was unacceptable and hated in his eyes. So I became extremely destructive with hate and blame towards myself.

For over ten years it never dawned on me my father's behavior might be caused by his experience in Viet Nam. When I did realize it, I became ashamed of myself and felt extremely guilty for all the years of condemnation when he was already in a living hell of guilt, remorse and hatred towards himself.

I can assure you that I have been deeply affected directly from the war in Viet Nam. I couldn't be excused from it because it came home with dad and lived in our house for a good portion of my life.

Today though, I am trying to learn and understand the destruction the war placed on our Viet Nam vets. It just tears me up inside to see the unmistakable misery within. I have both seen it with my own eyes and have felt the pain of confusion and guilt my father felt.

I will never forget the craziness and insane past behavior of both myself and my father. However, my awareness and acceptance is now the biggest asset I have. I am working on all those feelings I have suppressed for several years and to me this is the best thing I can do for myself. I need to keep trying to love him for who he is and where he's been, and to understand I'm not responsible any longer for his behavior that so deeply affected me.

Women's Voices

Edited by Rick Ritter and Bobbie Depew

A collection of quotes from non-veteran women in 1982 about the subject of Viet Nam and its aftermath:

"It seems as though to 'justify' the deaths, the only way left is to make people learn from the Viet Nam War. If I could *make* people learn from Nam, then the deaths would not be completely in vain. The only way I feel I can do anything is to organize and try to educate on the Nam experience. To somehow find a way to let surviving vets know that the shit haunting them is not just in their heads, so to speak. That their feelings are valid ones that have to come out and be re-channeled."

• • • • •

"Rape does not need any elaborate political or socio-economic motivation beyond a simple and general disregard for the bodily integrity of women, plain and simple. The very intensity of maleness that the military demand can only be seen as the beginnings of the power addiction that ultimately leads to female subjugation—rape."

• • • • •

"I looked at my younger brother today, hoping that by some lull of history, or some sense on his own part, he might be kept out of the military. At 13, peer pressure to conform to society's ideal about what young men are supposed to do is already stifling him in many ways. I only hope, with my encouragement, he can remain strong enough to speak his own, unique truth aloud even when it is difficult."

• • • • •

"In the elite fighting groups the incidence of rape was higher, but this does not seem incredible given the John Wayne image that many of these groups internalize. Since rape is a power and violence trip, it makes sense to me that those elite in terms of power and prestige would seek to retain that power by putting down those women they fought daily."

• • • • •

"It makes me sick to know what the Army or services in general deem necessary to make a 'man' out of human beings, male and female. My sister told me in her last letter that the Army told her she was a soldier now, and *nothing else!*"

• • • • •

"Many people have said that the military is a good experience for people and that it makes 'men' out of 'boys'. I really can't say that I'm very aware of the nature or the means by which the military achieves these goals, but I guess that ever since I've had an adult concept of what the military was I have disapproved of the stance that it has taken on the subject of masculinity. Many of my brother's high school friends went into the military after graduation; most of them into the Marines. When they came home on leave, it quickly became painfully evident that the way they viewed me was not the same."

• • • • •

"One of the first reactions that my two older brothers had was, "Why do you want to know all of that nasty stuff anyway? Why don't women leave well enough alone? Why do they want to know about blood and gore? Why don't they just keep *out* of it?" But I'm tired of being patted on the head, given earplugs, and told to go sit in a corner. I'm here to learn about what war does to people, what the roots are, what I can do about it—and how it affects me! I think that my brothers' attitudes are centered on their ego/masculinity problems, and I don't really think that I'll ever get through to them. But I'm going to fight all that I can to keep that far-off, frightening gleam out of my younger brother's eyes when the topic of guns, bombs, warriors and war arises. I want to feel that there's one *man* who doesn't need to fight to prove it to me."

• • • • •

"At the end of the war, when I was a junior or senior in high school, I remember reading an advertisement in all the major young women's magazines. 'Tough is easy,' it stated, 'tender takes a little doing.' I wondered why it was in the magazines I was reading. Why not print that in *Sports Illustrated*, or *Field and Stream*. Why not inform the men?

• • • • •

"I was afraid, for while, that I was sticking my nose into things that were none of my business; that I was too eager to learn about man's part of the world. That in striving to understand as much as I could about the war, about what it's like to be a soldier, about bringing the war home, I was learning about things that women aren't supposed to know. I was frightened that one day some well-meaning person would stick a knife in my back because I 'knew too much'."

• • • • •

"I believe that women are often affected adversely to a serious degree because they are often mis- or ill-informed—and men often are the main perpetrators of those painful experiences. I believe that to be strong and aware that we *need* to be better informed."

• • • • •

"It has been speculated that the V.C. held rape a more serious offense due to the position of women in the equality in fighting the war, and due to the necessary upholding of both the men's and women's morale as a single, guerrilla fighting unit. This idea, as well as the virtual nonexistence of rape by the V.C., seemed incomprehensible to the American fighting forces; somehow that doesn't seem ironic at all."

• • • • •

"Rape may also be used as a punishment by the victor to somehow further mar the property of the defeated nation; it denies the defeated men's ability to defend 'their' women—which has long been a strong suit of men's pride. It further humiliates the men involved if they are forced to watch, which seems to remain quite common. And to all of this we find ourselves in the same incredible circle as before; the rights of property have been abused and the property herself is held responsible."

· · · · ·

"The war seems to have only been real for the vets and the Vietnamese people. The vets not being able to relate to their friends, just other vets, doesn't say much for the American public. The feeling that they had to live up to everyone's expectations of being a soldier-hero..."

· · · · ·

"A socialized warrior is programmed almost unknowingly into somewhat of an animal. Kill and act on command! Reward—being a hero, a man. It really scares the hell out of me to understand how a socialized warrior has been dehumanized, thus what he has been turned into. His rights have been completely removed without his permission."

· · · · ·

<table>
<tr><td>

12
</td><td>

They Never Got Used to War: Women Who Served in Viet Nam
</td></tr>
</table>

Women At War

By Carol Tannehill

September 11, 1993. The United States lost in Viet Nam, but the nurses who served there won honor by helping others and simply surviving. They never got used to war; Midwestern women went fresh off the farm to the rice paddies of Southeast Asia. They came back from Viet Nam wiser—and sadder.

Cheryl German-Chung still can smell Viet Nam. When she stepped off the plane in 1968, it hit her hard—an unyielding wall of odor that mingled with stifling humidity and merciless heat. Bev Thompson smelled it, too: rotten fish. Jeanne Tagtmeyer noticed only hot air.

They were Midwestern farm girls, fresh out of nursing school, when they took off in military transports for plywood hospitals in Long Binh, Tuy Hoa and Cam Ranh Bay. They were hungry for adventure and itching to test their nursing skills on something besides officers' ingrown toenails and routine tonsillectomies. What little they knew about the Tonkin Gulf, the Viet Cong and the Tet Offensive, they had heard on the TV news.

What they encountered "in country," though, was not what they expected. Nor was the joyless reception they met when they returned home 12 months later.

In the 25 years since they flew out of war-ravaged Viet Nam, the three Hoosier nurses, who remain strangers, have struggled to forge new lives, to put behind them what most Americans had already forgotten. But a soon-to-be- dedicated bronze memorial to women who served is stirring up memories of the steamy Asian country that taught them what nursing —and self-reliance—are all about.

11,000 Women Served

German-Chung, Tagtmeyer and Thompson were among 11,000 women who served one-year tours of duty in Viet Nam during the war, August 1964 to January 1973. More than 250,000 others served elsewhere at that time. Most of the women were nurses in the Army, Navy and Air Force, but others served as physicians, physical therapists, air traffic controllers, communications specialists and intelligence officers. Almost all of them volunteered.

Tagtmeyer, 47, asked to go to Viet Nam. She had grown up on a farm in Columbia City, the town where she lives today. She joined the Air Force in

November 1968, when she was 23 and newly graduated from St. Joseph Nursing School. Her first plane ride took her to Chanute Air Force Base near Rantoul, Ill. Her second, in August 1969, took her 10,000 miles away to a military hospital at Cam Ranh.

"I guess I thought I could do anything for a year. It seemed like an adventure, like the epitome of nursing," she says. "When I was a child, I looked up to (American Red Cross founder) Clara Barton. I thought in Viet Nam I could be like her."

Thompson, too, had never strayed far from her childhood home in rural St. Francis, a tiny burg in the northwest corner of Kansas. Until she took her nurse's training at Asbury Hospital in Salina, she had never been more than 80 miles from her childhood home. She was not even 21 when her mother reluctantly signed permission papers so she could enlist in the Army.

"In those days, women who joined the military were considered whores, camp followers," Thompson says. "But my mother vicariously wished me an adventure." Thompson, 47, went through basic training in 1967 at Fort Benning, GA. In 1968, she headed for the 91st Evacuation Hospital, which ministered to the civilian war casualties in Tuy Hoa.

Schererville resident German-Chung, 47, also was seeking thrills when she said goodbye to the family farmhouse on Hathaway Road, where her mother, Virginia German, still lives. The Huntertown High School graduate joined the Army in 1968. By 1969, she was performing triage on wounded soldiers at the 93rd Evacuation Hospital in Long Binh.

Another World

To these Midwesterners fresh off the farm, Viet Nam seemed like another world. For one thing, there was an enemy. Far from the pomp and parades of their American training camps, the bases in Viet Nam faced real shells and sniper fire. Tagtmeyer's hospital was bombarded several times a month. Soldiers fired their guns into the perimeter to prevent Viet Cong soldiers from getting close.

For another, it was a land of strange contrasts. The sight of swaying palms, glistening beaches and blue seas seemed a mirage among the shanty towns of the military's wooden "hooches," wire fences and villagers' makeshift huts.

Military personnel dined on plentiful lobsters, giant shrimp and tropical fruit while the Vietnamese survived on bowls of plain, white rice. Villagers in ragged shirts and rubber-soled "Ho Chi Minhs" toted water alongside straight lines of Boy Scouts and little Catholic girls in crisp white blouses. And there were strangers everywhere.

The South Vietnamese had suffered greatly. Few whole families existed anymore; the war had scattered them. Their houses were little more than huts over dirt floors. And they had come to tolerate whichever foreigners—the Japanese had occupied Viet Nam during World War II, and the French had gained control after that—were in their country at the time.

"There was a language barrier, of course," says Thompson, who cared for Vietnamese patients from nearby villages. "I probably learned no more than 10 (Vietnamese) words, but we communicated very well. It's not hard to get across the idea of 'face,' 'hands' or 'eat.' For 'good,' you just rub your tummy and smile a lot. We all understood. They were just people, like you and me."

In time, the South Vietnamese joyfully welcomed the American nurses. Teen-age "mamasans" washed the nurses' clothes, shined their combat boots and combed their hair. They taught Thompson to be less naive: The Darvon pills she passed out so freely to moaning Vietnamese patients brought $6 each on the black market, they confided.

The nurses, in turn, paid their mamasans $7 a month and doled out American goodies. Thompson even gifted her mamasan with a frilly baby-doll nightgown imported from Kansas.

"She never wore it. She just sat there and stroked it," Thompson recalls. "I wondered how long it would be before some GI bought it through the black market and sent it to his girlfriend back in the United States."

The nurses quickly became accustomed to life in Viet Nam, German-Chung says. But they never got used to war.

'Tight Feeling In Your Gut'

"You learned to live with the heat and the smell. Fear of the unknown became less. But fear of not being good enough took its place," she says. "As a surgical intensive-care nurse, I was always worried I wouldn't catch something that could save a life. The tight feeling in your gut only worsened; it never got better."

The women in Viet Nam were the most young and inexperienced ever to serve in wartime. The training was scant. The conditions were bleak.

"I'd been working in a nursery, for heaven's sake," German-Chung says. "I had had no exposure to war-injured."

Their methods were unorthodox. Feverish malaria patients soaked in the ocean. Inexperienced surgeons frequently phoned their instructors overseas for advice. Sterile was as clean as you could make it.

The hours were grueling: 16 hours on, 16 hours off. And sometimes they saw suffering that they were not prepared to see. Tagtmeyer, who rarely cared for soldiers from the front lines, saw the effects of sharp bamboo punji sticks and land mines. German-Chung remembers seeing corpsmen remove live explosives from the abdomen of a soldier who'd committed suicide with his grenade launcher. And Thompson cared for a Vietnamese villager, nicknamed "Crispy Critter," who had been burned with Napalm over 90 percent of his body. Surgeons crafted him a thumb from his big toe. They circumcised him to get enough skin to rebuild his eyelids.

"No matter what we asked him to go through, he did it with a smile," Thompson says. "He was just happy to be alive. Because of him, I realized how wimpy the people were in America. I didn't want to fluff their pillows anymore. Instead of being a handmaiden, I wanted to really help people who needed it." Long after the medical procedures were finished, the nurses encouraged emotional healing as well.

During her evening shift, Tagtmeyer gave a lot of back rubs and told a lot of bedtime stories. *The Three Bears, Little Red Riding Hood*, whatever the soldiers wanted. It sounds strange, but it reminded them of better times. I'd tell the stories, and we'd laugh and have a good time. But sometimes they got pretty quiet, and I knew they were dealing with their own kind of grief and loneliness."

German-Chung recalls chatting with a fellow nurse about sex. "I asked a young soldier who was very, very ill if he'd overheard our conversation. He nodded and smiled—as much as you can smile with an endotracheal tube. I realized that maybe I had allowed him to go back and imagine being with his wife or his girlfriend for a while. I realized that for the short time that the soldiers were there, I was everything to them: their mother, their lover, their sister."

Breaking The Tension

In the midst of war, there were happy times, too. Nurses spent their free time napping on sunny white beaches, dancing in the makeshift officers' club and eating bountiful seafood dinners.

While waiting for the choppers to come, they broke the tension with practical jokes. They propped water buckets on door frames and covered toilet seats with Saran Wrap.

On holidays, they grabbed cups of hot chocolate, scrambled to the roofs of their hooches and watched the soldiers shoot off a stunning show of tracers.

Their brief vacations were spent in the world's most exotic places. In Hong Kong, Thompson shopped for handmade outfits of silk and linen at Kmart prices. She visited castles, shrines and Buddhist temples. She sampled bird's nest soup. Not bad for a young woman who'd never been out of Kansas before.

Coming Home

After one year of service each, American nurses left Viet Nam with little sense of the political implications of their service. It was harder to adjust to coming home than it was to adjust to going overseas, Tagtmeyer says. "I think we all felt a little lost. Everybody thought we'd win the war, but it didn't happen. Everyone had fought, but it hadn't achieved anything," says Tagtmeyer, who also served a couple of years in Taiwan.

"It was sad to see them loading everything up to leave in 1973. When I flew over Cam Ranh Bay on my way home, it was deserted. It looked beautiful and quiet, but it was sad, too."

What awaited the nurses at home was sadder. Tagtmeyer recalls taking courses at Purdue University in West Lafayette, where students protested the war and bad-mouthed returning military personnel. Thompson discovered that nobody was interested in her war stories. German-Chung met women who kept their service a secret.

"Many were—and are—afraid of the reaction," German-Chung says. "There's a great misconception about what women did over there in Viet Nam. Somehow, I guess, people think that we were over there killing babies and raping women instead of caring for the sick and wounded."

The three nurses went on with their lives. Tagtmeyer works in the newborn nursery at St. Joseph Medical Center. She and her husband, Mark, have two daughters: Mary Christie, 15, and Sarah, 4. Thompson, who moved to Fort Wayne from St. Louis four years ago, is a psychiatric nurse at Park Center. She and her husband, who also served in Viet Nam, have three sons: Chris, 11; Clinton, 9; and Colin, 7. German-Chung, who moved to Schererville two years ago, is an operating- room nurse at St. Anthony Medical Center in Crown Point.

Lately, news reports about a bronze statue sculpted by Santa Fe artist Glenna Goodacre have brought the memories flooding back. On Nov. 11, members of the Viet Nam Women's Memorial Project will gather in Washington, D.C., to dedicate the statue honoring women who served in the military during the Viet Nam War.

German-Chung and her husband, David, will stand proudly in the capital during the dedication. Tagtmeyer will quietly acknowledge the event in Indiana. Thompson will probably ignore the occasion altogether.

"My husband and I went to see the wall (Viet Nam Memorial)," Thompson says. "He cried while he was pointing out names of people he knew. That's not for me. I just try to remember the good times, and get on with living."

"That's exactly what the monument celebrates," German-Chung says. "Most monuments are put up to remember the dead. If you step on a land mine, your suffering is over in a moment. But if you come back, you must live with that for the rest of your life. Surviving a war is just as much an honor as dying."

Schedule Of Events

In honor of the Viet Nam Women's Memorial, which can be seen at Southtown Mall tomorrow, an hour long program will be held. It will include a proclamation by Mayor Paul Helmke, a presentation by a representative for Senator Dan Coats' office, and music and exhibitions by several area drill teams.

Noon	Sky diving exhibition by the Cloud Busters
12:15 p.m	Prayer by Chaplain Cephas D. Williamson, Chief of Chaplains at Fort Wayne's Veterans Affairs Hospital
12:18 p.m.	Presentation of Colors by Indiana Veterans of Foreign Wars Color Guard
12:20 p.m.	Opening speech by Jane Carson of the Viet Nam Women's Memorial Project
12:30 p.m.	Speech by Patricia Battista, Women Veterans state coordinator
12:40 p.m.	Speech by 1st Lt. Bernadette Sanner, Viet Nam veteran from the U.S. Air Force
12:55 p.m.	Retirement of the colors by the Indiana VFW Color Guard

BOLD in BRONZE: The Viet Nam Women's Memorial will be on display noon-5 p.m. tomorrow near the Firestone Tire Center in the parking lot at Southtown Mall. The 6-foot-tall bronze statue, created by Santa Fe, N.M., artist Glenna Goodacre, is traveling to 21 cities between Aug. 28 and Sept. 18 so that the public can see the multi-figure sculpture that depicts three military women, one of whom cradles a wounded soldier.

Schererville resident David Chung, who served in Viet Nam, will transport the statue by truck from Santa Fe to Pentagon City, Va.

The statue was commissioned by Diane Carlson Evans, an Army nurse who served in Viet Nam and who founded the Viet Nam Women's Memorial Project. After 10 years of raising money and support for the memorial, Carlson and other female veterans will see it dedicated in Nov. 11 in Washington, DC.

CELEBRATING SURVIVAL: Cheryl German-Chung served as a nurse in Long Binh, Viet Nam. She and her husband, David Chung, another Viet Nam vet whom she met in Indiana a few years ago, plan to attend the Nov. 11 dedication of the Viet Nam Women's Memorial in Washington.

ASIAN ADVENTURE: Bev Thompson was looking for excitement when she left her rural Kansas home in 1967 and joined the Army. She found it in Tuy Hoa, where she was stationed a year later. She met her husband, Mike Thompson during training at Fort Benning, Ga. Among her wartime souvenirs is a vegetable pod boat given to her by a Vietnamese child.

BACK RUBS AND BEDTIME STORIES: Jeanne Tagtmeyer thought serving in Viet Nam would be the "epitome of nursing," but she discovered her friendship was just as important to soldiers as her medical care. Her scrapbook of memories from the 12th Air Force Hospital in Cam Ranh includes a postcard from "Peanuts" creator Charles Schulz.

One Woman's Experience In Viet Nam

To the best of my memory, we women lived in a compound consisting of three 2-story buildings for sleeping quarters. Each story had 4 or 5 rooms with one bathroom consisting of sinks and commodes only. The first floor of one of the building contained CQ area, which was also First Sergeant's office and a mailroom, supply room, shower room and laundry.

The first building, second floor, 1st room, just above the CQ area, was my room, which I shared with 2 or 3 girls, depending on the turnover. This room contained the regular military issue bedsteads of which there were four. There were foot lockers for each individual, a wall locker and we shared dressers.

When I walked out onto the balcony of my room, I could look down on the pavilion where parties took place and movies were shown. It was a large slab of cement with a sloping roof and no sides. Picnic tables and benches were there for comfort although they were hard comfort.

All these structures were enclosed by one, big wooden 8 to 9 foot fence with concertina wire rolled up the outside and coming across the top. A security guard had a little shack just outside the walk-in gate where he searched people coming in and out, mostly the Vietnamese maids.

The night of our first actual attack while I was there occurred during TET. Rumors had been flying that we would get attacked during TET, because the installation had been hit during the last TET, also. For weeks prior the brass set off sirens, drilled us on how to get the bunkers and counted the time it took the protective troops to reach our area. I remember the platoon tried to lessen the time with every practice. Our part was to scramble and get to the bunkers as fast as possible. The bunkers were on the ends of each building. They were structures built above ground with sand bags encasing them. Each bunker had small wooden benches and you had to stoop as you entered. As we entered the bunkers, we carried what Uncle Sam considered essential for us to have. These were helmets, canteens of fresh water and Oscar, our gas mask.

When the siren went off, all these crazy women in pajamas, and not all of them in flannel (!) would go running to the bunkers from all directions. I remember one young lady went scurrying to the bunker with short, flimsy, bright pink, baby doll pajamas with a helmet hovering precariously on top of gigantic hair rollers.

Back to the night question, it had been a night like many others: you worked until 7 p.m., got to the club at 7:15 p.m., did a bit of drinking and danced if a band had been brought in, arrived back at the barracks, hit the showers, and were in bed by 11:30 p.m. and asleep by 11:35 p.m. The only thing different this time was that the sounds started before the siren went off at 2:00 a.m.

I awoke to the sound of the building creaking, glass breaking, and the ground exploding nearby. You could hear the whistle and the Kaaaaaboom!

This was different and I knew it instinctively. This certainly was not outgoing artillery!

I remember screaming across the darkened room at my roommate, "Chris, this is different, what in hell is going on?" I remember hearing her call to me, and then her voice, which was always so steady before, sounded scared like mine, but she said firmly, "Get your stuff and let's get out of here." She had had more time in country and I needed no second opinion. Terror took over. I would feel this over and over again but that first time is never quite the same. My object? Get to those bunkers!

I couldn't find my damn glasses. I was lost without them, and I remember groping here and there trying to find them. At last I located them under my bed. I had my robe on, thongs on my feet, and my helmet, canteen and Oscar were clutched in my arms. I was the last one to leave the room.

For the months since I had lived there, I had always used the steps closest to the CQ area. I used those that night despite the fact that we were told to use the second set at the end of the balcony during an attack. Panic gripped me and all I remember thinking at that time was, "Get to the bunkers, the bunkers, the bunkers."

Once in the bunker, I huddled up in my corner position and waited until the shakes stopped and my breathing returned to normal. In those first moments while we waited we all must have felt something just like the residents of London who were bombed during the blitz … and me? I prayed so hard and said many, many Hail Marys. It was a moment in time when you realize: this is it, this is the end, I am only 20 years of age and my life has been cut short. The waiting seemed never ending, but we were unable to do anything but wait. Our lives depended on God, on a platoon of protective troops, and luck. We had no weapons, but our bare hands and our courage to protect ourselves if the worst happened. And believe me, at that time you thought of only the worst.

It must have been a half hour or so after that my pulse quieted down from the triple time it had been working. The First Sergeant came around then took headcount and asked, "Who broke the water cooler?" Now that my nerves had steadied, I was almost afraid to speak up for fear I would be in trouble for the accident: but like George Washington, I would not tell a lie, so I answered, "I did, First Sergeant." I explained how it happened. Needless to say that accident got me a lot of ribbing from the rest of the troops over the following months. It took about 4 months to replace that cooler. First Sergeant asked me if I was all right, and my reply was "Fine."… Fine? Umph! How could one be fine when under earthen filled sandbags, your knees are knocking, your heart is pounding, and there is a girl hysterically crying right across from you, not to mention the noise of artillery both incoming and outgoing and the sounds of choppers filling the night.

Toward dawn we were allowed out for a breather. The artillery was mostly outgoing and in the distance now, concentrated on the farthest perimeter on the other side of the headquarters building. One could see the lights of the explosions and the wisps of gas as it floated on the breeze towards the enemy positions. Hueys crossed the installation making a flight pattern over our quarters on their way to the evac hospital. The sun was just coming up and I was walking around trying to tell myself over and over again that I was alive! I was OK! I even chatted with some of the guards who had arrived around 30 minutes after the action started when I was hiding away in my hole certain that I was in my final hour with no way to defend myself.

When one of the girls mentioned I was limping, I realized my feet hurt, particularly the left one. I put my finger under my heel and it came away with blood all over it. It looked worse than it really was. I went to the First Sergeant and with alcohol, iodine and tweezers, she pulled slivers of glass from the bottom of my feet. It happened when I broke the water cooler all those hours before. I still have a scar on the bottom of my left foot from that accident as a reminder of that night.

By mid-morning, I was dressed and at work even though fighting was still going on over the perimeter. The enemy had been turned back. The only problem was that not everyone would be going back to work ever again. Richard died while he slept as the first round had come in. The deputy commander died in his bunker from a direct hit.

The next day, the usual piece of paper was circulated regarding body counts of VC who had broken through our lines. The curious comment had been added that the dead VC carried can openers. These were in preparation for the C-rations they had been promised if they overran us.

The after-effects are now dreams that disturb my nights, dreams that re-live those nights of artillery exploding all around. At times I reach safety and at times I don't. Sometimes I am confronted by the black pajama-clad figures. Sometimes I survive. Sometimes I don't.

<table>
<tr><td>

13

</td><td>

The Viet Nam Warrior:
His Experience, and Implications
for Psychotherapy

By Stephen Howard, M.D.

</td></tr>
</table>

The psychodynamic experience of the Viet Nam trooper is described and emotionally evoked by the author, who is both a psychiatrist and a combat veteran of that war. It is shown how that experience continues to affect the lives of these men. The special implications of that experience for psychotherapy are then discussed.

Reproduced with permission of the Association for the Advancement of Psychotherapy.

Howard, MD, S. (1976).The Viet Nam warrior: His experience and implications for psychotherapy. *American Journal of Psychotherapy*. XXX, 121-135.

INTRODUCTION

This will be a most unscientific paper; much of it will be subjective and experiential, and more than half of it will be written in the first person.

In January of 1973, I delivered a paper at the Boston University Medical Center, where I was then an Instructor in Psychiatry. The paper was entitled "A Psychiatrist Views the Viet Nam Experience." It was based on my own experience as an infantry surgeon, and it left me and many members of my audience shaken and upset. It was a good paper; I had intended to revise it for publication. Between the press of events in my life and the anxiety which my combat experience still bears for me, I never did so.

Now many of the old names are in the news again. Quang Tri has fallen. Hue, bought with the blood of men in my outfit, flies the Viet Cong flag from the Citadel. Da Nang, the base of our Marine operations, was surrendered without a fight. The list goes on, and Saigon itself will probably have fallen before this paper can be published[1]. As the cities fall, my feelings again rise. I experience the old anguish, the burning rage, the sense of having been used. I feel the bitter vindication of having been right when I would have preferred not to be. Even the nightmares have returned, though with greatly diminished intensity.

I read the newspapers, I speak with other veterans; I listen to my patients, and discover that I am not alone. As will be pointed out later, marked delays in the psychological reactions to this war are common. I am certain

---

[1] April 28: As I finish the final draft of this paper, President Minh announces the surrender of the Saigon government. It is over. I am in tears with pain and bitterness. This paper was submitted in May 1975.

that other therapists are hearing what I am hearing and experiencing. I feel that the material in this paper is needed now.

Following this introduction, the paper is in two parts. First, the experience itself; this part is a slight rewrite of the original spoken address, and is an attempt to share that experience with others. In the second part I will become a little more objective and clinical, and try to offer suggestions to the therapist based on an understanding of the experiential realities.

I. THE EXPERIENCE

When asked to speak on Viet Nam, I very deliberately chose the title to stress the word "experience." This will not be a political paper nor a terribly analytic one, but an attempt to convey to you as best I can some of the aspects of the experience on a subjective level, personal to me and to the men with whom I shared that experience.

Before approaching the subject proper, I would like to share with you a present experience. I knew last summer that I would be standing here speaking with you today; I had five months' advance knowledge; yet I found myself endlessly procrastinating, and did not shut myself up in my study for serious work until a few weeks ago. When I finally did so, organizing my notes and beginning to write, I knew then that I had not simply been procrastinating; I felt a terrible chill of anxiety, all of the anxiety and horror which came with opening myself again to that experience so that I might try to share it with you. That anxiety persisted throughout the writing, and is still with me today. I have discussed my experience with friends, lovers, with my therapist; yet the anxiety persists. I suspect it always will; to this day I find it difficult and sometimes painful to see a war movie, and if it is not exceptionally good I will go out of my way to avoid it. Many conflicts have been resolved, time has had an effect, my understanding of events is deeper; yet experience takes its toll, and some scars are always easily reopened.

I hope these remarks are met not with sympathy, as they might be, but as an opening point for the sharing of an experience extremely difficult to communicate to those who may not have encountered it themselves.

Having been drafted in 1961, in 1968 I received my orders for Viet Nam. I served there as a battalion surgeon in the field with the Marine infantry in the I-Corps, the northernmost part of South Viet Nam, just below the so-called Demilitarized Zone. I had the dubious opportunity of taking part in the siege of Khe Sanh (which some of you may remember from Life Magazine and from David Douglas Duncan's remarkable photographic reports); and also in the defense of the Rock Pile, Ton Son Lam, and the second great battle for Kon Thein, at which I was wounded. So I draw upon my own direct experience, and upon the thoughts, emotions, and anxieties of the men who directly or indirectly shared their feelings and perceptions with me. I cannot address myself to the experience of the behind-the-lines noncombatant soldiers, with what must have been their unspeakable boredom and gnawing guilt; my own experience was that of combat.

Combat

There is so much to relate of the combat experience that it is difficult to know where to begin. Perhaps the most useful starting point would be to focus on the massive sense of depersonalization of the combat trooper. He is torn from everything that is familiar and comforting to him: his family and friends, his country, even the familiar routine of stateside barracks life; his normal hopes and troubles and ways of relating. He finds himself in a strange Asian country, knowing nothing of its language, history, or meanings, surrounded by desolation and threatened with death; he is the alien; the very word "alienation" takes on a depth of emotional impact unplumbed by most philosophers and psychologists. He is a non-person, an alien, a thing expected to function, while everything around him is strange and lacking in meaning. His view of his surroundings is startlingly expressed in the phrases "The Nam" and "The World"; Viet Nam is, in his perception and experience, someplace removed from the real world. And the excruciating boredom which he frequently must endure in the hiatus between military operations, along with the deprivation of privacy, only reinforces his experience of himself as a thing which is either performing in a prescribed way or waiting in the machine shop until called upon to do so.

This vast sense of depersonalization is further elevated by two factors. The first of these is the nature of modern warfare: it is usually fought at a distance; even rifles and grenades are frequently aimed at targets 100 meters or more away, the enemy soldiers are figures rather than people, and hand-to-hand struggle with another man is rare—I experienced it myself only once in my tour of duty. One fires, and one may be firing at a man, a movement, or a shadow. If it is a man and the attacker sees him go down, is he dead, wounded, or merely taking cover? Recently, in discussing Viet Nam with a patient, I asked him if he had ever killed anyone. His answer was, "I once fired at an old man across a river." Hardly the highly personalized life-and-death heroics we read about in the epic accounts of warfare.

The second device adding to the sense of depersonalization is the consciously and unconsciously perpetuated use of a language of slang and euphemisms more suited to the discussion of objects and mechanical events than to anything having to do with human beings. A few simple examples: the Asians are "gooks" or "charlies," terms which immediately disqualify them as human beings who love, hate, live, hope, and die; no one really dies, but is "zapped," "wasted," or KIA—meaning killed in action. And there are no attacks or blood battles, there is merely "contact." There seem to be no words at all for danger, fear, and so on; indeed a form of Newspeak.

A poignant example of this is a radio message received one day while I was on duty at the battalion command center. I still have a copy, and it reads as follows:

Alpha six to Walnut, contact hours one three zero five at one three seven zero two, moderate exchange, probable company november victor alpha break, twelve november victor alpha kilo india alpha break break, friendlies two kilo india alpha, thirteen repeat one three whiskey india alpha, evac. Following november november echo from desig coord, may need arty or air.

This could be a computer printout, so let me translate it into English for you. Alpha Company is on patrol, and the company captain is reporting to battalion headquarters that at a certain place designated by the map coordinates, they ran into a company of North Vietnamese soldiers. Of our own men, 2 were killed and 13 wounded: these have been medically evacuated. Alpha Company is now pursuing them north northeast, and is worried enough about what it may run into that they are warning us that they may need artillery or even air support. Consider: where in that mechanical message was the blood, the death and pain, the fear of men tracking other men through an unknown jungle, and the stark terror of walking into an ambush or some other fierce danger? No, there are only KIA's, coordinates, and the report of a "moderate exchange."

Under this burden of loneliness, alienation, depersonalization and fear, one might well ask: how then do men function, how can they meet what is demanded of them without giving way to despair and hopelessness? The military would like us to believe it to be a matter of morale, but I find this hard to believe. Morale rests on two pillars: good leadership, and belief in that for which one is fighting. The first of these qualities is so glaring in its absence that this will likely be noted by military historians as the most poorly conceived, planned, and led war in which we have ever engaged. I speak not only of the top levels—though who will ever think of Westmoreland or Abrams along with Eisenhower or U. S. Grant or Robert E. Lee—but also of the middle and lower levels of leadership. Nowhere but in Viet Nam have I seen so blatant an application of the Peter Principle of incompetence. This is borne witness by the incredible number of "fraggings," of officers killed or wounded by men under their own command.

As to the matter of belief or faith in a cause, I think a few words will suffice. With the exception of a tiny minority, the junior enlisted men (even in 1968) saw only futility and senselessness in the war, and the same statement could be made for the junior officers. These men had only one reason to fight—simple survival. The enemy was the enemy only because he threatened their lives, not because of any sense of purpose or any understanding of opposing political ideas. The contempt they expressed toward Viet Nam and its people flatly belies the idea of American boys fighting for democracy, Vietnamese self-determination, or any other ideological purpose. Much the same feelings emerged more quietly from the middle-level officers when it was possible to get them to express their views. Like the basically apolitical senior enlisted men, they were professionals doing a job they had been sent to do, and they tried to pay obedience, if not respect, to their seniors. This is hardly the picture of a high-morale army dedicated to a purpose.

So these were men fighting for survival, their own individual survival and that of the group on which they were dependent. But this does not answer the question I raised: by what maneuvers, by what mechanisms, were they able to do this in the face of their own terror, their sense of futility, their depersonalization, alienation, and loneliness? Or to put it differently and more simply, what is a man's experience of danger in combat, and how is this thing we call courage possible?

One crucial element is the fantasy and desire in each of us-but especially in the young—for invulnerability. Add to this the presence of real and frequent danger, and the desire easily becomes a quasi-delusional belief in one's invulnerability. This, of course, requires affirmation by the massive use of counterphobic maneuvers, and the meeting of danger with denial of almost psychotic proportions. If my use of language seems rather strong, this is entirely intentional—for I can find no other way to begin to convey an experience that is itself of a nearly insane quality.

Another element adding to the ability to be courageous is the intense wish to prove oneself. While our society continues to emphasize physical courage as a masculine virtue—for better or for worse—technology and the nature of modern life generally make physical courage superfluous. It is only in combat that most young men are put to the test, and few can resist this opportunity to prove what they believe to be their masculinity. It also becomes terribly important to offer this proof to their comrades; I shall have more to say about that shortly.

While aggressiveness is also a prized virtue taught to most young men, the ultimate in aggression—the opportunity to kill—is nowhere else permitted. Yet this urge, whether innate or acquired, is in most men so powerful that immediately before the approach of combat there is an anticipatory thrill accompanying or even overriding one's fear. I have experienced this myself, and have seen it in other men's faces and spoken with them about it.

I think that this is an appropriate moment to take up briefly the subject of killing. Probably most people have asked themselves at one time or another, "Could I kill another human being?" With one reservation, the answer to this question is a very definite "yes." The combination of self-preservation, all of our aggressive drives, and the permission granted by the circumstances, makes it possible for even the most gentle and humane person to kill. In the anticipation of combat, it is not unusual for men to indulge in elaborate wish-fantasies of destruction. The guilt which accompanies this is effectively isolated, and rarely emerges until one is out of the war zone. Even then it usually emerges in indirect ways, through participation in antiwar movements, and even more universally, in anxiety dreams.

I spoke of one reservation in answering "yes" to the question of ability to kill. I did see a few men who genuinely were unable to kill, and who would even permit their own destruction first. A tiny handful honestly had such powerful moral or religious objections that they would not kill, but I am talking about the others: those for whom such action was psychologically impossible. These men would come to my attention when they were sent by their company commanders, usually after a refusal to go out on patrol with their units. Whatever reasons they gave, one thing always emerged clearly in my evaluation of them: to a man they were latent or borderline schizophrenics. On some level they knew the danger to themselves of killing: that that act would release the primitive world-destroying rage inside of them, and their already fragile ego structure would be entirely overwhelmed. Naturally I had them evacuated to a hospital for full psychiatric evaluation, and all were sent stateside. These were the men who could not kill; all others could, however distasteful it might be.

I mentioned that I would have more to say about friends and comrades. It is difficult to describe to one who has not experienced it the power of the strange friendships and the comraderies which grow up quickly among men in combat. Part of the strangeness is in the power and rapidity of these friendships, and an even greater strangeness is that when death arrives, mourning lasts but a few minutes if it occurs at all. It emerges frequently in the universal after-dreams of the combat trooper, along with guilt, but it is not consciously felt at the time. After seeing and experiencing these friendships, one is able to look more closely and see that what is occurring is a powerful pseudointimacy; the surface feelings of a powerful love which one desperately needs for sustenance, and beneath that the withholding of oneself from the buddy who may die today or next week.

Traditionally, one of the things which motivates men in battle is the prospect of glory. But there is little or no glory in the mechanized, depersonalized jungles of modern warfare. Everyone knows this, but few wish to tolerate it; so compensation is made by bragging and telling stories, at first to one another, and later to anyone who will listen. Few soldiers can return home from combat and resist telling endless war stories.

The Real World

I would like to turn attention to another and very different aspect of the Viet Nam experience: the soldier's experience of home while he is 12,000 miles away from it, and his contact is through sporadic and unsatisfactory letters. He is again in "The Nam," somewhere outside the known universe, and the "real world" is questionable in its reality. Home is a psychological anchor, very real yet unreal, and the unreality is terrifying in its threat to leave the trooper completely adrift. As a result, this experience of unreality is denied and repressed; the sense of desperation, of isolation and alienation, the terrible need for a feeling of contact with something real and human, produces an overwhelming insistence on creating and recreating a sense of being somehow in touch with the world of home. An enormous amount of leisure time is spent in thinking and talking about experiences back home, in making plans for return and in dreaming about what it will be like when one arrives home, whether these are lifetime plans such as career and marriage, or simply the intent, as one master sergeant kept telling me, to "plunk down with my beer and fish the hell out of the nearest river."

The other aspect of being forcefully isolated from home is, of course, life without women. For the rifleman on the line, his contact with women is rare. When it does occur it is transient, artificial, almost always with prostitutes;

there is no opportunity for warmth, intimacy, or sharing; there is nothing sustained, and certainly no possibility of any meaningful dialogic relationship. The lack of these things, the absence of tenderness, and the more general sexual deprivation, have several important and unfortunate effects. The first of these is an even further increase in the sense of depersonalization -and if you are growing tired of hearing the word, please try to imagine what it is like to live constantly with the feeling.

The second unfortunate effect is that men quickly begin to lose any perspective of women as human beings with whom one may share experience, sexual or otherwise. Tenderness is lost, sex is reduced to sheer physical lust, and women become nothing more than fantasies for shaking that lust. This is all too common in our society anyway, and the conditions of war tend to promote it to the extreme degree. Many men never lose this outlook.

The third effect is also based on a socially fostered myth of masculinity— that to be a man means, in its crudest terms, fighting and fucking. This mythos is, of course, fostered by the military, and the younger men in particular are likely to believe in it. Thus, removal of the opportunity of sexually asserting one's masculinity feeds further into the need to fight. On a more analytic level, verbal slips, dreams, fantasies, and many expressions commonly used in the bunkers indicate a confusion, a blurring of the distinction between gun and phallus, to the extent that orgasmic release is sometimes experienced in the very act of committing violence.

At this point my anxiety level begins to rise again, and I would like to shift the focus slightly. In discussing women in this context, we should think also about the women—wives and girl friends—who have been left at home.

Here, too, I could repeat the remarks I made about the feelings of home: the desperate need for an anchor, the feeling of unreality, and the exaggerated insistence that that security is real and solid. Against this insistence— more or less real, more or less fantasy, but always bolstered by need— against this insistence stand several hard realities. People die at home, too: perhaps my wife or lover will be taken by disease or accident while I am helpless, 12,000 miles away. Barring this, relationships have a way of becoming tenuous with lack of contact and sharing, and this is especially true of the young and unmarried. The loneliness, the lack of sustenance, and another factor which I will mention in a moment, all tend to promote acting out, with the dangers that poses to the partnership. We should remember, too, that war is fought more by boys, by teenagers, than by men, and so the girl at home is not unlikely to simply find someone else. The effect of a "Dear John" letter can be devastating, and I have seen more than one suicide precipitated by such an event.

I said I would mention another factor, and that is anger. Many men will avail themselves of opportunities for sexual encounters, yet I never knew one to write home to his wife about it. But many times men would come to me or to the chaplain, deeply upset. They had received tearful, apologetic letters, describing—sometimes vividly—an affair the woman had had, and begging the man's forgiveness. Sometimes this would happen several times with the same woman, and often the vividness of the descriptions was startling. The first two or three times I took it at face value, but quickly realized that there was a terribly punitive aspect in this phenomenon. These women were angry, full of rage at having been deserted while husband or boyfriend went off to have a good time playing war. While I am certain that this rage and the consequent acting out-acting out not simply in having an affair but in writing about it-was largely unconscious, it had a devastating effect on these men. Many reacted with anger, many with guilt or depression, a few obsessionally avoided their feelings; but it was clear that all were deeply hurt. One man even said to me, "If she had to get laid, let her have it. I'm not doing her any good now. But why did she have to tell me about it?" I did not feel inclined to answer that question.

The Return

Feeling that I have at least touched on the most important aspects of the combat ordeal itself, I might have chosen to end here. However, there is another aspect of my subject that is little touched upon, and I feel it is important to attempt to share this too with you. The neglected aspect I refer to is the experience of the combat veteran returning home.

I will begin by very briefly touching on the aftermath of two subjects I have already discussed. The first is friendship, and it is no surprise that the seemingly deep and intimate relationships quietly vanish upon return stateside. Letters are not written, visits are not made, and even in those rare instances where attempts are made, the friendship no longer has a solid base of support; indeed, one wishes to escape from the shared experience which formed the relationship.

Second, there are the effects of family life. I have already mentioned the dangers to lovers and spouses of separation, growing apart, abandonment, and anger, and often of mutual or unilateral acting out. Needless to say, these problems are intensified if there were already weak points in the partnership prior to the enforced separation. And if there are young children, the course of a year has rendered the father practically a stranger through his absence during crucial developmental periods.

In addition, the veteran is carrying the burden of an experience so alien to ordinary life that he finds an almost unbridgeable gap in communication with parents, wives, and other significant people in his life. They can at best sympathize; he feels that they cannot understand. Only new-made friends who have been there can understand, and if the friendship is real, the two men will compulsively spend hours sharing it; they are close enough to understand, but since they did not undergo the ordeal together, there is enough distance to make the sharing tolerable and provide a valuable contact and catharsis. A current friend and I, who served in adjacent units but never met over there, could not get together for the first two years of our friendship without sooner or later talking about the war.

There now begins that universal phenomenon of men returning from modern warfare: the after-dream. This is a painful yet healing process, in which the individual at last has the opportunity to discharge some of the repressed affects of his experience, to relive-in dream language at least-some of the anguishing events in which emotion was stifled. He is now free to experience his guilt over killing, his grief for his lost comrades, and that phenomenon described so well from study of the concentration camps-survivor's guilt. Yet the dream distortions are often weak or even absent, and when present are rarely very effective; hence most of these dreams are anxiety-dreams, They usually persist for several months and in very disguised forms may often be seen years later in the analysis of the individual's dreams. Even today, when I examine my own dreams, it is surprising how often some disguised reference to a particularly traumatic war event turns up.

Finally, one characteristic which shows up with great frequency in the returnee is his rebelliousness. While this it not often understood, it should come as no surprise to us. He has risked life, body, and mind in an adventure he did not approve of or even understand. He has been dominated by authority which appears to him both incompetent and uncaring. He has seen men die, and perhaps he himself has been wounded, maimed, or become drug addicted, and he can make no sense of it.

The trooper home from this war receives no accolades, no parades, no congratulations other than those for sheer survival. The society he was supposedly fighting for offers him no thanks, no status, no special respect. Indeed it is just the opposite. He hears again and again that men are fighting and dying needlessly, and knows that he and his comrades have been those men. No one says, "I am proud of you." He is met with the uncomfortable reactions of people who do not know what to say, or worse yet angrily demand of him, "How could you have gone?" Everything contributes to increase his guilt and his sense of alienation from the society he was supposed to have served.

He is an angry man; he is a pariah. He is a nonhero soldier, however brave he has been. What can we expect but a fierce resistance to all authority? He is depleted of the normal masochism which helps so much to make compromise and conciliation possible. He is a wounded, angry, and estranged man who has no place in the society that sent him to war. And we have done this to him.

I began this paper with a terrible sense of anxiety. I end it now by sharing with you my sense of helplessness, my frustration, and my rage.

II. IMPLICATIONS FOR PSYCHOTHERAPY

Initial Therapeutic Considerations

As a society, we might like to follow President Ford's suggestion, "putting Viet Nam behind us" and looking to the future. I hope we will not put it behind us to the extent that we again refuse to learn from history. But for the Viet Nam veteran, "putting it behind us" is no simple matter. He must live with his experience, and every reminder reawakens old difficulties.

Some of the earlier psychiatric literature on the subject[2] presents the finding of a lower incidence of psychiatric casualties in this war than in previous ones. This is factually true but misleading. In World War II, for example, the soldier was in "for the duration." The dangers and stresses continued on and on with no finite end point. If he was to become a psychiatric casualty this was most likely to occur while' he was still with his unit!. The man in Viet Nam was returned home after a 12· or 13-month rotation resulted in a time-limited stress in which the serious sequelae often did not appear until long after the trooper left the combat zone. His nonwelcome home adds bitterly to these sequelae.

The Viet Nam veteran continues to experience a vast sense of depersonalization, isolation, and conviction of the impossibility of encountering any genuine understanding of his experience. In addition, these men as a group manifest an extraordinary assortment of aggressive and destructive thoughts, though their reactions are generally internalized[3]. In my experience, the combination of these factors most commonly manifests itself in a vast repression of affect, and in a mild but stubbornly chronic depression and dissatisfaction. Before almost anything else can be dealt with, the individual will need help in "derepression," in regaining contact with a wide range of emotions, many of which are quite painful.

This initial derepression involves the usual approaches to dealing with blocked affect: pointing out and challenging defenses: giving the patient "permission" to feel, building an accepting and accepted therapeutic relationship. But in the case of the troubled combat veteran, several additional features must be considered.

The first of these is the unusually strong authority transference which is projected onto the therapist. It is not that such a transference is unusual; rather it is the strength of the suspiciousness which is carried over from every uncaring or incompetent officer and sergeant; this must be confronted and dealt with early in the relationship. The therapist must be prepared to endure a great deal of distrust and unearned resentment.

The second feature is closely aligned with the first. It is important that full respect be paid to the external and phenomenological realities of indifference, lack of human caring, and the feeling of having been used and betrayed. It is hoped that the therapist comes to care in a genuine manner, and this contrasts sharply with the veteran's experience and expectations. As Chessick[4] nicely points out, caring cannot be forced on the patient; it is only as transference distortions are untangled that he can clearly perceive the existential reality of the human concern. The therapist's recognition and validation of the experience of indifference and betrayal can go far toward making possible recognition of the caring.

---

[2] Bourne, P. G. Man, *Stress, and Viet Nam.* Little Brown, Boston, Mass., 1970.

[3] Strange, R. E., and Brown, D. E. "Home from the War: A Study of Psychiatric Problems in Viet Nam Returnees." *Am. J. Psychiat.,* 127: 488, 1970.

[4] Chessick, R. D. Psychotherapeutic Interaction. *Am. J. Psychother.,* 28: 243, 1974.

Along with the general derepression of affect, these men need-even more than most-the sanction to experience and express "unmanly" emotions: tenderness, wonder, gentle love, passivity. They must be helped to unlearn the pattern of "tough masculinity" which they may have grown up with, and which the military has intentionally reinforced. It may be very difficult for them to understand that it is adult and manly to cry, to offer comfort, to fear, to grieve, to touch lovingly, to protect and to wish to be sheltered.

As these things are learned, as the enforced roles break down, a side result is that the man can then permit women to be human beings in his eyes, to be partners and to share, to be respected and cherished. Many of us today are concerned with overcoming the rigidity of traditional sex roles, for ourselves and our patients. The combat veteran often needs help with this even more than the rest of us.

The Therapeutic Relationship

Once derepression of affect is well under way, the depression and chronic dissatisfaction tend to lift, and are replaced by anxiety, anger, and resentment. This occurs, of course, along with the full range of emotions and conflicts to which anyone might be subject. As in any other therapeutic endeavor, the nature of the dyadic relationship becomes extremely crucial, in both its transference and its reality aspects.

To the extent that the emotions and conflicts are directly related to the combat experience, something above and beyond the usual therapeutic relationship obtains. For however much the neurotic (that is, transference) elements are uncovered and worked through, the experience remains. This experience carries a staggering burden of anguish, horror, and guilt stemming from real acts and events. This existential reality cannot be analyzed and resolved like a neurotic conflict. Much less can it be rationalized or comforted away, for the veteran will feel-correctly-that this is nothing more than a convenient escape from his own discomfort and that of the therapist. What he really needs is a way to tolerate this anguish, and he cannot learn that if the therapist is unwilling to accept and to experience with the veteran his anxiety, horror, rage, guilt, and anguish. The therapeutic alliance is usually seen as the ground on which treatment becomes possible. But to the extent that the veteran is haunted by these profound existential disturbances, the therapeutic alliance is itself the treatment. It is impossible to exaggerate the importance of the sharing relationship with the therapist, which requires not only a nonjudgmental attitude in the classical sense, but the ability and willingness to "experience-with," and often to be a real nonrole-playing person.

These experiences are not only painful, but carry overtones which are moral, political, and philosophical. The therapist, if he/she is to deal with these people, must be willing to monitor the counter-transference with unusual honesty and willingness to question oneself and one's values. Of special concern are the therapist's aggressive and destructive impulses, as well as the human impulse to project onto others characteristics which we would prefer not to recognize in ourselves.

In particular, the ability and even desire to kill, of which I have spoken, must be recognized by the therapist. An affective as well as intellectual recognition is essential; and this must occur not only in terms of the client, but in terms of the therapist's capacity for similar acts under similar conditions. If the therapist is unwilling to do this, then the "good" therapist is set against the "bad" patient, and the former will be ineffective or destructive in the treatment of Viet Nam combat veterans.

Some Notes on Guilt

Sarah Haley [5] discusses some special considerations dealing with the veteran who reports the commission of atrocities. Her thoughts are much to the point and are recommended to the reader; but I would like to go a step further. It is important not to distinguish too strongly between "normal" combat killing on the one hand, and murder and atrocity on the other. Of course they are different and our moral sense finds the former infinitely more acceptable. But subjectively, any killing can be experienced as an atrocity by the killer, even when committed in self-defense. In combat the emotion is repressed, one is "doing what is necessary"; but later the guilt may be of enormous proportions.

I have said it is important not to rationalize or comfort away the guilt. However, it is equally important to understand the context in which the guilt-producing acts occurred. Viet Nam was a war in which only a small number believed. Yet we performed as warriors. Even a subjectively unjustified and meaningless war produces a psychology of survival. Under the overwhelming threat of annihilation, our priorities regress to the survival state; all higher priorities, all ethical and moral considerations lose relevance, and only the survival of the individual and the immediate group retain significance. The therapist must recognize this real human reaction and help the veteran to do so. In understanding this, the soldier can at last place in context some of his actions which he cannot comprehend or accept in any other way.

Once the "murders" are placed in context of the psychology of survival, and this is given reality by the therapist's implicit or explicit acknowledgment of his/her own potential murderousness, there is no longer a split between "good" therapist and "bad" patient. The therapist is then in the position to ally him/herself with the part of the patient that sees his acts as ego-alien. The guilt is not now gone; but it has a context that makes it understandable and tolerable.

Therapy in Groups

Group experiences can be extraordinarily valuable. In the context of a group composed of combat veterans, an intense kind of sharing can take place. The veteran feels that here at last the phenomenology of his experience can be appreciated directly rather than intellectually or vicariously.

---

5 Haley, S. A. "When the Patient Reports Atrocities." *Arch. Gen. Psychiat.*, 30: 191, 1974.

He quickly feels that he is not being judged or evaluated, but related to. It is now possible-and, I believe, very necessary-to steer the group away from analysis, politics, or the telling of war stories, and toward the direct expression of affect.

With the help and mutual support in the group, the individual de-represses affect very quickly, and the group members discover, often with astonishment, the commonality of their feelings. Many of these are "forbidden" feelings which now lose their forbiddingness. They can be experienced, expressed, shared, sanctioned; they are allowed release, placed in a human perspective, and the group members help each other to find ways of understanding and tolerating their horror, guilt, rage, and so on.

It is strongly suggested that, if at all possible, the group leaders be trained therapists who are themselves combat veterans, and who are willing to share their own feelings. If such people are not available, the next best (and still effective) leaders are nonveterans who are in touch with their own destructiveness, have been involved with other aggressive behavior, and are willing to share affectively. There is little room in such a group for the classical "objective" therapist.

The therapist-veteran who shares of himself not only engenders trust and facilitates the permeability of the feeling of isolation; he is also in an excellent position to lead the group toward the creative sharing of affect which is so important[6].

It may be hoped that the therapist-veteran will have worked through his own difficulties to a greater extent than the other members of the group. But one of the points I am making, illustrated by my own experience, is that the feelings engendered by the experience of combat are never completely resolved, and must be dealt with on a life-long basis. So the therapist-veteran, by becoming a member of the group and again dealing with his own anguish, provides a model, a sense of hope, and a guide for the others.

The Way Back

As I began the sharing of the experience with anxiety and ended it with helplessness and frustration and rage, so the Viet Nam veteran proceeds with his own healing. When all else is said and done, he is left feeling unheard, impotent and used. At this time in 1975, as Viet Nam crumbles and the futility of the war is driven in upon us again, the rage and bitterness return.

It is important that this not be brushed aside or "therapized." The veteran needs an appreciation and a validation of his feelings and their source. He has received this in only very limited ways, and the therapist who is unprepared or unwilling to offer this should consider whether he/she is the appropriate person to meet this individual's needs. To the extent that the therapist experiences anger, outrage, and other unpleasant reactions to the war and the material presented by the patient, it may be extremely thera-

---

6 Borus, J. F. "Re-entry: Adjustment Issues Facing the Viet Nam Veteran." *Arch. Gen. Psychiat.*, 28: 501, 1973.

peutic that this be shared with the patient. Through the therapist as representative of society, the veteran is thus given the opportunity to take a step out of his bitterness and isolation.

Summary

The combat experience is a unique and strange one, and this is truer of Viet Nam than of other wars. The psychodynamic experience is described and emotionally evoked by the author, who is both a psychiatrist and a Viet Nam combat veteran. In the context of the shared experience, the implications for psychotherapy are discussed. Of extreme importance are the special nature of the therapeutic relationship, the need for unusually honest examination of the countertransference and the therapist's own potential for violence, and the management of guilt and anguish stemming from real events.

14	# Ideals, Death, Betrayal Are Central to PTSD Theme ## By Roger Melton

If my devils are to leave me, I am afraid
my angels will take flight as well.
— Rainer Maria Rilke (1907)

Underlying the complete range of post-traumatic stress disorder (PTSD) symptomology is a desolate, lonely rage; a rage so devastating that it may, unless resolved, eventually lead to total annihilation of the self, and death. If veterans cannot find the help that can release them from the haunted grip of memory, pain, and Viet Nam, their lives may only follow the same downward spiral toward oblivion that has already claimed the fates of too many of their fellow soldiers. Anger, without direction or purpose, turns on itself. Life, without meaning, is only dead-end solitaire. Against the massive injustices of war, the veteran needs to know there was a value beneath the madness; that the death and maiming meant something beyond politics, greed, and deception. Douglas MacArthur's belief that "old soldiers never die; they just fade away" was perverted by the war in Viet Nam. Veterans of that war never fade away. They self-destruct.

Alienation, isolation, withdrawal, and depression are individual aspects of confounded rage The soldier who went to Viet Nam grew up in a society which taught him a firm set of moral ideals and values which emphasized individual freedom, a strong sense of justice, and respect for the rights of the oppressed. Each soldier who went to Viet Nam was the recipient of an educational process which valued the defense of freedom as an ideal principle. The valuing of ethical and moral principles did not have to be part of any conscious understanding; it was deeply imbedded in the American character. One of the most profound tragedies of Viet Nam was the betrayal of those ideals reflecting the finest aspects of that character.

For the individual soldier, Viet Nam put the lie to reason, purpose and justice. The mad logic of that war shattered and distorted the true meaning of freedom, morality and fairness. Once held ideals vanished against the reality of pain, guilt and agony. Soldiers were compelled to fight for the most brutal ideal—survival. It seems such a meager justification. It implies selfishness, rather than heroism; fear rather than courage; cowardice, rather than sacrifice. But survival is the reality of all war. Battlefields have no flags, only the bodies dead and wounded. High ideals have no meaning against the terror of ambush. In the final and most practical analysis, all wars are fought for the possession of dirt. Soldiers do not fight to defend god and country, but to save themselves and as many of their friends as possible. And amidst brutal reality, where is the shame in that? Is it wrong to protect yourself and your fellow soldier from too soon destruction? Where is the madness in that, or the guilt?

One of the most common beliefs expressed by Viet Nam veterans is that the war made them old before their time. Their average age was 19, yet the war confronted them with issues normally dealt with at the end of life. Before their time, they were compelled to confront the meaning of death, hopelessness, and despair. The burden of what they saw and did shattered the structured expectations of their youth, where they had been taught to believe in reason and justice. Combat was a world in which every aspect of their learned belief systems was assaulted and ruptured. Viet Nam forced them to realize the absurdity of materialistic reason and the destructive outcome of purely logical truth. it compelled them toward a search which most men and women only begin as they approach old age and death. Reality, for them, can no longer be defined within the confines of social adjustment and psychic comfort. For them the rules of normal life have ceased to apply. They have experienced the shattering of reality's normal expectations. In the most practical sense, they have found themselves driven toward a search for meaning which goes far deeper than the simple demand characteristics of the average life. Viet Nam forced them beyond easy meaning. What did their confrontation with death, betrayal, and despair mean? How can they create meaning out of mad reality? How can they be brought to see that their survival did have value: that they did fulfill an ideal far greater than the stupidity of that war?

No man is born with a set of tools. They are learned and their learning is dependent upon family, culture, and society. The sense of betrayal which many Viet Nam veterans feel seems to result directly from the apparent mockery of the nation whose ideals they fought to defend. The intense rage felt by Viet Nam veterans is the result of that perceived betrayal. A monument has been built, the press and media seem more supportive, and many people Seem willing to listen, but the veteran senses that something more is needed. The nation has to face itself, and its responsibility for Viet Nam, before it can ever honestly face the men and women it sent to that war. And the veteran, having witnessed the truth was the lie of Viet Nam, is not willing to accept shallow answers or comfortable apologies. They have earned and deserve honesty, integrity and respect.

When counseling Viet Nam veterans, deal with the meaning of ideals and betrayal. Focus on the value of survival. And if there is one essential fact which we all can convey to every Viet Nam veteran, it is that no one died in vain. The soldiers of that insane war may not have been allowed to fight for victory, nor even been given the right to decide that Viet Nam was worth fighting for, but they all fought and served, as best they could, to protect themselves and their friends. And that is an ideal which puts all others to shame.

15 The War Without Mercy
By Nick Rizzo

In 1968, as many people laid
their heads to sleep and dream
their dreams of tomorrow.
The Viet Nam Vet at 12 at night,
was struggling thru the pitch black
jungle in South East Asia.
To come home to still more
torment. To the home of the brave
And the land off the free.

Dedicated to My Son

About the Author

Nick Rizzo was born in 1948 in Fort Wayne, IN and graduated from Central H.S. in 1966. He attended Chicago Academy of fine arts in 1972. He joined the Viet Nam Veterans Art Group in Chicago in 1986, where they still house a few of his paintings. This essay was written in 1981.

Introduction

I spent two years in the United States Army and those two years were a lifetime. This story is going to attempt to explain the way I felt at different times of the war. Then and now—I only know what happened to me, so that's the part I will tell as best I can. It hurts to write about some of these things. I really do not want to think about them, and there are some things I could never tell anyone.

I mainly write this for my son who will go out into the world one day, and maybe understand it a little better than I did. Each soldier in the war did not experience something unique, but generally, there were similarities. The words cannot and do not really describe the feelings I had and the bitterness inside. But if one can get just an idea that will be good enough.

The way I was changed mentally at different times of the war felt utterly shocking. Still today, I have these touches of change in me. Very rarely do you see a movie or read a book about the lower ranking people in the service, or in life. It is so often the view of the man on top, the officer.

The great numbers of men who died were not officers. It is the men who carried out the orders who died. A good point man was worth a dozen or so Lieutenants or for that matter, a General or two. There were a lot of guys who did not get rank in Viet Nam and really deserved it. There were men who left the Army as Privates, just as they had come in as Privates. These men were very good soldiers but they did not get along with the Army. You cannot

Illus. by Tyler Mills, 2006

fight a war where everyone is an officer. Who would do all the dirty work? Who?

It is a team effort to fight a war. A war is not won by one good General. A war is won by the brains and guts of men who were everyday people on the street, and by public support. We never did have that. The fighting man took all the blame for the war.

Don't get me wrong, there were some good officers, whether they were lifers or not. The point is, without the everyday man, where would the world be? The rich could not be rich and the Generals could not fight a war. I think the everyday people deserve much more than they are getting. I personally saved five men from getting killed from friendly fire. I got nothing for it. The Lieutenant and I saved many lives and we got nothing for that either. If an officer gets killed or leaves, there is always another officer ready to take over and do the same things all over again. He sometimes gets PFCs killed...

If you have the guts and the brains, and you can get them to work under fire, then maybe you will make it...

The Road to Viet Nam

I will start from the beginning. As I graduated from high school in the year 1966, like a lot of other guys, I went looking for a job. Looking for a job when you weigh 110 pounds is not easy.

I was not a good student; there was something in me that did not like to study. So, I blame myself for my poor education. Every place I went, they told me I was not tall enough and not heavy enough to work in their factories. At that time, it really upset and disgusted me, starting out my adult life in this way. I finally found a job, but the pay was not very good. It didn't really matter because before long I was drafted. Get this, everyone told me it was my patriotic duty to serve my country. So, I was off to Indianapolis, Indiana to be sworn into the US Army.

This is how it went: since I was poor and hadn't gone to college, I went to the draft. There were those who did not go because they really thought we did not belong in Viet Nam. But, there were those who did not go because they were cowards. In the beginning, some people started saying we had no business in Viet Nam, but it did not take long before the idea got around and it became a good excuse.

Most of us who were drafted were poor white people, blacks, and Hispanics. I never met one politician's son in Viet Nam. How fair is this? Draft the guys who did not go to college? After all, they are just about worthless. Our lives didn't mean that much. To us or our parents... I wonder whose idea it was to draft our dumb asses? I wonder what they thought? Maybe, they figured we did not have anything to contribute to life?

Off to boot camp. At the time, I thought, God, two more years to go before I get out. That's the way we all felt. While in Basic, I made a friend named Dave Platt. We became very close. He was from a city not far from mine. Dave got married soon and his wife came down. Even after Dave was married, I would often sleep in their apartment with them. Dave and I sort of laughed together at the Army all through it. We listened though, because they said if we didn't pay attention we could end up dead.

Sure enough, on a cool November day, we left from Ft. Lewis, Washington to go to a country halfway around the world, Viet Nam. We were on our way to fight for our country and our last day home we spent doing shit jobs for the officers. Dave and I had KP.

We got aboard a jumbo jet and swoosh, we were off. We soon found ourselves being herded off that plane. The first thing I remember was that hot humid air. It had a different smell to it. Welcome to Viet Nam.

Dave and I were assigned to 6th Battalion, 14th Artillery Regiment at Pleiku. However, the first thing we needed to do was to find our way to Kontum at a place called "Landing Zone Mary Lou." We were told that someone was coming to pick us up to go LZ Mary Lou, so we waited and waited. Nobody ever came so we asked which direction it was and someone pointed North. We started walking and soon got picked up by a three-wheeled scooter truck. We climbed in back with the two other GIs already on board. As we put-putted down the road, the four of us chatted. As we talked, a motorbike passed going the other direction and one guy burst out kind of loud and said that, "The gook gave me the finger." He turned to ask his friend, "Should I grease him?" The other fellow said "No." and the guy began to calm down. I thought to myself, man, that was kind of cruel.

We finally arrived at LZ Marry Lou. I went to a gun section and Dave went to Fire Direction Control, that's where the infantry called for artillery support from the four big cannon. The first thing I did was sweep the gun pad clean. I looked up at the sky and it was clear, peaceful, and blue. The sun shone down on my face. It was hot and the afternoon was slow and lazy. I had been in country for three days now and I had seen neither hide nor hair of the bad guys.

Nighttime came drifting in, and we all went to bed. It was somewhere between 3 AM and 4 AM when a field phone rang and everyone jumped out of bed.I sort of half-assed woke up when someone tapped me on the foot. Hell, I thought it was some kind of fire drill. Someone said, "Come on, fire mission." I kind of slowly walked out to the gun pit where the cannon sat. Just as I got there, KAWOOM, that big, ugly, nasty thing went off. It was a muzzle blast. That's when fire wraps around the whole gun. It feels like you are getting slapped all over your body. It hurts.

I said to myself, "God, this is miserable." They wake me up at who knows when and then they expect a guy to do all this heavy work half-asleep. I just did not like it. Someone soon pointed me in the right direction and I put contact detonators on 200 pound bullets. This was my job for a few weeks. Then the First Sergeant came looking for a radio operator for a Forward Observer team. I knew I did not like what I was doing, so I volunteered.

Forward Observer

They sent me to Forward Observer school so I could learn my new job. Well, I was the only one out of fifteen officers and draftees who got 100% on the test at the end of the seven days. The dear old Army sent me to S2 (Intelligence and Security) to work in an office where they had big maps and radios. You know, I had to have a Secret clearance for that. It was real nice. I had my own room. I had my own Jeep. I would have had it made, but I did not like it there. I figured I knew a lot of guys who did not have a choice, and so I told my officer there to tell them I wanted to go out in the field, meaning *the jungle*. They thought I was nuts and maybe I was. I figured, *hell, I am here, I want to fight the enemy.* That is what they trained me for and I was a bit curious too. So a day or so went by and I went back to LZ Mary Lou.

A Lieutenant named Franco Di Tullio was waiting there for me. He was about five feet eight inches tall and had black curly hair, sort of a heavyset guy. He looked more like Henry Kissinger than a soldier. He said he was drafted and decided to go in as an officer for the money. He was not a lifer Lieutenant. He was getting out when his time was over. He seemed like a pretty nice guy. He was an Italian from Boston. I guess the Army thought we would make a good pair since we were both Italian. After we hee-hawed around awhile, we finally got a rucksack, a radio, and a gun and we went to the chopper pad. The chopper came in and landed and we were off. It was kind of neat, just like in the movies. I had no fear of getting killed or wounded, or anything at this time. To me, it was just one day closer to home.

We flew for awhile and the chopper started to bank and then made a steep plunge toward the ground. At that time, I was still not scared, just excited and ready to go. Somewhere in Pleiku Province, the chopper hovered over the ground about seven or eight feet. The pilot said, "Go." Hell, I was still waiting for the chopper to land. Then I heard the Lieutenant say "Jump." I thought they were both nuts. I looked down and there was all kinds of stuff to land on like sticks and rocks.

Well, I can't remember, but I think I closed my eyes and shit, when I hit, I thought I would never get up again. God Almighty, did it hurt. I thought being in a gun section was tough, well this just about takes the cake. I then knew in my mind I wanted to go home, and I mean I wanted to go home right now. But, as I picked myself up, I knew that couldn't be.

As we got over the first shock, I saw a South Vietnamese soldier waving at us to follow him. We were walking so fast it was unbelievable. I said, "God, how am I going to keep up with these people." We did, but it was tough. The next thing I saw was a big area of thorns. I said to myself, "They are not going to go through them are they?" And sure enough, right through them. They ripped at my clothes and skin, I was going nuts. We just bulldozed our way through there.

Just when I thought the end of the thorns was near, they kept coming. About 200 yards of thorns. I was hot, dirty, thirsty, and tired before we stopped that night. For the next three days, I would be finding and picking thorns out of my body. We were out three days on that mission, but it seemed more like three weeks. We did not see hide nor hair of the enemy. I was kind of disappointed.

Second Mission

No sooner did we get back to our base camp when the Lieutenant came and got me. He said, "Let's go." We were off again. They told me at the FO school that we were guaranteed two days rest before we had to go on another mission. I found out it was more like two minutes. It was and out-and-out lie. The first of many, I would discover.

Lieutenant Di Tullio and I traveled from Ben Het by the Laos border and down to the Cambodian border to Ban Me Thuet. Time seemed to feel like it moved very slowly. Long days and long nights. We ate freeze-dried food. You add boiling hot water to it and eat it. Well, in the comforts of your own home it might be OK, but not where we were. If a guy could build a fire or burn plastic explosives for a fire, it was alright. But, still with boiling hot water it took more than ten minutes to soak in. We usually didn't have ten minutes, so we had to eat it while it was still crunchy. After being out in the jungle for five or six days eating crunchy, nasty food, a guy could get pretty sick of that stuff.

Always hot, thirsty, hungry, and tired, always going uphill or downhill with sixty pounds on my back, try that for a week and see how you end up. After about three days, you would have had all you could handle and there were some that could not handle it. When things got dull, you could always count on the enemy for a few exciting moments.

I was in the Central Highlands, the terrain was hilly, like I said, but you just don't walk up these hills. Many were so steep that we had to hang on to the roots and trees. We actually had to climb up the roots and trees from the bottom to three-quarters of the way up the hill. The hills were covered with bamboo most of the time, thirty feet or taller. In some places, it was so thick we had to chop our way through it. Then, it got real tough traveling. It was slow and hard and a living nightmare. When we would go into a valley or between hills sometimes there would not be a bit of breeze. It would feel like I could not breathe because of the high humidity. I guess I remember this so well because we stopped long enough to cook a water buffalo.

We were walking along a lake or rice paddy, I really don't know which one, and one guy took a shot at a buffalo and then a couple more of us shot at it. It took quite a few shots to kill it, which really surprised me. I shot it in the head five or six times myself. It started charging us and it rolled over and died.

A day or so passed and we came to a river that was too deep to walk through and too far to go around. It was the only place to cross. As we approached the river, it had a cliff-like edge dropping down six feet or so. The bank on the other side was a mirror image. The river was a good ten to twelve feet across. There was a bridge, which was a log about six inches across, roughly the diameter of the lower part of your leg. Stuck in the bottom part of the river were what is known as punji stakes. They looked to be about 2-½ feet long and had points on the end of each stake. They were under and beside the log, spaced about two or three inches apart. I would say that if one slipped off the log, he would stick like wet clay to a wall.

As we looked at the stakes, the Lieutenant came up to me and said, "Riz, I can't do it." Meaning he could not walk over the log. With a pack and a rifle, it wasn't the easiest thing to do. As one pictured himself falling on these things, well, it gets to you. The Lieutenant said, "Can you do it, Riz?"

"Sure, it's easy," I said. I didn't blink an eyelid and told him there was nothing to it. That was about the only time he needed any confidence. He was stocky and probably never had to do much balancing before. With the idea of punji stakes down there, it would give any man trouble.

As he kept saying to me, "I can't do it, Riz." I said, "Sure you can, watch me. Put your rifle out for balance, don't look down into the water, just look where your feet are going to be and walk fast."

He asked me if I would go first and show him how to do it. As I got to the middle of the bridge, I had to look down at the stakes and for just a second, I started to lose my balance, not all the way, but just enough. As I looked down there and saw the stakes, I really did get scared. I made it across. Now it was the Lieutenant's turn. As he started over the log, I grit my teeth and he somehow made it across as well. We continued on our way.

That same day we were walking next to a dry riverbed when the point man spotted a Viet Cong soldier. The Lieutenant and I took a few shots at him but missed. He was only in sight for a few seconds and was moving fast. The Lieutenant and I were always up front, ten to twenty feet behind the point man. We did not belong anywhere near that close, but that's where we walked.

I said to myself at this point, "Boy, this is fun." I was ready for action. The days passed by and we spotted four North Vietnamese soldiers coming down a trail, so we set up a quick ambush. We waited until they were about 150 yards away and we opened up on them, a rare opportunity. All of that shooting and one got away. We blew them off their feet. The one that got away we chased into a patch of bamboo. Looking from a distance it appeared like a big square of trees.

We got on all four sides and then lit fires and watched for him. We never saw him come out. I tell you by now the game was really getting fun in a way. I mean, I got kind of bloodthirsty.

We came off that mission and went to a small outpost that night. An NVA sapper tried to get in but was killed at the perimeter by an ARVN soldier. The one who killed him came up to me with his hands dripping in blood, and as I sat there eating my breakfast, he wiped the blood on my cheeks and my forehead. He told me that the blood on my cheeks and forehead would keep me safe. Well, I didn't know about that, but what the hell, if it did work it would be worth it. Another guy came up to me and showed me an ear he had cut off. They told me that without the parts of the body, the enemy would not go to heaven. Then also, you could get money for scalps and ears too. That was another reason they took ears, like a body count.

Firefight

My first firefight was a real eye-opener. The first time, things always seemed to be the most drastic, scary, or devastating for a soldier. The Lieutenant always made us walk up front behind the point man or very close so we could do our job (observation) better. So here we were about ten meters apart and wammm, pop, pop! We hit the ground and the Lieutenant and I were caught with almost no cover. Or should I say, the only cover we had was the underbrush and the bullets were hitting all over the place.

The Lieutenant says, "See that tree, Rizz?"

"Yeah."

"We will try to roll our way over to the tree and keep firing as you are rolling. We will go on the count of two."

I think perhaps I was only shooting the sky as I rolled, I have no idea really. But we made it behind the tree for cover. I handed the Lieutenant the handset of my radio and he called in the support. Since I was now in an upright position, I fired a few more rounds and the Lieutenant said for the first time, "Keep your head down, Rizz, it's gonna be close!" As I lay there halfscared out of my mind, the artillery rounds come screaming down and the shooting stopped. We got up and kept a-going.

Lean Mean Fighting Machine

This was the beginning of becoming a "lean, mean fighting machine" which everyone would always joke about. We were lean because we hardly got to eat, and as far as being a fighting machine, I would personally experience most aspects of this as missions came and went: torture, murder, battles, ambushes, interrogation, fear, and of course bloodthirst and anger. Not too much happy stuff is in there!

As we kept on going, my sub-brain seemed to always know that I wanted to survive no matter what. It told my body to go on, or as I put it, "Do or die." Time in Vietnam seemed to be like the money exchange of one dollar equals five-thousand Dong. For example, one day in Nam was like ten days back home. As we slithered our way through time, I became bloodthirsty. Still more alert than scared, I wanted to kill just about anything or anybody, and it was fun.

I try not to talk about or even think about this time in my life. I talk very little about that state of mind, because if I were to say that to someone who does not understand the situation they might get the idea to try something like that. So I have told very few people that it was fun, I just say that I got bloodthirsty. To this day, that is one thought that I have to control amongst the a few other happy little things that rumble around in my mind.

I went back to the rear area one time to get paid and the payclerk asked me, "How can you keep going out on those missions?".

"For my country?" I said

"If you ever run across a pistol, I'll buy it off ya. An enemy pistol that is."

I stopped at the door, turned, and said, "Why don't you get your own souvenirs?" and kept on going.

Other Forces in Country

As part of our job, the Lieutenant and I were often choppered into the jungle and we met up with different soldiers, like the Green Berets, mercenaries, and the Australian soldiers. Out of all of them, I liked the Australians the best. The officers were very nice and they'd talk to me and the Lieutenant. The Green Berets would only do business. You know, my Lieutenant was smarter than most of the Green Beret officers. Not that the Green Berets are bad soldiers, but the best fighting men as a whole were the men who joined the Marines or the men that got drafted. These were the people who kept everything moving. Like my friend Dave.

This one time we went on a mission with about twelve mercenaries and these guys had strings of ears around their necks. We jumped out of the chopper and met up with them. At first, there was no one around and then like magic they appeared out of the underbrush. And, as they came out I first noticed those strings of ears. That was the first time I ever saw it and it was really spooky.

The people we worked with were sometimes different, but the weather and terrain was always the same. Walking all day, sweat rolling off my head and all over my body, it would give me a bath. The night would ooze in and depending on where we were, sometimes the temperature would drop and it would feel real cold at night. It was probably only fifty or sixty degrees Fahrenheit, but because it was so hot during the day the contrast was extreme. I would shake from being cold clear up until morning. There has been many a day when my mind would flash back to those nights and it still disturbs me greatly.

The Dead Forest

This brings to mind a time when we were traveling through the green Hell, and entered an area where I swore to the heavens that there was not a living thing in there. I think to best describe it, I'd have to say that every bush and tree was dead. There were no bugs, there was nothing, the air felt dead. Everything was gray in color. It might not have actually been gray, but that is what it looked like to me. It was like being in another time zone within another time zone. That night we stayed there and just as I was lying down a big dead tree limb came crashing down. I looked up and moved out of the way just in time and it hit right in the spot where I'd been standing.

The next day, I was sitting right out at the edge of the dead treeline and somebody yelled. I looked over my right shoulder and I saw this big tree falling toward me. I leaned forward just in time and boom, it hit right where I had been sitting. I really didn't worry about it though. I had other things to think about.

One of the most shitty-ass things a person can run into is those mosquitoes. I tell you those mosquitoes were *yuck*! In places they were so thick they tried to fly into my ears and eyes and mouth. I woke up one morning with three inches of mosquito bites around my waist. My shirttail had pulled out overnight. I always wondered in the back of my mind whether I would get malaria.

Firefights and Bombs

We were always moving up and moving down, hill after hill, wondering when we would meet the enemy. Always ready, always ready to do our "Patriotic Job," God Bless America. When we met the enemy, the firefights would last for a few seconds or minutes. Sometimes there were hand grenades thrown and sometimes just shooting. Sometimes the enemy would be 400 yards away and sometimes twenty feet. Well, maybe a little further than that. If you have ever been in a firefight, you would understand how scared a guy could really get. Those bullets hammering at you like rain, bouncing off the bamboo as it ricochets off of different things. It really enlightens your whole being.

This happened to the Lieutenant and me in Pleiku Province. There was a small ridge in an open area, and as we walked along this ridge the enemy opened up on us. Taking cover, I turned my body along the same way as the ridge, which was about six inches tall. That is all the cover I had. As I hit the ground I could see the bullets hitting the dirt all around me. The Lieutenant yelled to me, "Riz, turn the same way I am." His head was pointed towards the way of the enemy. It makes a smaller target that way. As I wheeled my body around, the bullets kept coming. They were hitting within inches of me. They were so close I knew I was going to get hit. The Lieutenant gave me the grid numbers and I called in 155 mm rounds on top of the enemy. It was over, they ran as part of their way of doing "hit and run".

Those moments seemed to be all in slow motion or maybe fast motion. Everything happens so fast, but the time during the firefights seems to go slowly.

I don't know which was worse, the firefights or the bombs. When we called for air strikes, the jet came over and dropped a 750 pound bomb and the same thing would happen. It would only take a second or two to explode, but as the shockwaves hit me it seemed to take forever. I could see the earth move up and down a foot or two and the trees move sideways a foot or two and then return to the original position. It seemed that when we got air strikes to cover us, we were in the error margin. This is very close to where the bomb could go off. Let me tell you, an M-121 10,000 pound bomb is not a toy. I mean, when they slammed home, the whole country knew it. It was like everything else in my mind was shut off as I watched and felt the shockwaves hit. It felt like a wind that came swooping past my body, then the earth shook and the trees shook and then a moment of silence before the surroundings came back to my head and I knew where I was again.

Marking Time

Moving up and down again on hills with an elevation of four to five-thousand feet, we would take a break at times and I got a chance to stop and take out my pocket calendar and mark off a few more days. If I was not care-

The Bamboo Wall, Nick J. Rizzo, 1981

ful, my mind would slip back into thoughts of home and what my family might be doing. I treasured those moments, just those few moments were so sweet and the feeling of wanting to go home so bad I was just aching in my heart and soul. It was just torture, God, did it hurt.

Then the Lieutenant would say, "Let's go, Riz." I was so stubborn that I wouldn't listen to him. He would have to come and pull on me or yell and the vision would trickle through my mind like water running from my fingers. I would burst back into reality and be very disappointed, but soon shove it back deep into my memory so I could concentrate on my job. With a little luck and hope, maybe I would see home again.

I was so far into that jungle, if anything had gone wrong, I would surely be there today still trying to get home. Nobody ever talked too much; we were always talking to ourselves.

As I recall, we had been out in the jungle for twelve days or so and were moving at a good clip. I went to talk to myself and I did not remember my name. I almost went berserk, into panic, but I controlled myself. I knew the Lieutenant knew my name but I was too embarrassed to ask. After five minutes or so, I did remember. What a relief!

By this time, the Lieutenant and I were really getting into the war. Each day that passed, our senses grew sharper. I was sleeping with my eyes open. I woke in the morning at the first sign of daylight. The light was dull gray at first and then shapes would focus in and then finally the color. With one hand on my gun all night and the other hand hung over my throat, I was as protected as I could be. We had spies and double-agents with us so we never knew whom to trust.

Incoming Mortars

There were days and nights when the enemy would mortar us three or four days in a row, and then not for a week. My mind would go into frenzy during those terrible, terrifying moments when the mortars shot out of the sky. I could see the air vibrate up and down with energy. It might have all been in my head, but that is what I saw and felt.

We'd be on one hill and the enemy on another, and we could hear the mortar tubes firing shells. That was part of the Lieutenant's job and mine as well: to stop the mortars. We had to listen in order to identify the origin and then look on our map and call for artillery support. We did a good job at stopping them too. Most of the time they would kill or wound one of our guys before we could stop it. But, that is the way that it was and that is what we had to live with.

The fear of the mortar was enough to unglue anyone. I remember the first time I got mortared real close. I was in a foxhole and as they came down and hit next to my hole, I was laughing and crying at the same time. My mind was being twisted by torture of death like twine being snapped one strand at a time.

I don't know which is worse, the bullets, the mortars, or the hand grenades. What I do know is they are all nasty and to think some people imagine that this sounds exciting. What it is, is devastating. They are acts of violence that tortured our minds for a year and they are everything but fun. Believe me. All of us were out there trying to live through this and it was not our choice.

After I got used to it, I realized that clawing at the dirt with my hands and fingernails was doing no good. So I just gritted my teeth and kept my mind dancing around the pressure I felt in my mind. God, if I could have had certain people with me at that time, then there would be no more war.

It is strange to me, but for the most part, the people who sent us to Viet Nam never have really had their lives on the line in a war. I really think the military personnel in Viet Nam did not know what they were doing. The people who sent us, lifers, were seldom in battle.

I knew the guys around me didn't want to be there. The majority of us said, "What the hell are we doing here anyway?" Of course, the lifers and the government had a different point of view.

The General

One time, the Lieutenant and I were waiting on a plane to go on a mission, and a General, mind you a two-start General, got off of this plane. I was standing there and we did not salute him.

He came over to us and the Lieutenant said to me, "Riz, go stand at the end of the runway."

He sent me away because he knew when that General started to give him hell, I would have cussed that General up one side and down the other, and maybe worse. But, the Lieutenant sent me away, so I had to stand there while this General yelled at my Lieutenant.

He asked my Lieutenant where his binoculars were. He said, "If you are a Forward Observer, where are your binoculars?"

Sure enough, on the next mission, my Lieutenant had a pair of binoculars. You see, where we were, it was all jungle and we did things by judging and listening. Nobody carried binoculars out there, they were useless. That is what generals know. If it wasn't binoculars, it was something else. I just cannot say enough about the ranking system over there. You gave a guy some stripes back in the rear and he thought he was a god.

If you want to have respect from a group of men, you must first be a man yourself. If you are a leader and you have led men into battle, I mean really led, then the respect is there for a lifetime. It is not the rank that gets respect. A real leader is willing to go first into battle and then he has the right to lead others.

Getting back to my story... Like the waves in the ocean, we would move, always moving and as time moved on. History was being made with each foot and hand climbing those big green hills that seemed to go on forever.

Of Heaven and Hell

Not always, but much of the time, enemy fire came completely unexpectedly. Like, we were just settling down for the night and a B-40 rocket came smashing into our perimeter and killed one guy. One guy we had to take time to carry to a place where we could chopper him out. Then we had to move on in that bee-stinging heat, very dirty, very thirsty. I would put my lips to my canteen to finish the last few drops of warm water. And, out came a mouthful of mud with the last few drops of water. You just sort of spit it out and go on your merry way. The sweat was rolling off my lips. I had learned to lick it as it came dripping down. Now, wanting to find the enemy, after burning a few villages and shooting the people and everything else, the power of holding the rifle in my hands felt good.

We would go into the villages and do whatever, and it made us feel like Gods. About this time, I was feeling really bloodthirsty. The only thing that ran through my head was to find and kill. All those things that I had learned about God and man in church and at home had gone from my mind. I no longer knew right from wrong. And, I did not care. After I had seen what others had done, I realized I was not much different.

I did not take any ears; I figured the person was dead. I did my job and that was enough. Today I feel kind of bad for some of those things, but it had to be done and that's what I was trained for. At first, it seemed cruel, but I always thought, that's why I was there. To this day, I do not repeat in my mind some of the things that I have seen or done.

I got into a car accident not long ago and my son was in the car with me. He was four years old. I picked him up off the street. He was not moving. I thought he was dead for a second or two. It took a lifetime, it seemed, to pick him up. After that, I knew what I had done in Viet Nam. I was lucky. My son only suffered a broken leg. Over in Viet Nam, I had shot villagers and NVA soldiers and together the Lieutenant and I are responsible for killing over 500 people and probably more.

It was different when we fought the NVA soldiers because they had rifles. For some reason, I was not killed nor wounded. Why and how, I still do not understand. I have had bullets come within three or four inches of my body and head countless times. That is not counting the bombs and mortars.

I had learned to kill through training and by being in Viet Nam. It did not happen overnight. When I die, I hope dearly to see God face to face and man to God so I can ask him and so I can tell him and so I can cuss him for what I have seen and done here. And, when I die before he sends me to hell, if he does not have a good reason, I will punch him in the face.

There was a saying that went around Viet Nam: *I know I'm going to heaven because I spent my time in hell.* It is only half right—we surely spent our time in hell but I really don't know if I'll make it to heaven.

We learned to blow villages to bits and not think anything of it. An average village was about four small city blocks in size.

The time would pass. The days and nights, those long sleepless hoary nights, God, it seemed like a lifetime. We started to see the enemy now. Or was it, he found us? The way it seemed to me, we kept getting the bad side of the deal more and more. Like a scales that was weighing something but heavier on the one side.

Ambush

This brings back the memory of a time when we were going into a village on a cool morning with fog so heavy I could cut it with a knife. We entered a small stream about five feet wide and three feet deep, it was cool water and I was already kind of scared. This was supposed to be an unfriendly village.

We crawled up on the bank and as we moved into position, I could see the outline of vegetation and the hooches. We waited for the fog to clear enough to see the village. The order was given to go in. Not knowing if we would be cut down by machine guns or not, we went in. We searched the hooches and found nothing. It was kind of a relief. We then sat down and ate breakfast. We were relaxed and had our bellies full, so we moved out. We just cleared the village when they hit us like a hammer. If you didn't hit the ground by the time you heard the first shot, you probably wouldn't get up again. They killed fifteen of our men that morning.

I guess it kind of gets to a guy after a while, like when all the men around you have their brains and guts blown out. Those minutes passed, but it seemed like time had stopped. The thoughts are still in my head and I don't think they will ever go away.

The sun shining down through the green bamboo looked like little specks of gold floating through the air. As I got up on one knee, I looked to the right first, and there were dead bodies lying all around with their stomachs ripped open. Then, I stood up all the way and looked to my left and about five years away, a guy had his brains blown out and they were lying on the ground. They were kind of purple and gray. As I looked down at them, I saw silence and knew that I didn't want to die that way.

I looked at the sun again. Getting over the shock of the ambush, the first thing I felt was the warmth of the sun and it felt good. I then took a deep breath and let it out again real slow. Then, I realized that I was still alive. As this all happened in a few moments, I returned to the insanity of war.

We chased after them. We rumbled down the hill, and they were waiting with mortars, and killed four more men. So, we went back up the hill and entered the village and killed everything that moved.

With very little sleep and empty stomachs, we wallowed through the jungle, every step of the way. The mental strain got terrible at times, then it got worse. I would say it was a hair's thickness from insanity most of the time.

Death of a Son

Once again death has rained
And chopped down someone's son.
Poured his blood on the jungle floor
God, what have they done?

Nick J. Rizzo, 1981

Illus. by Tyler Mills, 2006

Arc Light

The Lieutenant and I worked well together. We argued from time to time, but mostly we got along well. He always took my opinion of situations seriously because both our lives depended upon it. I remember one time the brass was going to put an Arc Light on one of these hills and we were on it. An Arc Light is when they drop tons of small bombs. The Special Forces people we were with said we should go down one side of the hill. There were two of them. The Lieutenant said we should go down the other side of the hill. If we picked the wrong side, we would surely be blown to pieces.

We had 30 minutes before the bombers would be in position. It takes 30 minutes to get down the hill. He argued with the Special Forces men and we decided to go the Lieutenant's way. As we reached the bottom of the hill, we took cover and it sounded like the bombs were right on top of us. As the bomber went over, the sky rumbled like thunder right on top of our heads. I jumped up to run even further, but of course you cannot outrun a bomb. So, I took cover.

My Lieutenant was right. He picked the right way. The Special Forces are the elite soldiers. But, I know who the real elite were. We were always there to do our 300 dollar-a-month job for the American dream, and we did it well.

A little more time passed and I was getting closer to going home. That everlasting torture of my mind, wanting to go home. A few weeks passed, and as we reached the top of a hill, we ran smack dab into an NVA patrol. The bullets started to fly. When it was all over at 7 am the next day, my Lieutenant had a flesh wound in the scalp. An AK-47 round hit him just under the hairline.

Meet Lt. Brass

One day after that, I came back into base camp and went back out with another Lieutenant. His name, we will say, was Lieutenant Brass. Lt. Di Tullio was always telling me about this guy and how he would brag all the time. I soon found out how he worked. We got mortar fire from the North Vietnamese and he showed me a little tiny red spot on his side. Hell, he could have poked himself with a stick or something. There was just a tiny red spot. I said to him, "Where is it, I don't see it?" I really did. He got really mad. I had to authenticate the wound so he could get his Purple Heart. But, he gave himself a Purple Heart for it anyways. That is one advantage of being an officer.

By this time, I had dysentery and felt exhausted all the time. I was not eating well. When the enemy is trying to kill you, you don't think all that much about food. And, without sleep either, one wears down pretty fast.

On my second and last mission with Lieutenant Brass, we were in Laos. Up in the northern part of Two Corps, we woke up to mortar fire coming at us with pinpoint accuracy. As we radioed for artillery support, the mortars kept coming down upon us. They told us they were not going to give us artillery support because they were going to send in a bomber. They told us to retreat. God Almighty, the air was just full of electricity. So, we started down the hill. The mortars kept coming and the air was vibrating to beat hell. I was scared half out of my mind. We had maybe a half-second between the *ssshhhhh*-sound of the mortar and the time it hit and to hope it hit someplace else.

The enemy got close enough to start shooting. We could hear them coming up the hill toward us, the bamboo crackling and the underbrush moving.

The South Vietnamese had these old propeller planes and they flew over to slow the NVA from coming up the hill, shooting 20mm rounds at them and dropping napalm. We finally made it down the hill and the enemy was off our backs. As we ran down the hill and on to a less steep hill, we heard the bomber go over and drop the bombs. There was a battalion of NVA soldiers but the bombs took care of them. We had made it by skin of our asses.

As we headed east on the Ho Chi Minh Trail, it took all day to walk to the pickup point. It was late afternoon when I looked up and saw a Jeep in the middle of the road. It was about a half mile away. I really don't know where the Jeep was, it was the Laos-Viet Nam border. Maybe that is only as far as they had mineswept the road.

We walked to the Jeep. As long as I live I will never forgive or forget those last 200 yards. I could see the Jeep in the middle of the road as I got closer. I saw two men inside the Jeep. I was tired and thirsty, of course. I was always tired and thirsty. I was dizzy and my rucksack on my back felt like 500 pounds. I was wobbling back and forth a little and I hadn't eaten for about seven days. Of course, I had dysentery, most definitely in bad shape.

This Lt. Brass was in fine shape. Of course, he was an officer and he got treated better than a PFC. They got good food when they were in the rear while I would have to pull guard duty if I was in the rear on an overnight stay. Even that happened only a few times. They almost always sent us right back into the jungle. When I remember back, Lt. Di Tullio and I went down to the lower part of Two Corps before we went on a mission. We got something to eat. This West Point lifer told the Lieutenant that I could not eat in the officer's mess hall and then the asshole walked away. There was no place else for me to get food. The Lieutenant gave me his hat, which had a bar on it, and I wore it into the mess hall. All of these officers were saluting me. We went in and ate and it was pretty nice. They had South Vietnamese working in the kitchen. You know, those lifers liked the idea of having those Vietnamese women working for them. They would shine their boots and then there were rumors that the ladies would stay all night with them. Well, that was just rumor. Getting back to the story, I guess those officers thought PFCs ran on air instead of food.

Back to the road... I was down to the last 100 yards of that road and I ran completely out of energy. I just could not go any more. The Lt. Brass was yelling, "Hurry up. Hurry up." He pulled away from me, I sped up. I just could not catch him. I finally got to the last 50 or 60 yards. Lt. Brass was now in the Jeep and still yelling at me. I said to myself, "I made it this far, I can go the rest." So with one arm I held my rifle and with the other I grabbed my pant leg and I told the other leg to step forward. It worked at about one-half mile an hour. Each time I told that leg to step forward, it did. All this time I heard Lt. Brass saying, "Hurry up. Hurry up." I knew one thing: I did not want to collapse in enemy territory, so I fought it in my mind every step of the way. I was in great pain and when I came within a few feet of the Jeep, I looked at the two men in it. I can't really say for sure, but as I recall on the right side of the Jeep was a two-star General or a Colonel. I thought it very strange for such a high ranking officer to be this far from his cement bunker.

I grabbed the Jeep and tried to get in, but I could not. I tried the second time, I could not. I tried a third time, I could not and on the fourth try, Lt. Brass lowered his dignity and pulled me in. I just barely got in and my legs were still hanging out when they took off like they were scared of something. As I adjusted myself and put my legs inside the jeep, they were talking about something but I could not understand. It took all of my energy just to be there.

The big hills looked more like a big green dragon as we sped away in the jeep. It was like the good guys riding off into the sunset, but we were headed east. It makes a guy wonder who the bad guys really were. I turned my head back to the front of the Jeep and hate for the career officer and the Army grew to the size and depth of an ocean in me.

You might think the story ends here, but hell no. I still had a few more months to go in Nam before I could go home. At this point in time, I was just glad to be alive. My mind was like a blank tape on a tape recorder, with a low or underlying hum of death and destruction as the rewinding of the tape. I had no time out there to rationalize or wonder, or just scream from fear. If I would have rebelled against the war, any time in Viet Nam, any more than I did, the career officer would surely have done me in, one way or another.

We were all in the same boat. We had no rank and we had no say on anything. We just had to take our chances with the lifers and the enemy and we could only hope for the best. I was smart enough to push them only so far and they were smart enough not to push me too far, for fear of losing their lives. Of course, they knew I had risked my life several times when they were just sitting on their dead asses doing their misdeeds.

Still in the Jeep, we drove to Ben Het or Dakto, I don't know for sure, to a medical unit. Lt. Brass told them to put me in the hospital. At least that is what he told me he was going to do. As I met him at the top of the underground bunker, he told me to go to the hospital. As I made my way down the steps, one at a time, there were some guys waiting for wounded to come in and one said to me. "Do you need any help?" I said "No." But, inside I was saying, "God, do I need help." I was thinking, I walked this far, I can walk the rest of the way.

Nobody Cares

As I walked into this one-room bunker, I noticed it had a table on the right with a desk and chair on the left. The medic told me to sit down and I did, while he tended to a baby. The child was dying and the baby's mother squatted on the table next to the baby. There was nothing he could do about it, the medic said. He stood there with his stethoscope to the baby's heart and I sat quietly and watched. The baby soon faded into death and the mother burst into tears, holding the baby in her arms. The medic moved away. Then, there was silence for a while. Through all that killing and seeing men wounded and dying, I was very sad to see this baby die and the memory of this has stuck in my mind all of this time. When you see something like this in real life, it makes a crazy mind even crazier.

War

Many Men have come and gone,
It's sad to see them die.
As I sat there in that black
arm chair, I could not say good-bye
So as I sat there, the little girl
died and silence filled the room,
War has stepped on someone again,
Oh, yes, it's sad to see
Because the War has stepped on me.

Nick J. Rizzo, 1981

The second thing the medic said to me was, "If you don't have a fever, I can't let you go into the hospital." I desperately needed to go. He gave me the thermometer and left for a minute or two. He came back in and said, "No fever." I had no fever, but I was three-fourths dead. It was actually below normal, so he took it again. No dice. I slowly got up and it felt like my mind was rolling around in my head like a ball of glass in oil. I bid the asshole goodbye.

I started up the steps, one by one, very slowly. On my way up the guys standing on both sides of me said again, "Do you need help?" I said "No," but God did I need help. I stopped and told them what happened and they understood. One guy said, "That's the Army for you." I walked away, looking for the mess hall to get something to eat.

As I got to the mess hall, they told me they were not serving until the proper time. I walked away toward the airfield. I ran into a South Vietnamese soldier who gave me three or four cans of fruit. I thanked him and he left. I sat there eating and said to myself, "Nobody cares." The medic didn't care, the Army didn't care, and I was all alone. I said to myself, "The hell with it, I'm going AWOL."

I didn't know where I was going, but I was going. I was through with this man's Army and if anyone got in my way I would surely cut him down with my rifle. I stood by the airfield when enemy mortar fire came screaming in. I just stood there while these other guys ran for cover. Hell, the mortars were a hundred yards away. I didn't give a damn. After the mortar attack was over, I decided to go back to my base camp and just sit out my remaining time. I have to say, if you were not there, you don't know how American soldiers treated other American soldiers when they had one stripe more than the other person.

Goodbye Lt. Di Tullio

I finally made it back to my base camp and after I was there a month or so, I found out my friend Dave and Lieutenant Di Tullio were going to Dakto with One Cannon. Lieutenant Di Tullio had told me that after six months in artillery, officers didn't have to go into the jungle with the infantry. He said he was going to Dakto to run the gun section there. I talked to him before he left. He told me he was going to die. I did not believe him. How could he have known? I looked at his face and it looked scared. I thought he was just talking, but as I look back on the situation he hardly ever said anything that was not true.

Lieutenant Di Tullio was one of the best Forward Observers in Viet Nam and definitely one of the smartest. I remember him telling me when we had first started out, he wanted a Purple Heart and a medal for bravery. That changed after a while. I never wanted a medal or anything else for myself and I cannot see why he ever did. I always laughed at him for saying that.

I remember another time I laughed at him. We were tromping through the green hell and he said, "Riz, I got a jungle sweater, it keeps you warm at night. I'll wear it one night and you can wear it the next night." I said "OK." So the next morning he forgot to take it off. Well, at 10 am and moving fast, if you stop they leave you behind. You have to go twice as fast to catch up. We had to stop, the Lieutenant was boiling over and I was laughing my ass off.

That was one of the very few times I thought something was funny. He said, "Don't laugh Riz, but I forgot to take off my sweater." I instantly cracked up. We finally got the shirt off and we were a good ways behind the others. We moved out and got about 60 yards away when he told me he had forgotten his rifle. He sort of begged me to go back and get it for him. So I did. I said, "How in the hell did you forget your rifle?" I was just kidding. I got the rifle and ran back. We finally caught up with the rest of the men. I laughed for the next three days about that. He gave the sweater away. He gave me some very good advice before he left for Dakto and that was the last time I ever saw him.

Missile Attack at Dakto

My other friend, Dave, the guy I came in country with, was going to Dakto also. I saw him the day before he left. I told him not to stay in the bunker the Army built for them. I told him to dig a foxhole and when they got hit by enemy fire, get in the foxhole. At the time, I was talking to Dave while he was sitting in a chair writing home. We were beside one of those sandbag bunkers. I told him this over and over. I think I squatted there for over an hour telling him to *dig a foxhole and sleep in it*. Then I got down on my knees and I begged him and tried to reason with him to dig a foxhole. I think I was on my knees for 35 minutes saying the same thing over and over.

Illus. by Tyler Mills, 2006

I had my hands together like I was praying and I was sitting there on my knees. I pleaded for him to dig a foxhole when he got there, over and over. I told him to promise me. After all of that, he finally said "Yes." They left. Dakto was getting hit by these six-foot tall BM-21 truck-launched 122mm rockets, an unbelievable sight to see. The lifers at that fire base were in concrete and steel bunkers.

Let me ask why the rest of the men were in sandbag bunkers?

They could have just as easily built concrete bunkers for the men shooting the guns. It would have saved more lives and more money in the long run. It is like I said, they don't care and they figure they can just draft another boy if one there got killed. *Five of them did.* In that sandbag bunker were five of my friends. So now, a guy really starts to question his ranking officers and his country and the people running it.

On June 4th, 1969, the bunker got hit by 122mm rockets. The point of a rocket was still sticking out of one man's back. He was still wiggling when the medic got to him. But, he was surely dead. 1st Lt. Franco A. Di Tullio (age 23) and my friend Corporal David B. Platt (age 21) were both blown to bits. All that was left was Dave's head and Lt. Di Tullio's head and three feet between the both of them and that was all.

I guess it was three or four days I walked around, out of my head, asking questions and wondering about it all. I did not see anything or feel the heat of the day during that time. The next thing I knew or could remember was a guy from Illinois coming up to me, he was also a friend, saying "Are you back with us, Riz?" I said to him, "I'm OK," and still today the pain is overwhelming.

Kontum City

It was time for my R and R (Rest and Recreation). I went to Bangkok. It was pretty nice. I came back from R and R and the lifers kept putting me in different gun sections because I did not do any work, and I was leaving the camp and going down to Kontum City. After R and R, I was feeling a lot better. I could walk and I could run, but I could not sit. The pain in my stomach hurt too badly in my sides, so I had to lie or stand. About this time I was smoking marijuana. I think in the circumstances it was actually keeping me out of trouble.

One night, I was smoking a joint dipped in opium, we called them Joss. I went into a bunker to get some rest and as I sat down, I felt no pain in my sides. I sat there and it felt like my teeth were sinking into my gums. I could see each individual movement of my hands as I moved them up and put them around my neck and started to choke myself. But, I realized what was happening and I stopped. A guy would either drink or smoke dope and I did not like alcohol so I used marijuana.

I would go downtown into Kontum City and get high. A friend and I were walking downtown and it was after curfew time or something and the MPs were chasing us through yards and houses. We jumped over a few fences and there stood six naked women. They were taking barrel showers after a hard day's work. We didn't have time to stop, we said "The MPs are chasing us," and they pointed to the outhouse. We went inside, breathing hard so we could not hold our breath and we were laughing at the same time. Boy, did it smell bad. As we looked out of a crack in the door, we saw the girls point in the wrong direction and the MPs ran off. We came out and thanked them and went on our way.

Another time this guy named Anderson and I were walking downtown and we decided to see the suburbs of Kontum. So, off we went. We got a mile or two out of the city and we were walking on this dirt road. The road curved off to the right and a little house sat on the left side of the road. We had been smoking marijuana and we were feeling pretty good. All of a sudden, about ten kids came running up to us. They were trying to pick our pockets and steal our money and watches. That happened a lot in the cities or wherever there were a lot of kids. But, this time it was a little different. They seemed to be just playing with us and not really wanting to take anything. We looked over at the little house and saw about five men standing around in the doorway. They had a strange look in their faces. All of a sudden it hit me and Anderson, this feeling of fear. It hit us like a wall. We figured we had better get out of there. We had no weapons and the feeling of danger was just looming in the air.

We tried to act normal and turned around. We didn't know, but I'm sure they were either NVA infiltrators or they were Viet Cong. They were probably hiding something very worthwhile when Anderson and I just accidentally ran into the situation. We sensed it at the time.

Earlier in the year, when I was going on operations, we followed a battalion of NVA soldiers into Pleiku City. The NVA would come down from the north on the Ho Chi Minh Trail then walk into Pleiku dressed like South Vietnamese.

Swim or Fight?

When I first came into country, Pleiku was not a very big city. When I left, it had grown to three or four times that size with NVA infiltrators. What I have always wondered is, why the American Army never did anything about it. They certainly knew what was happening there. I guess the lifers were busy building their swimming pool at Artillery Hill, 6th Battalion of the 14th Field Artillery.

I remember I came in from a mission and I was trying to stay away from the lifers so I would go for a walk until the Lieutenant called for me. I came across a guy building a cement swimming pool. It was just about done. I said to myself as I walked around the pool, "What in the hell is a swimming pool doing in the middle of a war?" He said it was for the officers and I walked away in deep disgust. I said to myself, "This is where all the money is going that was supposed to be for food and other needs: the things that were so badly needed where the fighting was going on." I tell you that is pretty sad to see, that kind of stuff. But it was there and there were even worse things going on.

Rebel Without A Cause

When I had ten or fifteen days to go before I could go home, this Captain cut orders for me and a couple of my friends to go to another unit, where things were pretty bad. A few men were killed and they needed replacements so they were fixing to send me, who had only a couple weeks left to go. Luckily, they needed the men so badly that they got someone who was closer. You see, if the lifers didn't like you or if a guy like me didn't see eye-to-eye with them, they tried to get rid of you, and they really didn't care how.

The career officers, especially the West Pointers, treated us like dirt. The food was ungodly awful and we had leftovers from leftovers day after day. Of course, the officers were taking the fresh food and black-marketing it.

A few of the guys got dysentery the same time I did and they got to go to the hospital. But, when I had it I was in the jungle in Laos. As the days came and went, I started thinking the enemy was not only out in the jungle, but right inside me. I was planning to blow a few of the career officers up to heaven, but they found my dynamite, lucky for them.

At times, when I was in the FO team, I would come back and get an hour or so of rest before leaving again and this Major (who would soon become a Colonel) would come in my bunker on the perimeter. I would be cleaning my rifle, something I did every chance I got, and this Major would come in and I looked at him. Then I looked back down and continued to clean my rifle.

He yelled at me, "Don't you salute officers?" I just sat there and very slowly saluted him. He yelled again, "You are supposed to stand up when an officer enters a building!" Well, I looked back up at him very slowly and I saluted him, very slowly. Now, this guy did this a few times and needless to say, we did not like each other very well.

I had my radio in the bunker and I would get on his frequency and cuss the son-of-a-bitch out and boy did he get mad. He couldn't prove it was me because there were a lot of radio transmitters around the perimeter. I just loved that part.

After I was done with the FO team, I was pulling guard duty one evening and this same lifer was driving past me in his Jeep. There were about twelve guys in the area standing around. I picked up a rock the size of a baseball, sighted it up, jumped behind a bunker, and let the rock fly. I never knew whether I hit him or not, but the next day I was in a perimeter bunker and a guy yelled at me to come out, someone wanted to see me. So, I stepped out the door and there were the twelve guys all staring at me.

I said something like, "What's going on here?"

Just then a 200 pound lifer stepped forward and said, "Come here."

So I came to the gutter in the road. He stepped into the gutter, where he belonged, and he was eyeball to eyeball with me, inches from my face. He opened his lifer mouth and said, "Did you throw a rock at me?"

I believe my words were, "What rock? I didn't throw any rock at you." He finally backed up and left. He knew I threw it and I knew I threw it. He was there with two officers so if I had said "Yes," he would surely have arrested me. He thought he would scare me into saying yes, but he didn't scare me one tiny bit.

After he left, everybody laughed their asses off at him. Well, this was the end of my army career. I was what you call *short*. I was short, five foot six, but short meant I had only had a few days before I could go home.

Last Trip to Pleiku

The day the CO told me it was time for me to go home, I could not believe it. On November 21st, 1969 I got aboard a little jeep with three other guys who were going home and a Sergeant whom I did not like. As we departed for Pleiku from the firing battery, I grabbed two of hand grenades. Of course, I still had my rifle for protection at this time. The Sergeant said to me, "Why don't you get rid of your grenades?"

At that point, I hated almost everything and everybody. All three other guys were talking and having a good time. I was silently staring off into the countryside. I thought to myself, I suppose I could do that. I had experience throwing these things. I had also had the experience of being on the wrong end of them. About this time, the Jeep slowed down a bit as we approached a village. My thoughts were: how should I get rid of them? I did not want to waste them so my next thought was that I would pull both pins and let them drop to the floor of the Jeep and jump out. Whatever happened, so be it.

But just at that time, I saw a bunch of Montagnards standing in a crowd. There were about 30 men, women, and children all standing in a group. I pulled the pins on both grenades. I took the first grenade and tossed it in the middle of the crowd. Then, as the truck passed them up, I threw the other one off to the side. You see, you learn those things. One thrown in the middle which they all saw and one thrown to the side which nobody saw.

I turned and looked at the other three guys and there was a silence in that truck bouncing down the road that was absolute. They were all just staring straight ahead and not a peep was heard the rest of the way to HQ.

As the truck moved on, I knew that I had been there too long and the way we were treated by our own American soldiers and what I had to do in the jungle, well, they were just another group of gooks and I didn't care anymore. I no longer knew right from wrong.

As I was processing out of the country on artillery hill, this corporal was looking at my records and he said to me, "You were an RTO in an FO team and you are only a PFC?"

"Yes."

He said, "Just a minute, I will get the Colonel." I stopped him in the middle of his sentence.

"Does this mean I will have to stay here another day?"

"Maybe a couple of days..."

I hesitated a second, mind you only a second, and I said in as few words as possible, "No, I'm going home." I knew my time was up and if I ever meant anything in my whole life, by God, I was getting on one of those jets come hell or high water.

I was leaving. After my year was over, and now when my time was up, they wanted to give me one more stripe or whatever, before I left. I fully deserved it. Lt. Di Tullio had put me in for Corporal four different times. There were clerk typists and guys that kissed rank ass, who got the stripes, while I was the one in the firing battery who risked his life and got nothing for it.

That shows you how the war was run. If I hadn't left when I did, I would probably not even have gotten an honorable discharge. If I would have rebelled any more than I did, they surely would have put me in prison. It was only a miracle that I did not kill any career officers. I had seen and done many things there. Too many to remember. My life was almost taken from me, many times. I did my share of taking too. I was going home and I wanted to see no more.

As I went through customs at Cam Ranh Bay, the MPs took a few of my souvenirs that I had gotten by sweat and fear and if you call it bravery, well, let me call it so. They took them and I could not do a damn thing about it because they threatened us with, "You won't get to go home."

Back in the USA

When that big jetliner lifted off the ground, I could not believe I was actually going home. I looked at the white beaches that looked sort of like snow as the plane pulled away. For the first time, I got an overall picture of the country, which was just sticking out of the ocean somewhere in the world. Those hills that I ran up and down and the dirt I ate: it was both down there and it was inside me. I gritted my teeth and took a deep breath, then started to cry. Not only did I cry because I was going home, but also for two men. Two very good men whom I knew personally and cared for were not going home. My friend Dave and Lieutenant Franco Di Tullio. Again, you might think the story ends here, but it does not.

On November 23rd 1969, I landed at Fort Lewis, Washington. They had real beds for us and a hot meal. They told us to sleep, and we did. There were about six of us in a room and as I woke up every half hour with the sweat rolling off my body from the nightmares of the war, I said to myself, "Wait, I am home, I am in the real world." I would roll over and hear the others moaning and talking and yelling in their sleep.

They gave us new uniforms and let us go. I headed for the airport to buy my ticket home. I was happy, but as I walked through the airport, the strangeness of a different country, different people, hit me. The color, the loud noises that were in reality not really that loud.

My whole body became silent. As I walked down the hallway, some girl yelled something nasty at me, but I ignored it. My mind was rolling like a glass ball in a bottle of oil. I switched off the excitement of war, but the probes of survival still remained like vestigial antennae. Home was only a stone's throw away, yet almost to the other side of the United States.

I flew into Chicago but had to wait overnight there for a connecting flight. So I stayed in a hotel room. I looked at the room and I said, "Wow, look at that bed!" I could not believe it. I decided to take a bath and as I was sitting in the tub of water I got thirsty. I said to myself, "Where am I going to get a drink of water?" Finally, I looked at the running water and laughed for about three minutes. I said to myself, "Hey, this water right here, I can drink it." I looked up at the sink and there sat a glass. I said to myself, "They think of everything."

Home Again

As I walked up to my parents' house, the trees and the bushes looked the same as I had left them and they looked mighty good. I went inside and my family was glad to see me and I was glad to see them. There were so many days when I thought I would never see them again.

At first, I had to sleep downstairs on the couch to keep my eye on the doors. But, after a day or so, I went to sleep in my own room. I often found myself wondering where I was going to get a drink of water as there was no stream nearby. I was still sleeping with my eyes open and my arm over my throat. I found myself reaching for my rifle at times. But, that habit was the first to go. There were the dreams in vivid color, but after a month or so they faded and did not occur as often. The nightmares still continue in 2006 although not as frequently.

Along with the nightmares come flashbacks. I have had them while driving my car and ignored red lights as a result. I was yanked out of it by the car horns going off all around me. Another time, I was out jogging and suddenly I found myself back in the war dragging a guy to safety. I awoke from that not knowing where I was, but still jogging down the road.

My sleeping habits were ruined. Loud noises, and the very low noises like the creaking of the floor, scared the hell out of me. The loud noises made me jump and the tiny noises made me stiffen my muscles and stop breathing. After coming home, I kept hearing enemy mortar fire for about the next three years. To this day, the little noises still scare me at night. I still stiffen my muscles and stop breathing so I can hear what is coming. Every night for eleven years I have done this.

In restaurants, I had to sit in the corner so I could keep an eye on everyone in the room. I could not stand to be in crowds and I had no goals that I can remember wanting to reach. I was an uncivilized person living in a civilized world. All of a sudden, from a world of killing and eating rice and living how people lived in the Stone Age, fearing for my life almost every day, to noises and people and restaurants and civilization.

What a sacrifice I had made, yet nobody even knew I was there. Several times, people I had met, friends of friends, would call me and other Viet Nam veterans "baby killers." They would actually get violent with their mouth. At the time, I had no defense. I wanted to tell them how it was, but I did not know how. So, I just kept quiet. Most of the time, the ones who would speak their minds were girls. I was taught not to hurt girls. I really didn't want to hurt anyone anyway, but there were times when I got pretty mad. These girls thought it was awful that children were being shot over there. Well, the facts are, it is either you or him who will die, and I did not want to die. But, these girls would speak their piece to me and other Viet Nam veterans, and boy they would really give it to us.

One of the many ways the American people showed their thanks to us were by calling us names on our return home. I only wish one of these people could have been there. To let them feel the feelings and think the thoughts of fear and sickness in their bellies when you see a guy lying there with his guts ripped out or his brains shot out. Or, climbing the endless hills, sweating and straining ever inch of the way at nineteen years old. Crying for mercy to anyone who would listen to get home in one piece. They turned us loose in a civilized society to wander around like dogs.

The Petitioner

In Chicago, I was walking downtown one day and this guy came up to me and said "Would I like to sign this petition?"

"What is it for?" I said.

"It is to stop the bombing in Viet Nam," he said.

I gave him a few choice words and walked into the street. Then, I got mad. I stopped right in the middle of the street and I heard nothing. As I stood there, my eyes searched for the guy but he was gone. I was going to kill him right there on the spot. Then, all of a sudden, I heard the horns from the cars. I was in the middle of the street and I said to myself, "What am I doing here?" And then I walked on.

You say he had a right to petition, which is true, but I remembered back in Viet Nam. Those bombs saved my life three or four times. I knew if they were stopped, some good men would die one way or the other and that is what made me so mad. I was not prepared to meet people like that, thanks to somebody.

Benefits

They gave us what they call "benefits" when we got home, like the guys who had fought in World War II, but I never saw any such benefits. It really bothers me that most employers don't even give a damn if I had fought for my country in Viet Nam. I think a blind person can see better than most people in this country as far as the Viet Nam veteran is concerned. It never helped me get a job although it was supposed to. Hell, on the money I was making on some jobs, there was no way in hell I could buy a car, let alone a house. All of this adds up in the mind of a man who went to war and came home wishing to do something with his life.

The government had made us numbers instead of men and they stripped me of my honor, duty, patriotism, my God, and knowing right from wrong. And, because of the Army, I took drugs.

They just about took everything from my mind that could be taken. But, I was stubborn, like many other guys who were lucky and we managed to survive the war and society thus far. We carried the war with us when we came home, that is how everyone knew what was going on. Without the veterans throwing their medals they had won in the war in Viet Nam over the fence in Washington, D.C., nobody would have taken as much notice as they did.

The news media carried the hero bit to the guys who went to Canada, and to the protestors. Some of the protesters were veterans. That is OK. But, others were merely scared they might have to put their life on the line. I am glad that they made the draft fairer.

I have problems from the war. I have mostly conquered them on my own. I do not feel sorry for myself. I have learned not to hate the Army or the government and I am proud to be an American.

The Vets' Center

Eleven years after I came home, they started a veteran center for the Viet Nam veterans. The people there know how to help you deal with the problems that come up almost daily as a result of the war. If the Vet Center had come along right after I came home, I would have been so much better off. It took the government so long to decide to put out money for a Veteran Center. It has helped me so much and the people there have helped a lot of other veterans with their problems and also with their paperwork.

I really wish everyone from President Johnson to the President's sons and daughters and wife and on and on down the line could have had a taste of Viet Nam as I did. When I drank the mud from my canteen I could just see Lady Bird Johnson standing there with her rucksack, gulping down her last bit of water saying, "Damn you, Lyndon B. Why the hell do we have to be here?" Couldn't you just picture that? I guess this ends my story. But, you know that war will probably never end.

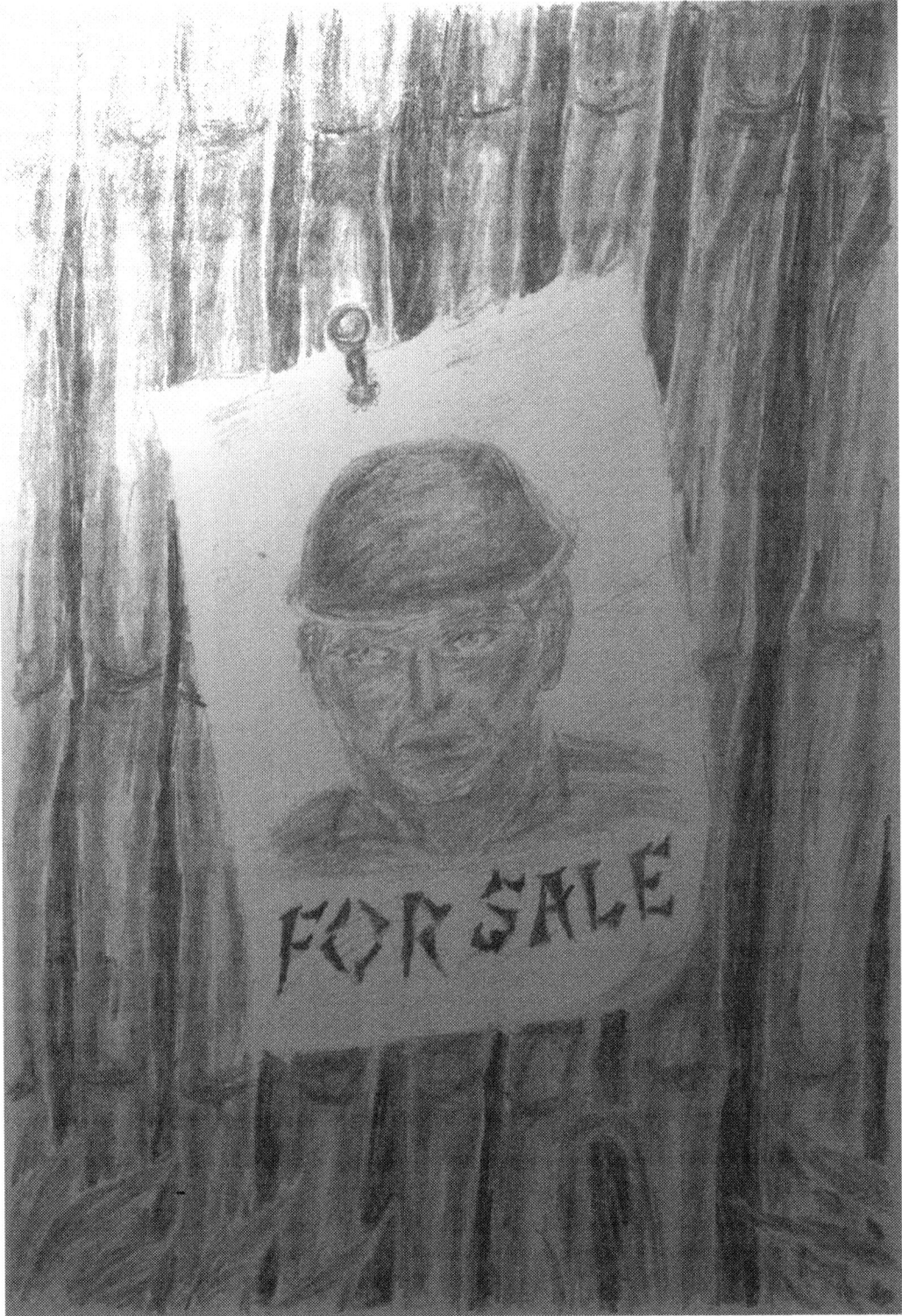

Illus. by Tyler Mills, 2006

<table>
<tr><td>

16

</td><td>

From Dakto to Detroit
By Jon Nordmeyer

</td></tr>
</table>

DETROIT, May 25, 1971—A few tenants living in the E.J. Jeffries Homes, a dreary public housing project in Cork town, an old Detroit neighborhood, can still remember Dwight Johnson as a little boy who lived in one of the rust-brown buildings with his mother and baby brother. They think it strange, after all that has happened to Dwight, to remember him as a gentle boy who hated to fight.

Dwight Johnson died one week from his 24th birthday, shot and killed as he tried to rob a grocery store a mile from his home. The store manager later told the police that a tall Negro had walked in shortly before midnight, drawn a revolver out of his topcoat and demanded money from the cash register.

The manager pulled his own pistol from under the counter and the two men struggled. Seven shots were fired.

Four and one-half hours later, on an operating table at Detroit General Hospital, Dwight (Skip) Johnson died from five gunshot wounds.

Ordinarily, the case would have been closed right there, a routine crime in a city where there were 13,583 armed robberies last year.

But when the detectives went through the dead man's wallet for identification, they found a small white card with its edges rubbed thin from wear. "Congressional Medal of Honor Society—United States of America," it said. "This certifies Dwight H. Johnson is a member of this society."

The news of the death of Sgt. Dwight Johnson shocked the black community of Detroit. Born out of wedlock when his mother was a teenager and raised on public welfare, he had been the good boy on his block in the dreary housing project, an altar boy and Explorer Scout, one of the few among the thousands of poor black youngsters in Detroit who had struggled against the grinding life of the ghetto and broken free, coming home from Viet Nam tall and strong and a hero.

The story of Dwight Johnson and his drift from hero in Dakto, Viet Nam to villain in Detroit is a difficult one to trace. The moments of revelation are rare. There were, of course, those two brief episodes that fixed public attention on him: 30 minutes of "uncommon valor" one cold morning in combat that earned him the nation's highest military decoration and the 30-second confrontation in the Detroit grocery that ended his life.

Oddly, they are moments of extreme violence, and everyone who knew Dwight Johnson—or thought they did—knew he was not a violent man.

CONGRESSIONAL MEDAL OF HONOR SOCIETY
UNITED STATES OF AMERICA

CHARTERED BY CONGRESS
AUGUST 14, 1958

This certifies that

Dwight H. Johnson
— —
is a member of this society

Secretary Treasurer   *President*

Now that the funeral is over and the out-of-town relatives have gone home and the family conferences that sought clues to explain Dwight's odd behavior have ended in bitter confusion, his mother can sit back and talk wistfully about the days when 'Skip' was a skinny kid who was chased home after school by the Corktown bullies.

"Mama," he would ask, "what do I do if they catch me?" His mother would place an arm around his thin shoulders and draw him close. "Skip," she would say, "Don't you fight, honey, and don't let them catch you." The boy would look downcast and worried. "Yes, Mama," he'd say.

"Dwight was a fabulous, all-around guy, bright and with a great sense of humor," reflected Barry Davis, an auburn-haired Californian who flew with his wife to Detroit when he heard on a news report that Dwight had been killed. Three others who had served with him in Viet Nam, all of them white, also came, not understanding what aberration had led to his death.

'Fighting Words'

"I can remember our first day at Fort Knox and Dwight was the only colored guy in our platoon," Barry Davis recalled. "So we're in formation and this wise guy from New Jersey says to Dwight, 'Hey, what's the initials N.A.A.C.P. stand for?

"And Dwight says, 'The National Association for the Advancement of Colored People.'

"And this wise guy from New Jersey says, 'Naw, that ain't it. It stands for Niggers Acting as Colored People.'

"And I said to myself, 'Wow, those are fighting words.' But Dwight just laughed. From then on he was just one of the guys. As it turned out, Dwight like this wise guy from New Jersey in the end as much as he liked anybody."

Most of the men who served with Sergeant Dwight Johnson remembered him that way—easy-going, hard to rattle, impossible to anger.

About Dakto

Dakto is a village in the central highlands of Viet Nam and in the so-called "tri-border" area where the borders of Viet Nam, Laos, and Cambodia all come together. Located just north of the Vietnamese town of Tan Canh -- nicknamed "Tin Can" by the American GIs, Dakto is populated by a Montagnard tribal people known as the Degar. It was viewed as a strategic area throughout the Viet Nam War because of its closeness to a major branch of the Ho Chi Minh Trail, which Hanoi maintained through the neighboring country of Laos. Dakto is in a lush region of forest covered mountains and deep valleys, with cool and refreshing streams in abundance. Yet the name will forever be associated with violence. In 1967 the mountains to the west of Dakto were the site of one of the bloodiest battles of the entire war, when the 173rd Airborne Brigade of the United States Army fought a lengthy engagement against major elements of the North Vietnamese regular army—the NVA. (Source: Wikipedia)

Another Side

But Stan Enders remembers him another way. Stan was the gunner in Skip's tank that morning in Viet Nam three years ago, during the fighting in Dakto.

"No one who was there could forget the sight of this guy taking on a whole battalion of North Vietnamese soldiers," Stan said as he stood in the sunshine outside the Faith memorial Church in Corktown three weeks ago, waiting for Skip's funeral service to begin.

Their platoon of four M48 tanks was racing down a road toward Dakto, in the Central Highlands near the Cambodian border and the Ho Chi Minh Trail when it was ambushed. Communist rockets knocked out two of the tanks immediately, and waves of foot soldiers sprang out of the nearby woods to attack the two tanks still in commission.

Skip hoisted himself out of the turret hatch and manned the mounted .50-caliber machine gun. He had been assigned to this tank only the night before. His old tank, and the crew he spent 11 months and 22 days with in Viet Nam and had never seen action before, was 60 feet away, burning.

"He was really close to those guys in that tank," Stan said. "He just couldn't sit still and watch it burn with them inside."

Skip ran through heavy crossfire to the tank and opened its hatch. He pulled out the first man he came across in the turret, burned but still alive, and got him to the ground just as the tank's artillery shells exploded, killing everyone left inside.

'Sort of Cracked Up'

"When the tank blew up, Dwight saw the bodies all burned and black, well, he just sort of cracked up," said Stan.

For 30 minutes, armed first with a .45 caliber pistol and then with a submachine gun, Skip hunted the Vietnamese on the ground, killing from five to 20 enemy soldiers, nobody knows for sure. When he ran out of ammunition, he killed one with the stock of the machine gun.

At one point he came face to face with a Communist soldier who squeezed the trigger on his weapon aimed point blank at him. The gun misfired and Skip killed him. But the soldier would come back to haunt him late at night in Detroit, in those dreams in which that anonymous soldier stood in front of him, the barrel of his AK-47 as big as a railroad tunnel, his finger on the trigger, slowly pressing it.

"When it was all over," Stan said, walking up the church steps as the funeral service got under way. "It took three men and three shots of morphine to hold Dwight down. He was raving. He tried to kill the prisoners we had rounded up. They took him away to a hospital in Pleiku in a straightjacket."

Stan saw Skip the next day. He had been released from the hospital, and came by to pick up his personal gear. His Viet Nam tour was over and he was going home.

No one would know anything about Dakto until 10 months later, at the White House Medal of Honor ceremony.

Sergeant Johnson returned home in early 1968, outwardly only little changed from the quiet boy named Skip who had grown up in Detroit and been drafted. Even when he and other black veterans came home and could not find a job, he seemed to take it in stride.

He had been discharged with $600 in his pocket, and it was enough to buy cigarettes and go out at night with his cousin, Tommy Tillman, and with Eddie Wright, a friend from the Jeffries Homes, and make the rounds to the Shadowbox or the Little Egypt, to drink a little beer and have a few dates.

And at home no one knew about the bad dreams he was having. They would have to learn about that later from an Army psychiatrist.

If anyone asked him about Viet Nam, he would just shake his head, or laugh and say, "Aw, man, nothing happened," and he would change the subject and talk about girls in Kuala Lumpur (Malaysia) where he went for R&R or the three-day pass he spent in Louisville, KY drinking too much whisky for the first time in his life and ending up in jail.

Out Before Tet

He returned home just as the Communist Tet offensive erupted in Viet Nam, and everyone talked about how lucky he had been to get out before things got hot. They teased him then about his lackluster military career.

"When he came home from Viet Nam, he was different, sure, I noticed it, all jumpy and nervous and he had to be doing something all the time, it seems," said Eddie Wright. "But mostly he was the same fun-time guy."

Carmen Berry, a close friend of Katrina May, the girl Skip started dating after his discharge, thought she detected nuances of change she attributed to the same mental letdown she had seen in other Viet Nam veterans.

"They get quiet," she said. "It's like they don't have too much to say about what it was like over there. Maybe it's because they've killed people and they don't really know why they killed them."

"The only thing that bugged me about Skip then," reflected his cousin Tommy, "and the one thing I thought was kind of strange and unlike him, was the pictures he brought back. He had a stack of pictures of dead people, you know, dead Vietnamese. Color slides."

In the fall he started looking for a job along with Tommy Tillman.

"We'd go down to the state employment agency every day and take a look at what was listed," his cousin recalled. "Skip was funny; he wouldn't try for any of the hard jobs. If we wrote down the name of a company that had a job that he didn't feel qualified for, he wouldn't even go into the place to ask about it. He'd just sit in the car while I went in

"Or if he did go in some place, he'd just sit and mumble a few words when they'd ask him questions. It was like he felt inferior. He'd give a terrible impression. But once we got back in the car, it was the same old Skip, laughing and joking."

A Pair of MPs

One day in October two military policemen came to his house. His mother saw the uniforms and before opening the door whispered urgently, "What did you do?"

"I didn't do nothing, honest, Ma," he answered.

The MPs asked Skip a few questions. They wanted to know what he was doing and if he had been arrested since his discharge. Fifteen minutes after they left, the telephone rang. It was a colonel calling from the Department of Defense in Washington. Sergeant Johnson was being awarded the Medal of Honor, he said. Could he and his family be in Washington on Nov. 19th so President Johnson could personally present the award?

Dwight Johnson receives Medal of Honor from LBJ. Source: LBJ Library

One week later on Nov. 19, 1968, they were all there in the White House, Skip tall and handsome in his dress-blue uniform, his mother, Katrina, and Tommy Tillman. The President gave a little speech. The national election was over, the Democrats had lost, but there were signs of movement at the Paris peace talks.

> *"Our hearts and our hopes are turned to peace as we assemble here in the East Room this morning," the President said. "All our efforts are being bent in its pursuit. But in this company we hear again, in our minds, the sound of distant battles."*

Five men received the Medal of Honor that morning. And when Sergeant Johnson stepped stiffly forward and the President looped the pale blue ribbon and sunburst medal around his neck, a citation was read that described his valor.

Later, in the receiving line, when his mother reached Skip, she saw tears streaming down his face.

"Honey," she whispered, "what are you crying about? You've made it back."

After he officially became a hero, it seemed that everyone in Detroit wanted to hire Dwight Johnson, the only living Medal of Honor winner in Michigan. Companies that had not been interested in a diffident ex-GI named Johnson suddenly found openings for Medal of Honor Winner Johnson.

Among those who wanted him was the United States Army.

"The brass wanted him in the Detroit recruiting office because—let's face it—here was a black Medal of Honor winner, and blacks are our biggest manpower pool in Detroit," said an Army employee who had worked with Skip after he rejoined the service a month after winning the medal. "Personally, I think a lot of promises were made to the guy that couldn't be kept. You got to remember that getting this guy back into the Army was a feather in the cap of a lot of people."

Events began moving quickly then for Skip. He married Katrina in January (the Ponchartrain Hotel gave the couple its bridal suite for their wedding night), and the newlyweds went to Washington in January as guests at the Nixon inaugural. Sergeant Johnson began a long series of personal appearances across Michigan in a public relations campaign mapped by the Army.

'A Hot Property'

In February 1969, 1,500 persons paid $10 a plate to attend a testimonial dinner for the hero in Detroit's Cobo Hall, co-sponsored by the Ford Motor Company and the Chamber of Commerce. A special guest was Gen. William C. Westmoreland, Army Chief of Staff and former commander of United States forces in Viet Nam.

"Dwight was a hot property back in those days," recalled Charles Bielak, a civilian information officer for the Army's recruiting operations in Detroit.

"I was getting calls for him all over the state. Of course, all this clamor didn't last. It reached a saturation point somewhere along the way and tapered off."

But while it lasted, Skip's life was frenetic. Lions Clubs... Rotary... American Legion. Detroit had a new hero. Tiger Stadium and meet the players. Sit at the dais with the white politicians. Be hailed by the black businessmen who would not have bothered to shake his hand before. Learn which fork to use for the salad. Say something intelligent to the reporters. Pick up the check for dinner for friends. Live like a man who had it made.

'Like a Couple of Kids'

But Leroy May, the hero's father-in-law could still see the child behind the man.

"Dwight and Katrina were a perfect match—they both had a lot of growing up to do," he said. "They didn't know how to handle all the attention they got it those days. They'd go out to supper so much Katrina complained she couldn't eat any more steak. I had to take them out and buy them hot dogs and soda pop. They were just like a couple of kids."

Bills started piling up. "They were in over their heads as soon as they were married," Mr. May said.

Everyone extended credit to the Medal of Honor winner. Even when he bought the wedding ring, the jeweler would not take a down payment. Take money from a hero? Not then. Later, the Johnsons discovered credit cards.

At first they lived in an $85-a-month apartment. But Katrina wanted a house. Skip signed a mortgage on a $16,000 house on the west side of Detroit. Monthly payments were $160.

'Ghetto Mentality'

In the spring of 1970, he wrote a bad check for $41.77 at a local market. The check was made good by a black leader in Detroit who was aghast that the Medal of Honor winner had gotten himself into a financial hole.

"I went to see him and told him he couldn't go on like this," said the man, a lawyer who asked to remain anonymous. "I said he was young and black and had the Medal of Honor. He could do anything he wanted. I tried to get him to think about college and law school. The black businessmen would pick up the tab. He wouldn't have any part of it."

Looking back on this meeting, the lawyer said he suspected Skip was burdened by a "ghetto mentality" that limited his horizons. His world had been a public housing project and schools a few blocks away. Now, suddenly, events had thrust him outside the security of his boyhood neighborhood into a world dominated by whites.

He was paralyzed, the lawyer speculated, by an inability to formulate a plan of action in this alien culture that he had been transported to by something that happened on the other side of the globe.

"What does he do when he's introduced to Bunkie Knudsen, the president of Ford?" asked the lawyer. "Does he come across strong and dynamic because he knows there is a $75,000-a-year job waiting for him if he makes a good impression? And what happens to him when he just stands there and fumbles and doesn't know if he should shake hands or just nod his head? He was forced to play a role he was never trained for and never anticipated."

Tommy Tillman remembers how Skip would take several friends downtown to the Ponchartrain Hotel for an expensive meal and sit fumbling with the silverware, watching the others to see what fork to use first. "I'd say to him, 'Shoot, man, what do you care? Go ahead and use anything you want.'

"I wondered how he must feel when he's the guest of honor at one of those fancy meetings he was all the time going to."

'A Nervous Stomach'

"It was all that rich food he was eating," said his father-in-law. His mother recalled that "Skip always did have a nervous stomach."

He began staying away from his job as a recruiter, missed appointments and speaking engagements. "It got so I had to pick him up myself and deliver him to a public appearance." Said Mr. Bielak, "I had to handcuff myself to the guy to get him someplace. It was embarrassing. I couldn't understand his attitude."

Last summer it was decided that Sergeant Johnson should report to Selfridge Air Force Base, not far from Detroit, for diagnosis of stomach complaints.

From Selfridge he was sent in September 1970 to Valley Forge Army Hospital in Pennsylvania. An Army psychiatrist later mulled over his notes on the patient and talked about them:

Maalox and bland diet prescribed. G.I. series conducted. Results negative. Subject given 30-day convalescent leave October 16th, 1970. Absent without leave until January 21st, 1971 when subject returned to Army hospital on own volition. Subsequent hearing recommended dismissal of A.W.O.L. charge and back pay reinstated. Subject agreed to undergo psychiatric evaluation. In cognizance of subject's outstanding record in Viet Nam, the division's chief psychiatrist placed in charge of the case. Preliminary analysis: Depression caused by post-Viet Nam adjustment problem.

In February 1971, Eddie Wright bumped into Skip on a Detroit street.

"Hey, man, where've you been?"

"I just got out of Valley Forge on a pass."

"How things going there?"

"They got me in the psycho ward."

"Huh, you got to be kidding."

"No, man, they think I'm crazy."

During the convalescent leave, Sergeant Johnson borrowed $4,992 from a Detroit credit union. In his wallet he had a cashier's check for $1,500, the back pay the Army had awarded him. Most of his time he spent at home on the pass but when he went out he would drive to the Jeffries Homes and play basketball with the teenagers after school.

New Friends

"He was a big man down there with the kids," recalled his cousin. "We had all lived in the project and had been on welfare, just like these kids there today, and we were like heroes because we had broken out of there. We had made it to the outside world, and to them we were big successes. We had made it.

"Skip was something special. He had that medal, and they were proud of him. He'd be down there five minutes and the kids would come around and say, 'Hey man, ain't you Dwight Johnson?'"

His old high school crowd was concerned about some of his new friends, though. "They were strung out on drugs and they just seemed to be hanging around Skip for his money," said his mother. "I asked him one night if he was taking anything, and he rolled up his sleeves and showed me there were no tracks [needle marks]. 'Ma,' he said, 'I'm not taking a thing.'"

On his return to the hospital, he began analysis with the chief attending psychiatrist.

Subject is bright. His Army G.T. rating is equivalent of 120 I.Q. In first interviews he does not volunteer information. He related he grew up in a Detroit ghetto and never knew his natural father. He sort of laughed when he said he was a "good boy" and did what was expected of him. The only time he can remember losing his temper as a youth was when neighborhood bullies picked on his younger brother. He was so incensed grownups had to drag him off the other boys. In general, there is evidence the subject learned to live up to the expectations of others while there was a build-up of anger he continually suppressed.

The Army hospital is actually in Phoenixville, PA, several miles from Valley Forge. It is the principal treatment center for psychiatric and orthopedic patients in the Northeast, with 1,200 beds now occupied.

Because of the large number of amputees and wheelchair patients, the hospital has only two floors and is spread over several acres. Long oak-floored corridors run in all directions, connected by covered walkways and arcades. Someone once measured the hospital and found there were seven miles of corridors in a maze-like jumble. To prevent patients from losing their way, wards are painted different colors.

Dressed in hospital blue denims, the warrior-hero walked the labyrinth late at night, wrestling with the problems that tormented his mind and drained his spirit.

"The first day Dwight arrived here, the hospital's sergeant major brought him to us," said Spec. 6 Herman Avery, a tall Negro with a flat face and close-set eyes who was master of the ward Dwight was first assigned to at the hospital. "It was the first time the sergeant major ever did that. We got the message. This guy was something special."

"Well, practically the first night he's here they dress him up and take him over to the Freedoms Foundation in Valley Forge to shake hands. When he got back he told me that if they ever did that again he would go A.W.O.L."

Further Evaluation

There was further psychiatric evaluation:

Subject expressed doubts over his decision to re-enter the Army as a recruiter. He felt the Army didn't honor its commitment to him. The public affairs were satisfactory to him at first, but he started to feel inadequate. People he would meet would pump his hand and slap his back and say, "Johnson, if you ever think about getting out of the Army, come look me up." On several occasions he contacted those individuals and they didn't remember him. It always took several minutes to remind them who he was.

Back in Detroiton leave on one occasion, his mother asked him to drive her to a doctor's appointment. In the office, an off-duty black Detroit policeman, Ronald Turner, recognized the Medal of Honor winner. When he asked for an account of his experience in Viet Nam, Skip replied: "Don't ask me anything about the medal. I don't even know how I won it."

Later, the policeman reported, Skip complained that he had been exploited by the Army. He told him that ever since he won the medal he had been set on a hero's path as an inspiration to black kids.

Others recalled how upset he had become when his recruiting talks at some black high schools in Detroit had been picketed by militants who called him an "electronic nigger," a robot the Army was using to recruit blacks for a war in Asia.

With his psychiatrist, he began to discuss his deeper anxieties:

Since coming home from Viet Nam the subject has had bad dreams. He didn't confide in his mother or wife, but entertained a lot of moral judgment as to what had happened at Dakto. Why had he been ordered to switch tanks the night before? Why was he spared and not the others? He experienced guilt about his survival. He wondered if he was sane. It made him sad and depressed.

Skip signed out of the hospital on March 28th, 1971 on a three-day pass to Philadelphia. The next day the newspapers and television were filled with reports of the conviction of First Lieutenant William L. Calley, Jr. on charges of murdering Vietnamese civilians. Skip turned up in Detroit a few days later and never returned to the Army hospital.

He settled in at home once again and dodged the telephone calls from the Army.

"How can you take punitive action against a Medal of Honor holder?" asked a major at the hospital who tried to convince him to return.

The Army did contact the Ford Motor Company, however, which had been letting Skip use a Thunderbird for the past two years. Ford picked up the car on the theory that without it he might be inconvenienced enough to return to the hospital. Instead, he cashed the cashier's check for $1,500, his

Army back pay, and bought a 1967 Mercury for $850. He changed his unlisted phone number to avoid the Army callers and a growing number of bill collectors.

By April 1971, his house mortgage had not been paid for the previous nine months, and foreclosing proceedings had been started. He owed payments on his credit union loan.

The car hand to go into a garage for brake repairs on Wednesday, April 28, and Skip was told it would cost $78.50 to get it out. The same day, Katrina entered a hospital for removal of an infected cyst and he told the admitting office clerk he would pay the $25 deposit the next day.

Lonely and depressed at home, Skip telephoned his cousin. "Let's go out and grab some beers," he said. But his cousin was busy.

He made another phone call that night and spoke to a friend in the Army. "I have a story I'm writing and I want you to peddle it for me," he said, "It starts out like this: "Sgt. Dwight Johnson is dead and his home has been wiped out..."

On April 30, Skip visited Katrina at the hospital. She said they were asking about the hospital deposit. He left at 5:30, promising to return later that evening with her hair curlers and bathrobe.

"He was just the same old Dwight, just kidding and teasing," his wife recalled. "When he was going, he said, 'Ain't you going to give me a little kiss good-by?' He said it like a little boy with his thumb in his mouth. So I kissed him and he went."

A Plea for a Ride

When Eddie Wright got home from work that night about 9 0'clock, he got a call from Skip. He said he needed a ride to pick up some money someone owed him and wanted to know if Eddie could get his stepfather to drive him. He said he would pay $15 for the ride.

Around 11 o'clock, Eddie, his mother, and his stepfather picked up Skip at his home. At his direction they drove west for about a mile to the corner of Orangelawn and Prest.

"Stop here," Skip told him, getting out of the car. "This guy lives down the street and I don't want him to see me coming."

The family waited in the car for 30 minutes. They became nervous, parked in a white neighborhood, and as Eddie explained later to the police, it may have looked odd for a car filled with blacks to be parked on a dark street. "So we pulled the car out under a streetlight so everybody could see us," he said.

At about 11:45 a police car pulled up sharply and two officers with drawn pistols got out. "What are you doing here?" they asked.

"We're waiting for a friend."

"What's his name?"

"Dwight Johnson."

"Dwight Johnson's on the floor of a grocery store around the corner," the officer said. "He's been shot."

'I'm Going to Kill You'

"I first hit him with two bullets," the manager, Charles Landeghem, said later. "But he just stood there, with the gun in his hand, and said, 'I'm going to kill you...'

"I kept pulling the trigger until my gun was empty."

Skip's psychiatrist recalled one of the interviews with him:

The subject remembered coming face to face with a Vietnamese with a gun. He can remember the soldier squeezing the trigger. The gun jammed. The subject has since engaged in some magical thinking about this episode. He also suffers guilt over surviving it, and later winning a high honor for the one time in his life when he lost complete control of himself. He asked: "What would happen if I lost control of myself in Detroit and behaved like I did in Viet Nam?" The prospect of such an event apparently was deeply disturbing to him.

The burial at Arlington National Cemetery took place on a muggy and overcast day. The grave, on a grassy slope about 200 yards east of the Kennedy Memorial, overlooks the Potomac and the Pentagon, gray and silent, to the south.

The Army honor guard, in dress blues, carried out its assignment with precision, the sixth burial of the day for the eight-man unit, while tourists took photographs at a discreet distance from the grieving family.

For a few days after the burial, the family weighed the possibility that Skip had been taking narcotics in the last few months of his life and the demands of drugs had sent him into the grocery store with a gun. But the autopsy turned up no trace of narcotics.

Eddie Wright and his family were released by homicide detectives after questioning, even after Eddie could not produce any plausible reason why his best friend had carried out a bizarre crime and implicated him at the same time.

The dead man's mother was the only one who uttered the words that no one else dared to speak. "Sometimes I wonder if Skip tired of this life and needed someone else to pull the trigger," she said late one night in the living room of her home, her eyes fixed on a large color photograph of her son, handsome in his uniform, with the pale blue ribbon of his country's highest military honor around his neck

[Ed. Note: You can learn more about Sgt. Dwight Johnson at http://www.aavw.org/served/homepage_djohnson.html]

The Healing Wall

Karin A. Hancuff

[Ed. Note: "THE WALL" came to Ft. Wayne in a traveling exhibition form in July 1998 and September 2001. 1,531 of the Viet Nam War dead were from the State of Indiana.]

I stood silently watching "THE WALL" being taken down, one panel at a time and placed in its special packing crate to be shipped to the next city. It was all I could do to keep from crying, it was like losing a very close friend, it hurt; it hurt quite a lot.

At first, I had been quite apprehensive and almost too afraid to see "THE WALL". I knew from my reading that it was very impressive, but I could not understand how it could be when I felt that it was only a big black tombstone. It could be eerie, but *not* impressive. How could anyone stand to look at it, let alone receive any healing from it?

I had volunteered to help with "THE WALL" to hopefully pay back the Vet Center for all the support Jeff and I received when he was having a tough time with delayed stress.

We attended six training sessions and the first session was about how to handle abusive people, due to drugs, alcohol, and sheer grief. After that first session I wanted to quit, it scared me to death! Just knowing it was possible to become abusive because of so much pain. It cannot be worth it, if all it is going to do is bring out the worst in people. Well, we did make it through all the sessions and we were asked to come the Friday before the opening to view "THE WALL." Hopefully, at this time each of us would try to handle our ghosts left from the war.

Friday as we pulled into the parking lot we could see "THE WALL" on a slight knoll. It had flood lights and viewing it almost took your breath away.

Jeff and I slowly walked the incline in silence. We held hands, squeezing gently as if saying to each other, "This is going to be hard, but we must, we must do it for us and for every name up there."

Most of the volunteers had arrived by then and one by one they climbed the hill to "THE WALL." Some found *the panel* with *their name* and stood in silence. I found *my panel* and I just stared at it; I could not go any further. I felt like running away. You do not know how much strength it took to get the courage to do what I knew I had to do, for my own sake as well as for my family.

I kept thinking there are an awful lot of names on my panel. Finally I started counting the lines 10-20-25-26-27-28-29. As I slowly ran my finger from left to right I read the names William D. Nelson, Gerald R. Peterson, then *David L. Merrill!*

As I read the name in my mind I started trembling. All the while thinking, "My cousin David, my God he is really listed on 'THE WALL'. My Dear Sweet Cousin David is legally, actually dead!!" I thought I had worked through this before, but I had not really faced it, I avoided it. My cousin was so young when he was killed. He did not have a chance yet at life, he cannot be dead. But, he most certainly was dead, there it was right in front of my eyes, listed by the government on a huge tombstone. I sobbed uncontrollably with such a gigantic lump in my throat I could barely breathe, and the pain, the pain in my heart was as if it had been completely broken. I had fleeting thoughts of people possibly staring at me, but I did not care. My poor David was on there and I had to mourn for him, apologize to him, and ask him for forgiveness about trying to forget him. He was only 23. I was a mother for the first time at 23, and David's fiancée buried her love at the age of 23.

It was just not fair; this damn wall is reminding everyone of lost loved ones. It does not hurt as much if you do not have to face it and "THE WALL," is forcing all the hurt, pain, and bitterness to come back.

While thinking this, I turned from my panel and started walking away. I could not help seeing each panel as I passed, which seemed to be getting larger and. larger with rows and rows of name after name... No, it was not! It was human being after human being, lives upon lives all lost for what? Disrespect, humiliation, shame, and forgotten, for the call of duty?

I was so angry that evening I did not even pay any attention to my husband, I did not know how he was handling anything. I just worried about myself and what I was feeling.

Saturday was the opening ceremony and people had already started coming to view "THE WALL," some left mementos such as flowers, flags and even *a pair of combat boots*. I thought that was a strange thing to remember someone by, but then I noticed painted on the toe, 'REMEMBER'. That one word made me *stop*. Stop thinking about myself and my own guilt about trying to forget my beloved cousin and start to realize that my thinking about "THE WALL" was not right. It was not a huge tombstone with no room for even a small epitaph; It was not a long black Hall between life and death but actually a bridge between loved ones and lost ones leading them closer to the truth, with healing and ultimately peace for all people concerned.

Some were very quiet in their grief and others quite demonstrative to the point of complete emotional breakdown. Others returned day after day slowly walking the length of the wall running their fingers across the names in complete silence. I seemed to understand their reason for this, they were trying to "Remember why, *why*, the names were forgotten, Why we turned our backs on all these souls. We were trying to say *why* I am sorry for attempting to deny our lost ones their honor, dignity, and righteous place on this earth."

As the days went by my husband and I seemed to change in our thoughts about the Nam experience. He seemed to be less resentful, and less angry through all this we became closer and began to heal our hurts. Strangely it seemed that the Viet Nam Memorial Wall had some sort of power over our emotions. We were not at all afraid to show them to each other or to members of the volunteer group. As the people came and shared with each of us their stories while we directed them to their name, they felt safe enough to openly weep and lean on us at times, and we seemed to have no fear of trusting in complete strangers. We wanted to touch, or hug and show that we cared and understood when they were in desperate need of support.

I grew so much emotionally during the visit of "THE WALL" from marching in the parade with our heads held high with pride, as tears of joy streamed down our faces, and finally getting the gratitude and respect from the people of our nation, with acceptance and pure love!!

The strange magnetism of "THE WALL" compelled many of us to pull longer shifts. There was something about it. We were never tired while there, always rejuvenated, maybe because of all the raw human emotions always present and just being a part of all the love being shown to the lost ones found on the wall. I am not sure what it was, but I do know that if the daily exposure did not affect you then the closing ceremony surely would have.

On Sunday, the last day of the exhibit, during the reading of the additional 110 names[1], I saw a dear friend of mine crying. With the appearance of just a few tears, I too started to sob. He had a right to weep, all the rows of names on this "WALL OF LOVE" and now more to add. *God please make us remember what happened so it is not forgotten and this horrible waste of precious human life will not happen again.*

We were asked after the closing ceremony to join hands along "THE WALL" and continue out to form an unbroken circle, as we all stood listening to Taps, many of our eyes filled with tears. You could tell by our determined expressions that we were not going to *forget to remember.*

Through memories of lost loved ones and everyone's love expressed by those who viewed "THE WALL" we have finally brought a lot of our soldiers home!

---

[1] In 1986, 110 names were added, the majority of which were added when the geographic criteria were enlarged to include those killed outside the war zone while on or in support of direct combat missions.

Symbol of the Valley of the Shadow
Michael Scrogin

The Viet Nam Veterans Memorial was dedicated in Washington, DC on November 11th. My family and I visited it a week later. When I first realized that I wanted to see the memorial, I wasn't sure why. But I knew I had to see it.

I did not serve in Viet Nam and have never served in the military. During the height of the war years I was in seminary and participated in occasional nonviolent protests against our involvement in Viet Nam. Three close friends did serve, however—three football teammates who, upon graduation from college, were either drafted or volunteered. Each was a casualty.

Bill Link, my best friend and college roommate, was shot through the neck while on patrol. He might have died, but he didn't. He completely recovered, is now married, has children and teaches school in Colorado. Don Newson was a teammate I knew less well. He was a quiet, steady young man. He went to Viet Nam as a Marine Lieutenant and lost a leg in fighting there. I don't know where Don is now. Rick Cooper was killed in Viet Nam. I pictured him on that raw November day—a tall, gawky, barely adequate athlete who laughed at everybody's jokes and was everybody's friend. He was drafted, trained away from his native harmlessness and sent as an Army squad leader to fight in the jungle. He is buried near his parents' home in Florissant, Missouri. I intended to look for Rick Cooper's name on the memorial and to stand before it for a moment wishing things were different.

I didn't do so, however, for the monument has a power of its own. Located in Constitution Gardens, with one end pointing to the Washington Monument and the other toward the Lincoln Memorial, the Viet Nam Veterans Memorial makes a statement different from that of either of these two. Its black granite face contrasts with the white marble of the monuments nearby. While the architectural tributes to Lincoln and Washington rise with pride of empire above the reflecting pool, the Viet Nam Memorial is set quietly and humbly into the earth. You walk up to the Lincoln Memorial; you have to take an elevator to go to the top of the Washington Monument. But to walk down a gently sloping ramp to that apex and glance to left and right—with only blackness and names visible—is to feel again the grip in which Viet Nam once held us all.

Even the way in which the names are ordered conjures up the chaos and confusion of the war. I had gone to this place thinking the names would surely be listed alphabetically. And they are, partly: they are alphabetized in groups according to dates of death. To find a particular name you must either know the date of death and then search out the panel and tread through the names to the one you seek, or turn to one of the park rangers who are stationed in three positions near the wall. Each ranger has an index the size of a Manhattan telephone directory listing names and other vital statistics (maybe more than one Rick Cooper died in Viet Nam.)

As is now well known because of the controversy that followed the choice, the design for the memorial was chosen by competition, and 2,573 artists and architects offered their ideas. The unanimous selection of the judges (all Viet Nam veterans) was the design of 21-year-old Yale University senior Maya Lin of Athens, Ohio. Lin's monument is catharsis; it cleanses and changes those who view it. It has the almost physical power to shift the observer from indifference to attention. What had been lost sight of—the war's vast cumulative waste—is brought before one's eyes.

The stone chevron has the power to hush those who stand before it. While I was at the memorial, a group of high schoolers on an outing came streaming noisily down the steps of the Lincoln Memorial. They ran and danced across the mall toward the Viet Nam Veterans Memorial, their voices loud with playful insults and laughter. When the leading edge of the group reached the memorial, they pulled up short and turned, signaling to those behind that they should be quiet, stop their running and playing. They knew instinctively that they were in the presence of the sacred—a place both fearsome and fascinating.

The memorial is a work of art, even of creation. It evokes so much. It is a wailing wall. It is a mirror; in fact, one sees oneself reflected in its polished surface. It is an altar littered with the evidence of burdens laid down. Roses and carnations were dropped before most panels. Lipstick gave testimony that many names had been kissed. Notes on scraps of paper were stuck between the panels: "Johnny, we still love you!" An MIA bracelet had been removed from a wrist, bent flat and inserted next to the name the bracelet carried. A garishly ugly plastic wreath hung on a wire stand before one panel, the words "For Our Son" glaring from the nylon bunting. Some people stood quietly, touching a name with the tips of their fingers—as if the letters were a kind of Braille that might yield a meaning to touch that they wouldn't to sight alone. It is a symbol of the valley of the shadow of death. It is a last, enduring body count. It is a book of the generations—even as the Bible lists generations: "And this is the book of the generations of the sons of Noah: Ham, Shem, Japheth." And this is the book of the generations of Viet Nam: Andrew, Robert, William. It is a sphinx that will endlessly pose its riddle to those who seek power and will, let us pray, devour those who cannot answer or who answer poorly. It is a scar upon the monumental landscape of our capital; like all scars, it is at once evidence of a wound's healing and a reminder of its hurt.

As I walked up the incline to leave the memorial, a well-dressed man from the National Parks Service was giving instructions to one of the uniformed park rangers assigned to the monument. There had been complaints about the drainage. With all the rain and the foot traffic, the lawn before the memorial was turning to mud. "If anyone asks," he said, "tell them that we're going to re-sod and that the drainage problem will soon be cleared up."

I could feel the suck and pop of the mud as I moved away, and words like swamp and tunnel and quagmire rang in my memory. Will it be cleared up soon? Or was the mud too part of Lin's moving and potent memorial? Elie Wiesel wrote "Poets exist so that the dead may vote." So do appropriate memorials to soldiers lost in battle.

	Viet Nam Redux:
# 18	# The Year of the Cock
	## By Nick Rizzo

Redux: 'bringing back'. This epithet was often applied to the goddess Fortuna in the sense that she was being invoked to protect the emperor on his return journey to Rome.   –David R. Sear

In the Year of the Cock (1993), after many years of nightmares and tears, I decided to go back to the place I swore to the heavens that if I got out alive I would never return. But, little did I know...

Would being counseled at the Vet Center in the 1980s give me the knowledge to cope and understand what had happened to me? Had I not gone to the Vet Center I would not be here today and then still even today it is a struggle. Everyday things like eating, sleeping, talking to people, going to restaurants, eating in public, listening to some people's bullshit...

I did not know I would have to fight every single thing of daily life when I returned home. For example, waking up at home on the sofa in the living room, I would almost jump right out of my skin when I reached out for my rifle to find it not there.

Little did I know at the time, that this was just the beginning of the nightmares of war. I can say that one's mind can play some very deadly games on oneself, so when you are young and want to survive, your mind and body do everything their power to survive, and I mean anything. It's up to you, as they say, your will to survive, period.

Why did I decide to back to Viet Nam in the Year of the Cock? Returning in 1993, before the US had good relations with Viet Nam, I entered a world much different from my own. It turns out I got back there just in time to see the war years of Viet Nam disappearing forever into the air. As far as history goes I enjoyed that, but as far as my mental state goes, I did not like or enjoy the trip.

As I walked down the streets, it was like my soul was walking behind me, remembering the things I had done and seen. I did do some good things while I was there, but those things do not out-shadow the bad. The bad always out-shadows the good.

Or should I say, for the most part I went back to Viet Nam to see the truth. The truth for myself through Nick Rizzo's eyes, and when I saw all the destruction and devastation of people's bodies and minds, I did not care for it at all. I thought this to myself as I looked at a man walking down the street with his motherfucking eyes melted shut.

What the hell is wrong with civilizations that would do this to people, and still in 1993 so many poor people who were walking the streets still hungry?

I thought that I had been a part of that, through no fault of my own, but still it is there.

Instead of fighting the war, I could now see all the horrible sites, up close and personal and on my own terms. Then add them to what I already have floating around in my head. Like the innocent people that I had killed because of my state of mind during the war.

Looking Back

The war had taken me from an innocent boy to a lean, mean fighting machine and I mean I could kill someone and walk away and think nothing of it. That is what I had turned into... This is another thing that I had to keep hold of for the rest of my life, like when someone makes ya' really angry. It's not fun to live with: to carry all this stuff around in my head is not an easy task.

So, in thinking many things like this, hoping to get rid of some of these things, I went back, or tried anyway, thinking maybe I could put a few of the pieces together. I was scared to go back for the reason that I thought I might lose my head, not that I was scared physically of the place.

As it turned out, several times I had to hold my head. I kept telling myself that "the people are friendly now", "the war is over" and other things like that. It turned out that I was so interested in the history part, and the people treated me so very nicely, that I did not have too many bad things to deal with.

Did going back do me any good? I guess it did. I saw the truth and many other things, but on the other hand I still have that anger and hate, and dreams, and memories, of the bad things that happened. So what I can say is that it kinda' equaled itself out. Am I a better person for going there? I can say yes.

Then there were those things that ya' just can't understand no matter how hard ya' try... In 1969, after being ripped through hell and back and losing my two best friends, on or about 10 in the morning I sat on a bunker looking out into a valley from our perimeter. I will say that if anything was really real, it was this. How or why it happened, I do not know, but I will say it really happened. As I sat looking into this valley I was put into some kind of a trance. I could not feel or talk at this moment. I stared straight ahead and the only way I can describe it is: a stream of gold flakes very quickly was lifted right from my brain. My head was kinda' tilted upward as this stream of gold dust shot up into the sky and all of a sudden was cut by some invisible thing, and part of the stream kept going up and the other part went back into my head, and as it came to a stop or as part of the stream came down in my mind, I thought "Stop, what is going on here?" I got angry, but there was nothing I could do.

Then a guy I knew came up to me and the next thing I saw was him waving his hand in front of my eyes. He was saying to me, "Are you ok, Rizz?" And I said to him, "Yes," but I knew I was not. I was angry on top of being angry. The only thing that I can think is that something took part of my soul that day in June 1969.

Valor of the South Vietnamese

One second... When you look back on your life you can surely see where you went wrong, did right, missed the "gold rush", and all the rest of that junk you wish that you had done differently.

I guess that is what you call history. In 1993, I decided to take a look back into my history, and so I did. Sometimes you see things that are good, and sometimes you see things that are bad, and sometimes you see the truth. I guess most of all I wanted to see the truth, because I did not know I was going to see it all.

I have heard a Viet Nam vet say, "Fighting in Viet Nam was like the movie Gulliver's Travels." I agree fully. As you go through life, you make many decisions and it takes only one second to change life with one decision. It's like a shot in the dark, and I sure know what that is like: bang, you're dead!

The war has been over for me now, for 24 years. When I finally got up the nerve and the money to go back to Viet Nam, it was before the US normalized relations with them in July 1995. I knew that there were veterans who went there before me in the 1980s and I am sure there were some business people also. They each have their own story, but this is mine.

During the war I slept, ate, and fought, with the South Vietnamese army. Being with the South Viets, I got a different perspective of the war. If you counted up numbers, there were only a small percentage of us who had the honor to do so.

The Americans, from what I saw, looked down on the South Viets and claimed many things that were simply not true. To their best ability, they tried to work with us and since we had the power and the money, and the fact that Americans had never lost a war, you can see why we dominated the situation. I had heard years ago that the South Viets were cowards, and one of the magazines had pictures of them not shooting back at the enemy. Just because you never saw any Americans cowering in pictures does not mean that there were none: there are cowards in all armies.

What most people do not know is: at the perimeters of many LZs and army bases were South Viets. At the bottom of the hill and hence at the first line of defense, the South Viets were at the famous siege of Khe San, with the US Marines at the top of the hill. Every week of the war, there were more South Viets than Americans killed.

In '69, the Lt. and I were sent out on a mission, to some godforsaken hill in the jungle. As we climbed our way up the hill, passing us going down the hill were the dead and wounded South Viets and there was a steady line of them. As we made our way up to the front, the enemy was pounding the mortar rounds home that day. We then got orders to go on the far side of the hill: the brass was going to try to sneak us in the back door. There were just a handful of us. Was I scared? I was quaking in my boots!

The underbrush was very thick and we could not see much of anything, so as we lay there waiting for orders to give it a go, the Lt. was telling me what was going on. He told me that the South Viets had been there for three days trying to take the hill. And as he spoke I could hear the choppers coming in and taking out the dead. Every three minutes, a chopper would come in and take out the dead and wounded. Since we had nothing else to do, we timed the choppers and sure enough every three minutes one came in and one left.

As I was lying there, more or less waiting to die, many things ran through my head and one was of my brother, who was at draft age and who came very close to getting drafted. My thinking at the time was, if taking this hill meant my brother would not have to come and do this, then by God I was going to take that hill on that day and I had no choice. So the way I saw it was: do or die. Period.

We lay out there for four hours before the brass called it off and told us to abort our mission. Every three minutes a Chinook chopper came in for the dead, and a chopper like that carries 30 men: that is a lot of dead. We were there for four hours. The South Viets who were way up that hill that day knew what was going on and they all still went up that hill. So much for cowards, huh?

The New Viet Nam

I had seen the old Viet Nam and now I was about to see the new. I had many questions. And of course, I was curious to. I was going there by myself and I did not speak the language, I knew a few words like "Where are the girls?" I had been lied to about many things in the past and I wanted to go look for myself. I did not know what to expect from them and from myself. The war had made a very big impact on me—even more than I had thought. I had been wondering about many things for many years.

So on an April day, the big plane came swooshing down again into Saigon. As the plane taxied to a rest, I could still see the hangars where the Americans had kept their choppers during the war. And at the same time I felt the rush of history hit me, what a feeling that was!

After a very long flight I felt woozy, stepping out of the jet. One thing for sure, it was still hot, but the funny smell was gone. I guess that must have been the smell of war. We got on a bus and it took us to the airport building. I got off the bus and as I did, there was a woman on a bench who asked me if there had been another plane that landed. I told her I did not see another plane. She looked and spoke American and it looked like she had been in Viet Nam awhile. You get a certain look after a long stay. She looked to be too young to have been in Viet Nam during the war, so I figured she must have been there on business.

So I walked through the doors and shit, there stood the enemy! I was stunned. I first started to panic, my blood pressure must have gone up a couple of notches. I was the only white person in the building and I did not speak their language. I got myself under control went through customs.

Most people who went to Viet Nam before me went with someone, or with some kind of goodwill group.

I remembered I had bought my plane ticket from a guy who got out of Viet Nam in '75 and he had made arrangements for a guy with a motorbike to pick me up on arrival. So I found him and off we went plowing through the streets full of motorbikes and people. The only rule I saw was "Just don't hit anyone." There were very few red lights working and nobody stopped for anything! Here I was in a place that I swore if I ever got out alive I would never come back to. Funny how things turn out? Ain't it.

Welcome Back to Saigon

At first I did not remember that I had even been in Saigon before, but when we pulled up to a hotel and went inside, I recalled having been there. I sat my backpack down as the interpreter asked for a room. I looked around and then realized during the war the Lt. and I had tried to get a room in this hotel, but the owner had turned us away because he did not like Americans. So at that point, I knew I would not get the room again and sure enough again I did not.

We then went to another hotel, the Miss Koiis Hotel. It was a nice place and the price was right too. It had a walk-in bath tub and cockroaches as big as small birds. In '93 nobody had any money to take care of the problem, but since then they have. I thought it was no big deal, when I took a shower I would squirt them with hot water and try to kill them before they got away, like a game.

After I made myself at home, I made plans to go to Kontum where my unit was during the war, which was north of Pleiku by about 40 miles. The next day, I was up early and rented a car to take me to Kontum. We got on Highway One, which runs all the way up to Hanoi. As we drove I saw a few sights left over from the war, and some things that I had not seen before.

My Second R&R

Driving through many small towns going north I looked out into landscape and it began to turn to white sand. The sand triggered my memory of Cam Ranh Bay (180 miles north of Saigon), where I first came into country in 1968. Thinking back, I remembered when I got off the jet there was a smell in the air that to this day I cannot describe or compare anything with.

Standing there on the air field with two or three other guys, I looked out into the hills and saw smoke rising in the distance. A guy who had been there for a spell told us that was where the fighting was going on. I looked at the smoke and thought to myself, how the hell are we going to win this war when all the enemy has to do is go around the other side of the hill? I thought, what a way to fight a war! Little did I know, little did I know, how very little did I know...

Then I remembered when I'd gone on R&R for the second time. Everyone was supposed to get two R&Rs, but things did not always work out that way—some guys got three R&Rs whereas some of us only got just one. The

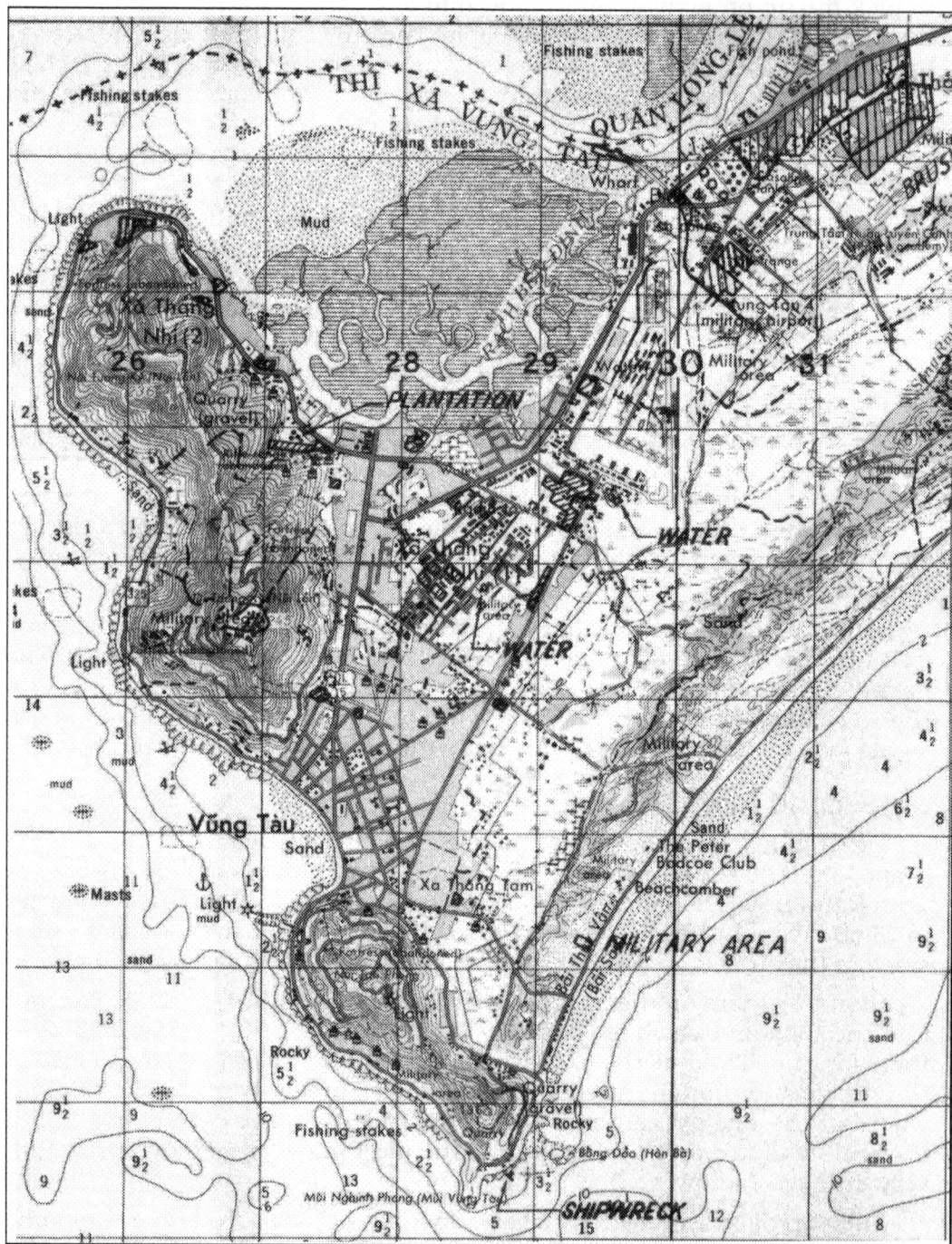

Vung Tau Peninsula (Courtesy: USGS)

old who ya' know, where you were stationed, regular politics, ass-kissing, deceiving the army, tricks, and that kinda' thing.

Anyway I got my second R&R but it was unauthorized, like AWOL, but not really AWOL because I did have papers. So at Cam Ranh Bay, I met up with another guy and we decided to go to Vung Tau[1]. We got off the plane at Vung Tau and right-off-the-bat there were MPs at the gate. We kinda' lucked out because the MP was from Indiana too and he told us that we would have to stay in the barracks till tomorrow when we could catch a plane back to our units.

So like two good little soldiers, we went to the barracks. But when we got there, we saw nobody, so we figured fuck it—we'll go downtown anyway. We started walking down the street when an old French car which was retrofitted into a cab pulled up and the driver asked if we needed a ride. So like two little good soldiers we got in and off we went. We got out of the cab and started walking down the street, which was very crowded. We found a store, bought some civilian clothes and kept going on to find a hotel for the night.

As we were walking and looking around, here came a Vietnamese woman down the street toward us. But she was different from the others—as she passed by, my head was only up to her waistline. She had to be at least seven feet tall or maybe even taller. Back then there were not too many people in the world that tall.

We found a hotel and then of course we got hungry. Across the street was a restaurant. When we came through the door a girl told me to come over and sit with her. She introduced herself as Mai Lin, whether that was her real name I have no idea, but she was pretty and very nice so what the hell—that was what we were there for. I sat down with her and we ordered some food. She ordered Chinese soup. I remember she tried to get me to eat some soup, but no thanks it looked to me there were little things swimming around in there and I was not about to eat it. They brought us some fortune cookies which we read, but I cannot remember what they said. They were tied with a little plastic string which I kept as a souvenir, and still have today.

We asked the girls if they would come to the hotel that night. We then got up to leave and the girl I was with pointed to a woman sitting at another table, who asked me to come over. She was a handsome woman (about thirty) and we talked for awhile and then she put her hand flat on the table. I saw that her ring finger was cut off at the first joint and she told me that when her husband got killed she cut it off. It sure looked like it had been cut off. She told me to come back later on that evening and she told me where to meet her.

I was very curious to hear what she had to say so I went back that evening. When I got there I waited a while, but the woman did not show up. Another woman came out of nowhere and told me that the first woman could

---

[1] Vung Tau is the first seaside resort for the elite in Vietnam. The first hotel, the Arduzer, was built in the 1870's and was a spa for the French leadership at the time. Over time, many more bungalows and vacation homes were built by the well-to-do of Saigon.

not come because she had something very important to do. Now this all seemed very strange to me, but I was so curious that I had to go and find out. But as it turned out, I never found out. The only thing I could figure was that she was a VC. I'll never know now. Those few minutes that I talked to her I felt a great deal of respect for her. She seemed to be very brave and intelligent, not just because of her finger, but it was her whole being. I got this feeling that she was a very brave woman and the only thing I can say is whoever she was I am glad I had the chance to meet her.

I went back to the hotel and the two girls we first met in the restaurant came later that night. We messed around a little and smoked some pot. The morning came early the next day as I awoke to slamming doors and girls screaming and running down the halls. Our two girls went running out of the room telling us that "The MPs are coming!" We quickly flushed our pot down the toilet. By that time, the MPs were two doors down so we decided to go out and climb down the balcony. We climbed down and the guy I was with went to the left and I went straight across the street.

I went into the restaurant and told the girls the MPs were after me. They pointed to the back of the room and just as I put one foot in motion the MPs grabbed me, and that was all she wrote. They took me out to the jeep and told me to spread my legs and put my hands on the jeep. Then they took everything out of my pockets. Among some of some other things I had a switchblade knife and they told me that it was illegal to have that kind of knife. However, they gave it back to me and put us on a plane back to our units with an Article 15. If I remember correctly if you get three Article 15s you're supposed to get court martialed, and that was my third, or was it my fourth? Anyway, they did not court-martial me.

Cam Ranh Bay

Well, they sent me back to Cam Ranh Bay to catch another plane. When I got there a guy came up to me and told me that the day before, the VC swam by the guards, who were sleeping on guard duty, and cut their throats as they slept. Then they went into the hospital and started shooting the wounded men in their beds. I asked him, "Didn't anyone have a rifle?" He told me that all the rifles were locked up. Boy, was I angry. I was thinking, darn if I'd been there, I probably could have saved someone's life.

For the most part, the men at Cam Ranh Bay were clerks and supply people and had no dealings with enemy soldiers. At night like that, the enemy causes confusion and then goes in and kills whoever they can. One has to use his head in those situations, but when the bullets start to fly it is a very difficult thing to do. So here I was again, driving past all the white sand of Cam Ranh and then I saw the sign that read "Cam Ranh Bay". But in '93, the bay was closed, so we kept on driving north.

I could see the coca bushes growing on the side or the road. I suppose it was for medical reasons? Still dodging the giant pot holes, we go further to Nha Trang beach, where we stopped to eat. The driver pulled the car underneath a sun roof. We got out and walked onto what looked like a big porch with tables and chairs under it. It was a restaurant overlooking the ocean.

As I sat there I felt the cool breeze coming off the sea. As the breeze hit, so did the memories. During the war, the Lt. and I stopped here to eat when we were on our way to Saigon, and I did not remember that until I sat there in that breeze on that day. On my way to Kontum, there were many stops that I did not remember until revisiting them in '93. Even now I remembered what I had to eat back then: I had lobster, and in '93 I also ordered lobster. Both times, the lobster it tasted like rubber so I didn't eat it. I think I did not remember the good things because the bad things overshadowed them. While sitting there waiting for my food, I got a very empty alone feeling and thought of the Lieutenant and how nice it would have been if he were here with me now. What a shame that all those men had to die! You know, if we'd have come over here as tourists in the first place, we could have saved the world a lot of grief.

After I'd finished eating, I walked out onto an old wooden pier that has probably been there for a century, but during the war it had barbed wire all around it. I then walked off the pier and onto the beach itself. When I looked out into the water, it was a brilliant blue color all the way up to about a foot to the shoreline. It was the bluest water I had ever seen. I could have never imagined how beautiful this water was until I saw it for the second time. During the war I remembered it as gray in color.

I then walked away from the beach and saw where the Americans had built a bunker and a trench running along the beach. Back then it was just a trench dug in the ground with sandbags and at the end of the trench was a bunker —also made of wood and sandbags—but now they were both cement.

What a strange world this is? If only I would have been at Dakto with my friends that day on June 4th, 1969, maybe all three of us would have been standing here today?

North on Highway One

We walked back to the car and drove north on Highway One. As we drove I did not see very many cars. Most of the traffic were motorbikes, lumber trucks, and every once in a while a bus or two. On the sides of the road were the Montagnards walking to their destinations, but nowadays I don't think I saw even one Montagnard woman topless. I guess that is progress for ya? Messin' things up... Civilization. I wonder who is really civilized in this world? That used to be kind of an extra treat to see the topless girls during the war.

I think it was a little after noon when the driver pulled over to rest, so I got out of the car and walked to the back of it when I saw a girl coming my way with a handful of coconuts and a machete knife. When I saw her I backed up about ten feet out of caution and reaction, but she just wanted to sell us some coconut juice. So we bought some; it was very good on a hot day like that. The way I see it, it's better to be safe than sorry, you just never can tell, can you?

Qui Nohn

I was glad to be riding in a car this time and it was late afternoon when we got to Qui Nohn. I got a room at the Sea Breeze Hotel. I took my backpack up to my room. Then me and the interpreter took a walk on the beach. As we walked I kept feeling something squishing under my feet at first I thought it was jellyfish, but when I looked down I saw it was human waste. When I looked down the beach, I saw many people out on the beach using it for a toilet. We just kept walking; I thought it was a good idea using the beach for a toilet. When high tide comes in it will all be washed away, I thought, kinda in tune with nature.

We finally got out of the toilet area and came across a group of people having some kind of ceremony. They were thanking Buddha for the fish they caught that day. I asked them "Do you catch a lot of fish?" And one of the men said, "Yes, we always catch a lot of fish."

That's where I crossed paths with Oong Bouy. She had long black hair, teeth as white a fresh fallen snow, tan skin, eyes that sparkled like diamonds and stars both, and a smile that could melt stone. She was ten years old, and spoke very good English. I stood there talking to her and we started to draw a crowd, who called themselves The Boat People. On further down the beach we ran into Oong's mother, who was packing fish of the day, she looked at me and said, "Do you want to help?" I promptly said "No," knowing that if I did I would end up smelling like dead fish... everyone laughed.

When I looked into Oong's face I wondered how many Oongs were killed during the war? What a shame that was. I heard a Vietnamese woman say, "Both sides lost." I agree, if you lost a son or a daughter it is a loss no matter the reason.

It was getting late, so we went back to the hotel. To do that, we had to go in-between people's houses. It seemed as we walked in-between the houses I could see the people getting ready for bed and I felt that it was kind of rude. We could see right into the rooms of most of the houses since they were open to the air. We made it back to the street and went back to the hotel.

Boot Hill

We got up early the next morning and headed for Pleiku, but first we had to go through the Ahn Khe area, which used to be "sin city" to some. If I recall right, that was where boot hill was, named by the Americans. It was a graveyard, I do not know if there were any Americans buried there or not.

During the war our unit sent three of us to Ahn Khe to a school where one learns to call artillery in on the bad guys. We spent the week there and after we were done with our class we were allowed to go downtown. This was a treat. I remember walking into town, and if I recall rightly, as we went into town on the left side of the road was boot hill.

As I walked by the graveyard there was a sign above it that read *boothill* and I got this scary feeling as I stared at it. The streets were very crowded and on the left side were tents full of those Vietcong girls. As we got to the entrance to one of the tents, a GI came running out at full speed, and right behind him came a girl. She had a 16 oz. Coke bottle and threw it at the GI, missing his head by a foot. I guess he forgot to pay for something and the only thing I got to say is he had better not show his face around there for a good long time.

Walking down the street further, a girl came out and grabbed my hat off my head and then ran into the building, hoping that I'd follow her in and do whatever comes to mind. I lost a good hat that day. Come to think about it, I lost a lot of hats that way! Here I was again, but we did not have time to stop at Ahn Khe. Do you suppose those tents are still there? Well I guess it doesn't matter anyway, I was not wearing a hat this time around.

Pleiku City

On to Pleiku... We got there in late afternoon. As we drove through what looked like a back entrance to a hotel and through a big gate, I got that strange feeling again. Like déjà vu, but still not remembering that I had been here before.

We got out of the car and walked inside. As I stepped down into the lobby, I was looking at the step and it seemed to kinda move upward to my eyes and I thought how strange, and stared at the step a little longer for some reason. They gave me room 202, so I climbed up the steps and got that strange feeling even stronger this time. I unlocked the door and stepped inside and then it hit me, there sat the big black armchair which was still torn. What were the chances those twenty years later I would get the same room I had during the war? I could not believe it, it was almost scary.

In '69, the Lt. and I were here to see a General and as we walked up those steps, he was telling me that I would like this General. The Lt. knew I hated lifers, and as he spoke to me he told me to keep an open mind. So the Lt. knocked on the door and the General said to come in so we did. There stood the general with a drink in his hand. We all shook hands and then the general asked if the Lt. wanted a drink. The Lt. said that he was on duty.

The general said, "It's OK," so the Lt. took the drink. Then the General offered me a drink and the Lt. quickly said that I was not old enough to drink.

The general then said, "If he is old enough to fight a war, then he is old enough to drink."

"No thanks, I do not drink," I said.

"That's good. That way you will not end up like me." He grinned sardonically.

Later on, the Lt. told me that the General was an alcoholic. We all sat down and started to talk, but I cannot remember what was said because I fell asleep in the black armchair. The Lt. woke me up and the General told me that I could have his room for the night. We all shook hands and he left.

The Lt. went to his room and I sat down on what appeared to be a real bed. Just kinda' sat there for awhile, feeling the bed. Then I lay down with my clothes on and my rifle beside me, just in case I would have to run out of the room shooting. You just never knew when or where the VC would attack.

It was about two in the morning when there was a ruckus outside at the gate. I got up and went out on the balcony. Everyone was out there as we all stood there watching. The officer who had a room next to me said something to me like "Where are you from?"

"It's OK, the guards are taking care of the problem," said the Lt. He knew if things got out of hand I would go down there myself. He knew me pretty well! Then I heard a woman's voice coming from the Lt.'s room. I guess all those officers were not too much different from the rest of us?

Well, here I was again... In 1993, but again alone. Still thinking how I should have been at Dakto on that horrible day in June of '69, which I will never forgive myself for. I started to take my clothes off for bed, but for some reason I stopped and left them on; I don't think I did it on purpose. Again here in '93 at two in the morning I got this overwhelming feeling that I should go out on the balcony. It was like I could not help myself, I just got up and went. I stood out there for a while thinking about the war. It seemed like I could hear the Lt.'s voice or something. I went back to bed and did not sleep much. It seemed like I was having nightmares, but I was not sleeping and I had very strong feeling that someone was watching me.

The next morning I walked down to the lobby and as I did I passed by some stuffed animals in a room off to the right. So I went in and looking around I saw a stuffed tiger that was still there since 1969 and still for sale.

Back on the road again, heading for Kontum, forty more miles and I'd be there. I was in Viet Nam for a year, but it seemed like a lifetime. As we got just outside of Kontum, I recognized some of the buildings that had dates on them starting with (I think) 1948, going all the way up to 1993. All these years I had wondered what they were all about, but never went inside to find out. I still don't know, I am sure it had something to do with history.

Eventually, it was lunch time so we stopped at a small restaurant to eat. After I ate, I walked onto the road and took a picture of a guy who had a cow in a sling and had a hammer in his hand. As I stood there watching, he came out of his yard with an angry look on his face. I pointed to my camera at him and he went back into his yard. I have no idea what that was all about.

Take Me to The River

We got into the car and off we went. I knew we were getting very close and the river should be coming up shortly. In Viet Nam, the river is a fun place where people swim, fish, wash their clothes, and gossip. Oh, and it's a good place to meet girls.

I recalled one time I went to the river with a guy in my unit to get shower water. He got the water and I waded in and started talking to a girl. While we were talking, everyone started to move out of the water. The girl I was talking to waved to me and said "didi," meaning I should get out of the water. There was a loud chatter from all the other women. I thought, "What the hell is going on here?" Then another GI told me that man-eating fish were coming down the river. Needless to say I picked up my pace a bit.

We walked up onto the bank of the river, where she introduced me to her mother the best she could. No one spoke anyone's language; they were Montagnards . I told them I wanted to take their picture. So as I got ready, the mother started to fix her hair... strange! Here I was ten thousand miles from home and looking at a more or less primitive culture, and this woman had to fix her hair. It seems that no matter where you go in this world that people are still all the same. Just as things were getting interesting, the guy I was with said, "It's time to go." When ya' gotta go, ya' gotta go.

Now, in '93, as I stood by the river, I saw that the old wooden bridge was gone. In its place was this big cement bridge; it looked funny sitting there with a small paved road coming up to it and a dirt road leading into the city. I guess they were anticipating other new roads in the near future. So there I stood in awe, I have found that seeing change is a very interesting process.

I walked down to the river's edge and was kinda' shocked . The river itself had shifted course a little bit there. I looked at the shoreline where I had taken the woman's picture by a large tree, but it was long gone. What a shame.

At the Gates of Kontum

I got back in the car and drove to the edge of the city where we had to stop at a lever gate. In '93 the Vietnamese kept a very close watch on their guests. The driver gave the guard some papers and they let us through. At the time, the authorities told me that I was the first person to visit the area since the war. They said that since I was there during the war, that they would let me go into the area. They knew that I was also a veteran. They have a respect for veterans over there, even enemy veterans.

There had been a person who was there about six months before me but he was arrested and sent home. I don't know what that guy was thinking. A white guy sticks out like a sore thumb up in that part of the country.

Anyway, as we drove through the gate, I looked to the right and there sat a new hotel. To the right of that was another tree. It was a small tree, but it had big branches on it and the branches ran parallel with the ground. This tree had a history to me: in '69 I sat there by an old bombed out temple, waiting for a ride back to Pleiku. A girl popped out of nowhere, wanting to make some money; she was a refugee from Laos. I asked her, "How did you get so far?" as she was now hundreds of miles from home. She told me she had walked, and now was going to Saigon.

She was a very nice girl and as I look back on it now it was a wonder that she was even sane after having her home bombed. So I decided, *why not?* At the time, where the hotel now sits, was a little wooded area. So we walked back there and I had a little R&R, then we walked back to where the tree was. We sat in the tree and she started to sing. I did not understand the words, but I recall the sound was very soothing and peaceful.

The way I saw it, the girl deserved more money that what I gave her. As I passed by the tree, the little wooded area was gone but the tree was still there. I just smiled as we went by. I was very pleased that they spared the tree. After all, there ain't enough trees to go around anymore, are there?

We drove to the police station to pick up the police chief. Because, as I said, in '93 no outsiders were allowed to go there unescorted. We finally found the spot where the LZ sat and I was a bit disappointed. The area was just newly bulldozed over and when I looked down the road, there were new red brick houses. It was all gone, long gone. I guess I had the idea that there would be something there of the past. Strange how your mind works.

I stood looking out into the countryside and remembered how our cannons would bark so loudly that they would shake up the area. Dust was raised all around the cannon for about fifty yards as it sent its projectile into the air. During the rainy season, sometimes the round would go off as it left the barrel of the cannon. But it would be far enough away so we were not in any real danger, it just kinda broke up the boredom.

Looking out into the valley to the west, recalling what went on here years ago… like how I was treated by the lifers and how I hated them with a passion. One time, when returning from a mission, I had just come through the gate when I saw an officer walking the other direction with a .45 caliber Colt pistol in his hand. Later, a guy came up to me and told me that the officer had shot the guy in the back.

I don't recall exactly what he told me, it was something about the guy who was shot went crazy and he was running away. I never did find out what the real story was, there were a lot of crazy guys over there and I was one of them. After risking my life many, many, many, times and then having to put up with all the lifer bullshit in the rear areas… well, things get to a guy after awhile.

That little story is just one out of I am sure many, many, terrible stories about how the lifers treated us. Many boys died at the hands of some lifer in one way or another, other than in combat. Stories which I am sure will never be told about all the misdeeds of the brass. I am talking about misdeeds where young men died. It is one thing when it is someone else's son, but when it is your son, or your husband, it is a whole different ball game.

In The Villes

There was only the stillness of the noonday, with bugs flying around and the ever-hot sun. I got back into the car with a breath of disappointment, then went to a village that was near the LZ that I had visited during the war.

In '69, our cannon had to leave the LZ and go out to where this ville was and support the infantry. So someone, the brass, picked a spot out near this ville. The captain sent me and a guy named Kline to go out with a half-track and plow down the weeds in a certain area. Kline was the driver and I was the shotgun. We drove to the spot and started to plow, getting the area ready for the cannon to come and shoot for the infantry. Well, as we plowed, in walked a string of Montagnard girls. So I told Kline to stop or he just stopped on his own, I can't remember. Anyway I pointed to one of the girls and waved to her to come up and ride with me. Of course, I had more than just a ride on my mind. As I pointed to the girl, they all kinda laughed and some of the other girls were telling her to come up. But she just smiled and kept walking. In the highlands, the people who live there always travel in a line on the trails.

During the war, when I went out on missions, I had the honor of seeing many villes and village people. I found them to be very interesting, especially the ones with the big tits. Anyway, after we got all the weeds cut down the rest of the unit came in. As they were digging in, I thought to myself *I hope we are not staying here for the night, this is a death trap.* I could feel it. By this time I had had a lot of experience with the enemy, and I knew that this was not a good place to spend the night without enough support. After the girls walked by us, I knew every VC in the area knew we were there.

So, after four hours of digging in, a chopper came in and a high ranking officer got out and told our captain to pack up and go back to our LZ. I was relieved. Here I was again... I stepped out of the car and started to walk through the ville. As I did, all the people started to follow me, like a flock of sheep. They were all very friendly, all but one, who was nursing a baby. She gave me a look and if looks could kill, I would have been dead ten times over. She did not have to say anything to me, I knew why. I knew very well why. Something we both would live with for the rest of our lives.

I started to turn to go back to the car when in walked a tall, very handsome woman dressed in black. She stopped right on the trail. I looked at her and she looked at me, just staring at each other. I got that real strong feeling that I knew this woman. She bowed her head and I did the same. I then turned around and went back to the car. As I did, the whole ville followed me.

I started to get in the car when the police chief told us that the village chief was coming to see me. I was expecting an old man but to my surprise he was about twenty. We shook hands and I was about to ask him some questions, but he was too young and wore a North Vietnamese hat. If one wanted the truth about something, he was not the one to ask. I said goodbye to everyone and took some pictures and left; it was well worth the trip.

Some people say we could have beaten the north. We could have if it were just the North Vietnamese. At the time, China was watching closely and if we would have started to beat the north, the Chinese would have brought more men into Viet Nam. There were already fighting Chinese in Viet Nam anyway. Sure, if we would have used the Big One there would not be much of a Viet Nam left. And then we would have had to bomb China... what would we have won? And of what cost to human life?

And what for? Just to put our way of life on someone else's lives, who have their own ways of life, long before the US was even born, is morally wrong. There are many people in Viet Nam who still hate the US. I sure don't blame them.

On the home front, as some called it at the time, there were a few senators and people who said it was wrong to be over there and they were right. Later came the bandwagon people, some who were just plain chicken, and like I have said before I had nothing against those people. Still, there was no excuse for the way we were treated when we got home.

For years, people called me names and told me how bad I was for fighting for my country. Clear up to 1997 I had a guy call me stupid for going into the tunnels during the war. I can only say, "Am I still angry?" Yes indeed, yes indeed...

Signs of the Times

As we were driving back to Saigon, in some of the small towns there were still leftovers from the war. In people's front yards were haystacks and stuck in the haystacks were poles and on top of the poles were things like ammo cans, army helmets, and other American belongings. I do not know why they had them stuck on poles like that.

Every so often I would see an old American truck or Jeep pass by us. Seeing the old trucks really brought back memories. Some would be beat to hell, jumping along on their last legs: no lights, part of the hood gone, but still goin'. I got this feeling of being proud of my country again, seeing them. After twenty years of hard driving, they still kept going. Then I would see an American jeep being driven by the Vietnamese soldiers and the jeep would be in mint condition and I would get angry. I wanted to shout out to the drivers and say, "That Jeep does not belong to you, bastards!" But, of course, it did.

We had abandoned the equipment as easily as we did the ARVN army, and am I angry about that! Yes, indeed. Regardless of the outcome of the war, I am still angry about that. Even angrier if we had in fact left American POWs there. In some of the old buildings, I could still see bullet holes in the walls.

Almost everywhere you could see barbed wire, which also brought back memories. One of the good memories happened when three of us were sitting on a berm. To help keep enemy mortar fire from doing so much damage, we had put a small hill just inside the perimeter barbed wire. I and two other guys were out there on the berm and smoking some pot. It was late into the night when we decided to go to bed. We all three stood up at the same time and went forward down the little hill. As we did, the hill was a little steeper than we remembered and also there was barbed wire right at the bottom. Two of us stopped in time, but the third guy kept going and ran into the wire.

He started yelling, "Lieutenant, I can't get off, I can't get off...!" while still standing up face-forward into the wire. He was stuck like glue so me and the other guy pulled him off the wire, and all the time we were laughing so hard we could hardly stand it. I never laughed so hard in my life! The guy was OK; he just had a few puncture marks in him to show for it.

The Booby Trap

We got back to Qui Nhon just before dark, dodging the potholes all the way . It was the same hotel we stayed at on the way to Kontum. I was tired, so I went to bed early. I was just dozing off when the driver came in and woke me up and was kinda pulling me out the door. As I slipped on my sandals I was thinking, "What the hell is going on?" I thought the interpreter was in some kind of trouble. The driver pulled me across a wooden plank over the gutter and we went into what looked like a bath house in a trailer park. But as I walked through the door and in-between the stringed beads hanging from the top of the door, my memory was jogged and I knew what the place was. It was a whorehouse.

It had been a long, long time since I'd been in one of those. During the war, there were many whorehouses in many of the cities. They stretched all the way down the streets, mixed in with bars. It also made me think of when the Lt. and I were out on a mission once. We were out walking next to a stream in an area where no-one seemed to be around. We came across two girls were splashing around in the water and looked to be having a lot of fun. As we walked by, they were waving us to come into the water. I thought to myself, or I might have been thinking out loud, because the Lt. promptly told me it was a trap. The girls would lure the GIs into the water and then jump out and run away. That would leave the GIs like sitting ducks. If the Lt. had not told me it was a trap, I would have fallen for it. It was hot, I was thirsty, and the girls were naked. Then it did dawn on me that the girls did look kinda strange out there all alone. Now I know how "booby trap" got its name.

Well, here I was again, caught in a booby trap. As I went inside, I saw the interpreter sitting at a table with a beer in one hand and a girl on his lap. The room was lit only with candle light. They told me sit down and have a Coke, so I sat down and another girl came in and sat down on my lap. I drank my Coke and told them I had better get back to the hotel. So with a bit of sweat on my bald forehead, I got up and did just that. Talking about reliving the past, that came pretty close...

The next morning, I got up just before sunrise, stood out on the balcony and watched the sun come up. As the orange glow hit my eyes, I thought to myself how lucky I had been in '69. Thinking about the enemy mortar attacks that I had suffered and lived through, each round whizzing down on top of me, 12 inches or so from my foxhole... And when I had no foxhole I would hit the ground and take cover the best I could and hope to hell my head would not be ripped off my body. Each round was a terrifying experience as I lay there waiting for one to hit me, and die... time and time again.

One round coming down on top of a guy like that could scare you so bad that it could put a guy in a mental state that he may never come out of. We would go out into the jungle for a week and catch enemy mortar fire every day, and sometimes every two hours. So, watching the sun come up, especially in Viet Nam, is a whole different sun for those who fought there.

On that morning in Qui Nhon, all those old feelings and memories came back to me. Not only the war, but present day thoughts: The pain of war and the pain of coming home to an unfriendly country, and the tears started to run. Each day as the white hot sun came up in the East and hit my eyes, I knew I had lived another day and as the red sun sank into the green foreground I knew I had to prepare my mind for the night... These thoughts were of the past, but not gone. Not by a long shot!

Back to Saigon

My reverie was interrupted as the driver knocked on the door. It was time to go on the road again to Saigon, dodging the potholes one more time. After a few hours of driving, we stopped at a bus station. Still there and in good shape was a water tower that the Americans had built. I walked down the road and saw a village, so I decided to go and take a look around.

The first house I came upon was the chief's house. He and his wife were both at home. They were tall, slim and good looking, dressed in very plain clothes, and seemed to be very nice. I sat down in their kitchen and we talked for a moment.

I then went further into the ville and ran into an old man and talked to him for a spell. He told me that during the war, that this ville was neutral. I don't know if that was true or not. A lot of villages tried to stay neutral, but if they got in the way of war there ain't no neutral about it. He then pointed to the hill across the highway and said that was where the American Screaming Eagles were camped. The hill next to it, he continued on, was the Korean compound. Then he told me that all around those two hills the VC were camped. I asked him, "Were there many VC around there?" and he pointed all around and that answered my question. The funny part of the story is the Americans probably didn't even know it!

Just like in Kontum and Pleiku, they had been around us. While we were out running around the jungle, they were sitting at our doorstep, pretty strange... Sitting there in the gold sun and a slight breeze, it felt so peaceful like nothing had ever happened there. It felt good sitting there not worrying about someone trying to blow your head off.

It was getting late, so we had to be on out way. As we drove, it got dark and the headlights of the car showed all the bugs flying across the highway. There were gazillions of them, and some were very large. We got into Saigon late, after ten sometime, and as we drove through the city I could see people in every crack and crevice: poor people, homeless, bums, some with clothes literally rotting off their own backs.

Driving down the streets, we went by a large crowed of people all yelling or making a great deal of noise. I thought to myself *what the hell is going on there?* I later found out that singing stars go there and sing. If you didn't have any money, you could still sit outside and listen. I found it to be very pleasing even though I did not understand the words. By the time I got to the hotel I was ready for bed. I fell fast asleep, which is something I never do!

At The Zoo

The next day I decided to go to the zoo. I bought my ticket and went in. The zoo was very dirty and rundown and the animals looked very hungry. As I walked, I came across a fish tank. I stood looking at the fish and that strange feeling came over me again. Then I remembered, in '69, me and the Lt. came here on our trip to Saigon. As I looked at the fish swim in '93, I remembered what had happened in '69: as the Lt. and I stood at the fish tank, one of the fish came up to the glass and it looked like it was looking at me.

The Lt. said, "I think that fish likes you, Rizz!" and we both laughed. Then, a guy with lottery tickets had come up to us and tried to get us to buy some. We did not buy any because we were leaving the next day and we would never have known if we won or not. I find it strange that Viet Nam had a lottery clear back in '69 and only within the last few years the US got them. Now in '93, they still had the lottery.

I moved on to the elephant cages. A girl yelled out to me, "You feed the elephants sugar cane?" I told her, "No, but you feed them and I will take your picture." I then started to pass on by, but for some reason that I cannot explain I stopped and went back to the girl. I told the interpreter to tell the girl I wanted to talk to her so he did. As we stood there, at first she just looked at me for two minutes without saying anything and then she told us to come back after the zoo was closed.

So later that evening we came back and we all went to a street bar and sat down and had a Coke. The owner of the bar sat down with us and talked with us. She spoke very good English. The girl's name was Li, she told me about her job and her family. She seemed very nice, but she only smiled one time that I remember.

As we walked back to the hotel, it was late at night and I could see all the poor people up close and personal: ragged, dirty, some without arms, some without legs, some without eyes, and some without a few of the above. Everywhere I looked I could see the talons of war. We would walk down the dark street and a beggar would come out of nowhere, and walk up to us and beg for money. It kinda scared me because at night it seemed that I *could* understand what the war did to these people. It was magnified and the memories came back to me of how I shot blindly into homes. Just before coming home, I had thrown hand grenades into a bunch of civilians outside a ville. I guess it all comes back to haunt ya. It did not matter if it was a war or whatever to them. They went home with mutilated bodies of horror for the rest of their lives and I end up with the horror of doing it.

Jungle Warfare

Kill the enemy, don't kill the innocent. Who was the innocent? Who was the enemy? The girl I had sex with the other day? No, that cannot be. Daytime—let's go downtown, nighttime—don't go downtown. Watch what you say to people, they might be spies. Don't drink all of your Coke, it might have ground up glass in the bottom of the bottle. We are the good guys, we don't kill prisoners? *What the hell is??* Boom boom—two more dead prisoners. It should have been named the "flip-flop war." My brain sure did a flip flop. We did the best we could with what we had. We went into the battle with our guts already hanging out. All we were waiting for was the bullet to hit…

Through no fault of our own, we were again taking the bullet when we got home. It was like killing us twice; I guess once was not enough. When ya walk down the street, you can tell the ones that hate you—the glare is unmistakable. I still carry the thoughts of yesteryear and now I carry the images of today in my hotel room. Every night I cried for hours, it hurt so bad.

It was time for me to go home, so Li hired two motorbikes to take us to the airport. Zipping through the streets, I was taking one last look at history's nightmare I thought I'd never see again. I got to the airport and went through customs and turned to wave at Li. But at first I could not pick her out, then as I looked there she stood, not moving a muscle and she had a terrifying look on her face. *What was that all about?* I waved to her again and got aboard the plane. It was very strange going there, and it was equally strange leaving.

Again as the jet lifted off, I was angry again. I had done my job, maybe too well in a flip flop war for a flip flop country. A war that had flipped me and then flopped me, searing my golden soul and taking part of it away. I peered through my soul and saw myself: I saw the lean mean fighting machine, in the Year of the Cock, 1993.

Nick J. Rizzo
2006

Illus. by Nick Rizzo, 2006

19	Poems (iv)

ALL I HAVE

I look at my child and I pray
My God, why does it have to be this way.

He's only a baby, so small and helpless too.
Why can't I bear the pain that he's going through.

I'm racking my brain, doing everything I can.
But Lord, I know, his life is in your hand.

Sometimes my heart is filled with so much hate,
Because I know where my child's pain originates.

It's so hard for me to stand here and see
my darling child is lying there suffering because of me.

I was involved in a war that should not have been.
It destroyed the lives of so many men.

Now my child has become a victim of my past.
God when will it end? When will the torment stop, and
the happiness begin?

It may sound as if I'm giving up, this I will not do.
I've got faith and I believe the Lord will see us both through.

I'm going to keep my hand in God's hand. He will show me the way.

With my child by my side and God as my guide, I know there will be a
brighter day.

S.J.

Steve Mason is the Poet-Laureate for the Viet Nam Veterans of America. He is also our conscience. He presented the following poem at the first National Convention of that organization on November 7th, 1983 in Washington, DC. Reprinted with Mr. Mason's permission.

VVA Founding Convention Poem

I have looked death in the eye
and spat blood
I have faced life squarely
and made love
I am a combat veteran
of Viet Nam
And not altogether certain
of my direction,
But sure of myself -
A delegate enroute
to a national convention
and proud to count for more
than my pain;

At 30,000 feet there are
no flat clouds
which point to the nation's
capitol
No calendars to enumerate
a just-right world
of sequential firmness
on-going below,
My unresolved hurt
makes it difficult
to look out this small
round window
And know beyond reason
what time and place
my mind suspends
outboard this aircraft -
I look to see
a mirrored on-board image
of myself
and question with a hard blink
and a sharp eye,
Where are my epaulettes?
Who took the hash marks
from my sleeve—
Damn—It's been a long time
between rides
A long time since I looked out
another aircraft window
and watched real life
Refracted across
the lawns of the world

Sat helpless as the thick,
plastic window
distorted the courage
of my innocence
So that I might
distinguish capitalist jungles
from communist jungles
at a distance of 6 miles
straight up...

I was a soldier/statesman
on that flight also
Gone to represent my government
in Viet Nam
and today I fly to Washington
to represent 35 former statesmen
from that earlier flight
Funny flights
Funny world—
And time won't make sense of it
But you and I will try...

And I stare unfocused
thru the blur
of bending light
and passing time
and use this porthole-like window
as a rewind button
To blink those just-post war years
back
and know the pain
from which my courage comes
And I begin to feel
the reality of war
debunk the illusion
of my upbringing
And I sense that I have quickly become
the shadow man I was
Detached, alone -
drowning in myself
Stranded like a pubic hair
in an airport urinal -
Those just-postwar years
when suicide was sad companion

to my nights
and sat at my bedside
writing notes with me 'til dawn
and never left a single one for
at dawn's early light
As if it had been spring
From the promise of my wall paper
in a long gone childhood dream
I would be rescued
by my cowboy, cut n' shoot
John Wayne rage—ha hah!
Yeah, if it was woeful suicide
that got me thru my nights
it was heroic rage
that swept me through my days
You know the kind
I thank God you and I
are men of passion

and I know that even
the poorest of records
of this madder
than mad world
will show that
Whether suicide or homicide
generally only one life
hangs in the balance,

But indifference manufactures
death on a planetary scale
and calls it something grand
occasionally putting it to music

Maybe that's why
there is no wallpaper
anywhere in the world
for an eight year old boy
with pictures of thin, bloodless
technocrats
waving briefcases
at passing taxicabs -
Maybe that's why there's cowboys
on the walls of America
But whether suicide or
homicide or genocide
one day we are all asked
to choose a "cide"

As this convention will ask
my conscience
which side it is on

(on other, more brave issues)
And I hope whatever my answer
it will echo in agreement with the
voices
of a thousand, thousand veterans

Ah, we can make it happen
you and I
we've still go it to do...
The plane pitched slightly
an errant right elbow
struck me from reverie
The onboard movie was
a romantic comedy,
But the man with
the too pink face
next to me
was pornographic—
Nobody seemed to notice, but me
as he masturbated
his pocket computer
with a fantastic combination
of obscene numbers:
2 of these
and one of those
3 of these and not a
single one of the others
combinations with bottom line results
not concerned with
the human condition
An occasional ecstatic sigh escaped
from his
credit card smile.

I leaned away from him
Back into my chair
And looking out the window
pushed the fast forward
to consider my own numbers

How about U.S. Rangers
jumping onto the airstrip
at 500 feet!

Do you have any idea
what that number marks, sucker?

I hit the rewind again
for a split second
and stopped at 229
Hey, you want numbers

I got numbers
How's 229 killed
young guys in Lebanon
who found out that death
is the only dream
from which you can't wake screaming
Put that in
your wafer-thin
designer computer
Mr. technocrat

and I'll talk to you, of tetrytol and
Primacord™
of lost legs
and long gone grunts

You know something
you sonofabitch
you don't look familiar to me
where were you
when we were in Viet Nam?
Funny, how many guys
"were ready to go "
whose numbers just
didn't come up
in the lottery

Funnier, most of the guys I knew
weren't ready to go—
but went anyway.
And then the heavy numbers
jumped at the windows
grabbed the wings
and shook the plane
like a cyclone
with the force
of their meaning:
58,000+ KIA
248,000 WIA
and then the nausea
which had nothing to do
with air sickness came
As the whispered whimperings
of my reptilian mind
clawed at the cortex
of my reason
"How many of us
did you leave behind?"
My balls turned to jelly
and the guy next to me
belched on his scotch.

You want higher math,
Computer-man?
If we left only one MIA/POW
behind—that number and its loss
are incalculable.

Thank goodness
the stewardess
told me to straighten up
for landing
And I thanked her
for her attendance
and especially
for "the real whole milk"
she smiled blankly
and I offered lamely
It was an inside joke, you see,
Knowing somewhere
there was an entire generation
of 40 year old stews
who knew what
"real whole milk"
was all about
(and I want to make love
to all of 'em.)

And the wheels
rumbled down
As I prepared
to hit the ground running
Shuffling to the exit door
I reminded myself to
vote as a representative
not as an individual
and that conscience
without balls
becomes guilt
Just as government
without philosophy
becomes only power

The door opened slow and wide
on the day of the Viet Nam Veterans
Blue and sweet
Men who have ratified
the constitution of this nation
with sweat and blood
And will now help
formulate its philosophy
with pride and truth

with profound respect   of our now grateful children...
for all our fallen comrades   STEVE MASON
and to the standing ovation

TODAY,

      I'M ONLY MOVING CLOUDS

TOMORROW,

      I'LL TRY MOUNTAINS

                        AUTHOR UNKNOWN

• • • • •

WE TURNED IN UPON OURSELVES,
WE LIVED AMONG OURSELVES,
AND WE BECAME AS TOUCHY AND SENSITIVE
AS MEN FLAYED ALIVE.

BUT HOW GREAT WAS THE DESPAIR WE FELT
AT BEING REJECTED BY OUR COUNTRY
AND HOW GREAT WAS OUR NEED FOR
FRATERNITY.

                        FRENCH CAPTAIN AT THE END OF
                        THE INDOCHINA WAR

Filmed About the Nam

In the words of Paul Wappenstein, the image of Viet Nam veterans has been tarnished by a generation of people who have grown up seeing only the "slick Hollywood productions... productions whose only purpose were to make money." If you have read the book thus far, you must consider that the truth of the war is not in any one person's experience. Nor can it be possible to encapsulate all of it in any one film. In the spirit of providing a fair and balanced view, we present the following suggested viewing list to provide an audiovisual experience for enhancing your understanding or recollection of the era.

American Survivors of Viet Nam: Still Coming Home. Documentary

Be Good, Smile Pretty (2003). Documentary. Tracy Droz Tragos heart-wrenching journey to understand her father's death in Viet Nam over 30 years later. Available from www.docudrama.com.

Coming Home (1978). Drama / Paraplegia. Jane Fonda, Jon Voight. Won 3 Oscars.

Diên Biên Phu (1992). Drama: An American reporter finds himself in the middle of the 57-day battle of Diên Biên Phu between the French army and the Viet Minh.

Frank: A Viet Nam Vet (1983)

Front Line (1981). Documentary from the point of view of the Vietnamese and one extraordinary Australian cameraman.

Great Santini, The (1979). Drama: Masculinity issues drama about a Marine commander.

Green Eyes (1977). Drama: disillusioned Vietnam veteran travels back to Southeast Asia in search among thousands of war orphans for the son he left behind.

Hearts and Minds (1974). Documentary. Oscar-winner.

Johnny Got His Gun (1971). Drama: Dalton Trumbo's WWI disability nightmare. Cannes Film Festival winner.

Killing Fields, The (1984). Roland Joffe. Viet Nam, Cambodia, and Pol Pot. Won 3 Oscars.

Let There be Light (1946). John Huston's documentary about PTSD in WWII. Third in a trilogy, suppressed by the government for 30 years.

Maya Lin: A Strong Clear Vision (1995). Documentary. Oscar-winning film about the Maya Lin, the artist who designed the Viet Nam Veterans Memorial. Available from www.docudrama.com.

Medal of Honor Rag (1982) (TV). Adaptation of a stage play about the final days of Medal of Honor winner Dwight Johnson. The play was most recently performed in Los Angeles by rapper "Heavy D" in July 2005.

Regret to Inform (1998). Documentary. Oscar-winning film about Viet Nam widow Barbara Sonneborn's emotional and extraordinary trip to Viet Nam. Available from www.docudrama.com.

Resting Place (2001). About the controversy over Dwight Johnson's burial.

Sticks and Bones (1973). Drama about a Viet Nam vet who returns blind.

Tribes (1970) - good piece on boot camp in the Marine Corps. Made-for-TV movie won 3 Emmys.

Vietnam: A Television History (1983). 11-hour documentary series, more about politics than battles.

Vietnam's Unseen War: Pictures from the Other Side (1985). National Geographic film.

Vietnam: The War at Home (1979)-Documentary on the antiwar movement at home. Oscar-nominated film.

Vietnam: The Ten Thousand Day War (1980). Peter Arnet's 16-hour documentary mini-series is the most comprehensive filmed account of the war.

Vietnam: Time of the Locust (1986). A collection of short films illustrates the horror of it all

Welcome Home, Johnny Bristol (1972) (TV). Martin Landau returns home as a tortured POW.

Guidelines for Watching Films

In preparation for each viewing session, sit comfortably. Let your attention move effortlessly, without strain, first to your body then to your breath. Simply inhale and exhale naturally. Follow your breath in this innocent, watchful way for a while. Notice any spots where there's tension or holding. As you grow aware of them, let your breath travel into these spots. To release tension you may experiment with "breathing into" any part of your body that feels strained. Never force your breath.

Your gentle attention is sufficient to help you become more present and balanced, as it spontaneously deepens and corrects your breathing if it is constricted. Experience your condition without inner criticizing or comment. If you notice yourself judging or narrating, simply listen to the tone of your inner dialog as you come back to your breath. Lay judgments and worries consciously aside.

As soon as you are calm and centered, start watching the movie. Most deeper insights arrive when you pay attention to the story and to yourself. While viewing, bring your inner attention to a holistic bodily awareness (felt sense). This means you are aware of "all of you" — head, heart, belly, etc. Once in a while you might notice your breathing from an inner vantage point — from your subtle, always-present intuitive core. Observe how the movie images, ideas, conversations and characters affect your breath. Don't analyze anything while you are watching. Be fully present with your experience.

Afterwards reflect on the following:

Do you remember whether your breathing changed throughout the movie? Could this be an indication that something threw you off balance? In all likelihood, what affects you in the film is similar to whatever unbalances you in your daily life.

Ask yourself: If a part of the film that moved you (positively or negatively) had been one of your dreams, how would you have understood the symbolism in it?

Notice what you liked and what you didn't like or even hated about the movie. Which characters or actions seemed especially attractive or unattractive to you? Did you identify with one or several characters?

Were there one or several characters in the movie that modeled behavior that you would like to emulate? Did they develop certain strengths or other capacities that you would like to develop as well?

Notice whether any aspect of the film was especially hard to watch. Could this be related to something that you might have repressed ("shadow")? Uncovering repressed aspects of our psyche can free up positive qualities and uncover our more whole and authentic self

Did you experience something that connected you to your inner wisdom or higher self as you watched the film?

It helps to write down your answers.

If some of the mentioned guidelines turn out to be useful, you might consider using them not only in "reel life" but also adapt them to "real life" because they are intended to make you become a better observer.

Excerpted with permission from www.CinemaTherapy.com by Birgit Wolz, PhD.

<table>
<tr><td rowspan="2">

Appendix

B

</td><td>

Viet Nam in the First Half
of the 20th Century

</td></tr>
</table>

The beginnings of American involvement in Viet Nam date back to 1819, when Captain John White sailed up the Dong Nai River to Saigon in search of trade. This first American in Viet Nam failed in his venture, but found, as Americans were to find out more than a hundred years later, that the Vietnamese are overly fond of paperwork. The Imperial inspectors who looked over his ship drew up 13 copies of the crew list and similarly recorded all arms on the vessel in a methodical manner.

Little was heard from this faraway country, however, until the closing days of WWII, when, the defeat of the Japanese occupying forces in the area seemed near. It was then that Franklin Delano Roosevelt and the U.S. military found themselves involved in the shadowy fight for control of a post-war Viet Nam.

Viet Nam: Land and People

In America we catch only television glimpses of Viet Nam—jungles, swamps, scattered villages, small huts. United States forces are fighting there[1], but the land seems strange and remote to us at home.

Viet Nam stretches along the eastern coast of the Indochinese peninsula, southeast of China's border, for 1200 miles—about the same distance as the coastline from New York to Florida. Long stretches of the coastline are straight, sandy beaches. Near the middle, Viet Nam is less than twenty-five miles across, but it widens irregularly to about 300 miles in the North and 130 miles in the South. The center of Viet Nam is highlands: tall mountains, plateaus, and narrow coastal plains. Sparsely populated, the mountainous land is traditionally feared by Vietnamese as the land of "bad waters and evil spirits." The climate is hot and humid throughout the country, though the North experiences more varieties of weather than the South. The summer monsoon winds bring most of the heavy annual rainfall

The bulk of the Vietnamese population of 35 million lives in villages scattered throughout the flat, fertile deltas of the Mekong River in the South, and of the Red River in the North. Only 10% of the population lives in urban areas. The Mekong and Red River deltas, and small river basins in the Central lowlands, which are the areas best suited for rice, make up only 13% of Viet

---

[1] Ed. Note: This text was written in 1967 and we have not updated any facts or statistics. You may assume that all data applies to the latter-half of the 1960s decade.

Nam's total land mass. Consequently, parts of the Mekong delta country have a population density of over 2,000 per square mile. The heavy rainfall and intense cultivation make Viet Nam one of the world's greatest rice-growing areas.

The life of the Vietnamese peasant has changed little over the last thousand years. He cultivates his crop according to age-old patterns and traditions. He understands his role and position in the social structure of this rice-producing culture: landowner, tenant, laborer, rice miller, merchant, or gleaner. Rituals, deities, and sacred holidays are connected with the cultivation of rice, and collective rituals ensure a good crop to the village or family. Life is unchanging, rooted in the endless cycle of preparing fields, planting, tending, irrigating, and harvesting.

Late in April or early in May, the southwest winds bring rain to the Mekong delta, signaling the beginning of the planting season. The seedbeds are meticulously prepared, harrowed and planted. Transplanting to the fields and harvesting are done by hand and involve long, monotonous hours. Hand-held scoops or foot-operated waterwheels are the tools of irrigation— technology comes very slowly to a traditionally rural society.

Ancient Viet Nam

Ancient Viet Nam (until 1000 A.D.) encompassed only a portion of the area that is now North Viet Nam. Most of its population was clustered in the Red River delta, and along the seacoast. To the south and west dwelled the Indianized civilizations of the Chams, who inhabited most of present-day central and southern Viet Nam, and the Khmers (Cambodians) who farmed and lived in the Mekong delta.

Before the arrival of Westerners, Viet Nam consisted of a loose confederation of self-sufficient villages. Life was extremely harsh in the famine-prone Red River delta. The land was overpopulated, the climate poor, floods frequent, and disaster always imminent. For common protection, village life was tightly organized in a paramilitary fashion, as in China. Great emphasis was placed on cooperation, and little on privacy or the rights of the individual. The villagers' code was group responsibility and self-sacrifice. These values were strengthened by a cultural tradition of family loyalty, respect for authority, and adherence to ancient custom.

Vietnamese social, cultural, and political institutions, unlike those of other Southeast Asian nations, bear the stamp of long and intensive Chinese influence. While most of Indochina was "Indianized"— i.e., affected by Indian culture, religion; and forms of political organization—natural territorial boundaries caused Viet Nam to be "Sinicized." Viet Nam was actually conquered by the Chinese and was ruled for over a millennium (111 B.C. to 939 A.D.) as a Chinese province, Giao Chi. Under Chinese rule the Vietnamese people learned improved methods of growing rice; increased food supplies led to population growth, and this, together with the problems of poor soil and floods, caused Vietnamese expansion along the Indochina coast.

Years of Chinese domination did not destroy but rather fostered the Vietnamese feeling of separate identity and desire for "Doc Lap" (independence).

From the Chinese came the very ideas of racial pride and manifest destiny which led to Vietnamese hostility, rebellion, and finally winning of independence from the Chinese in 939 AD. China continued to exert considerable influence over the Vietnamese royalty, however, who fashioned themselves on Chinese models, paid tribute to China, and occasionally called in Chinese armies for help when rebellion threatened.

With independence from Chinese rule came Vietnamese expansion to the south and west, which was to continue intermittently for the next 800 years. The Vietnamese were feared by their neighbors, and fairly early got the reputation of being aggressive and expansionistic. In their march to the south, they defeated and totally absorbed the Chams, an Indianized culture that governed parts of what today is central and Southern Viet Nam. Their conquest of the Khmers' territory in the south was halted only by the arrival of the French in the nineteenth century. The effects of ancient Vietnamese expansionism are still noticeable today, in the hostility between Vietnamese and the Laotians and Cambodians.

The Arrival of the West

Western influence and colonial rule came in 1859 when the French moved into Saigon. It took the French twelve years to pacify the central and northern regions of Viet Nam, though armed resistance from certain sects did not die out for over fifty years. For administrative reasons the French divided Viet Nam into three colonies: Tonkin (North), Annam (Central), and Cochinchina (South). They brought much that was beneficial to Viet Nam in the way of roads and economic techniques, but their Western ideas about the place of the individual, the nature of government, and, the necessity for progress struck at the roots of the authoritarian and traditional society of Viet Nam. French trained administrators replaced the Vietnamese mandarinate; French justice replaced the more flexible and paternalistic attitudes of the village elders. The Emperors and their bureaucracies, having become only ornaments of the French-run government, lost the respect of their people, thus weakening the Confucian structure of authority.

Where a framework of traditional loyalties is in collapse, new ideologies can find adherents and mass movements usually thrive. Viet Nam was no exception. As French influence pervaded Viet Nam, young people flocked to the cities, eager to learn modem ideas and ways of life, in order to assuage the feeling of cultural and national inferiority Viet Nam suffered under French domination. Religious sects and political groupings—Christianity, Socialism, Communism, Buddhism, Nationalism—gained members by offering hopes for the reassertion of Vietnamese identity. The underlying mood of the times was anti-colonial, anti-Western, and nationalistic. This was particularly true in the North, where the tradition of nationalistic revolt against a foreign overlord was strongest.

In the 1920's, several nationalist groups emerged in opposition to the French. Some of these, moderate Western-style reform groups, demanded improvements and liberalization of French rule. Their pressure was ignored by the conservative and fearful French colonials, who often could not see the

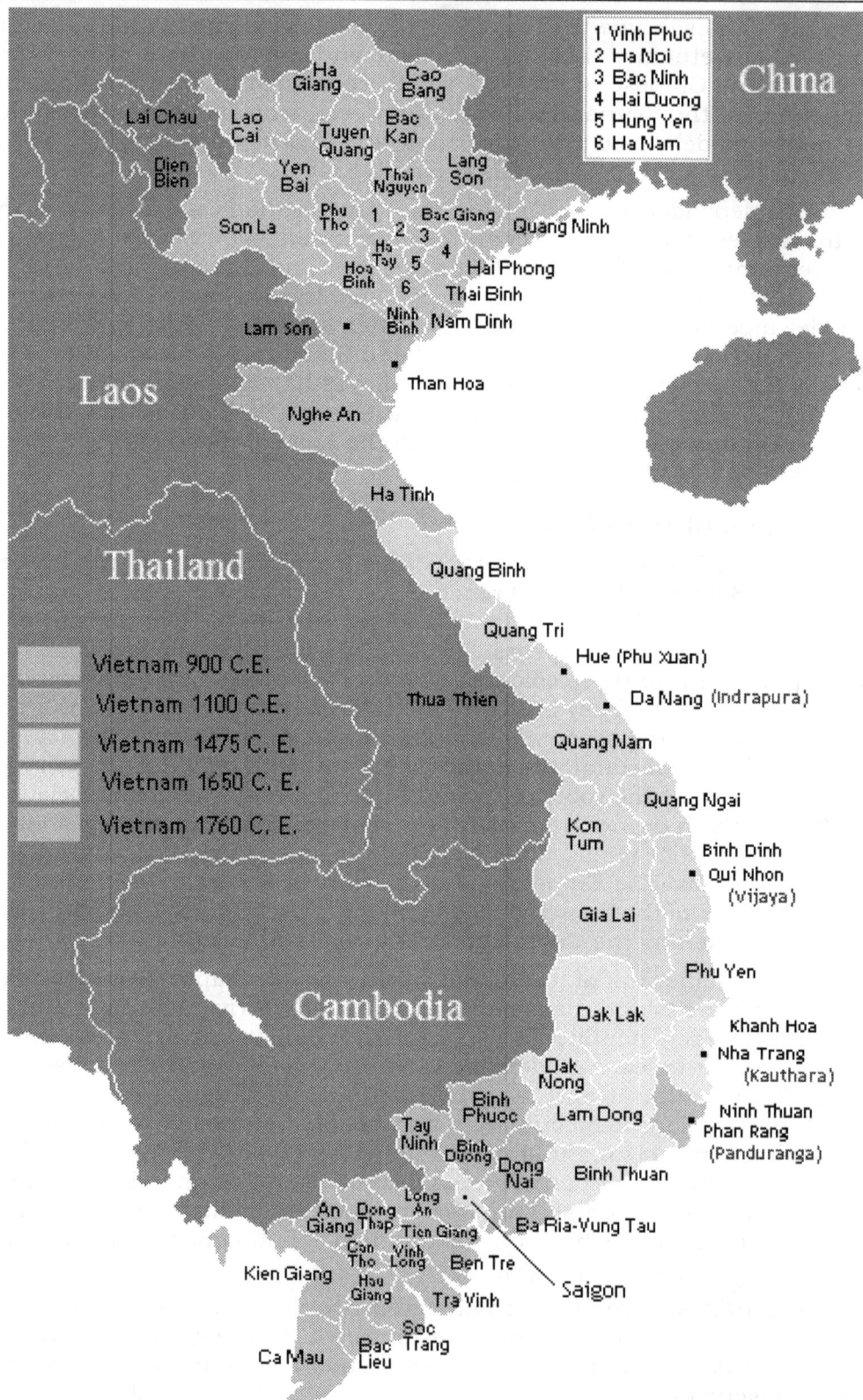

1 Vinh Phuc
2 Ha Noi
3 Bac Ninh
4 Hai Duong
5 Hung Yen
6 Ha Nam

China

Ha Giang
Cao Bang
Lai Chau
Lao Cai
Tuyen Quang
Bac Kan
Dien Bien
Yen Bai
Thai Nguyen
Lang Son
Son La
Phu Tho
Bac Giang
Quang Ninh
Ha Tay
Hoa Binh
Hai Phong
Thai Binh
Ninh Binh
Nam Dinh
Lam Son
Than Hoa
Laos
Nghe An
Ha Tinh
Thailand
Quang Binh
Quang Tri
Hue (Phu Xuan)
Thua Thien
Da Nang (Indrapura)
Quang Nam
Quang Ngai
Kon Tum
Binh Dinh
Qui Nhon (Vijaya)
Gia Lai
Phu Yen
Cambodia
Dak Lak
Khanh Hoa
Nha Trang (Kauthara)
Dak Nong
Lam Dong
Ninh Thuan
Phan Rang (Panduranga)
Binh Phuoc
Tay Ninh
Binh Duong
Dong Nai
Binh Thuan
An Giang
Dong Thap
Long An
Tien Giang
Ba Ria-Vung Tau
Con Tho
Vinh Long
Ben Tre
Kien Giang
Hau Giang
Saigon
Tra Vinh
Ca Mau
Bac Lieu
Soc Trang

Vietnam 900 C.E.
Vietnam 1100 C.E.
Vietnam 1475 C. E.
Vietnam 1650 C. E.
Vietnam 1760 C. E.

difference between reformists, socialists, and communists. The failure of the moderates led to organizations more in the traditional Vietnamese political pattern: militant and clandestine. Vietnamese royalty had never trifled with rebels: captured rebel leaders had been traditionally tortured, dismembered, boiled in oil. Clandestine activity was the rule, not the exception... neither in ancient times nor under the French was a loyal opposition permitted. All opposition in an authoritarian, communally-based society such as Viet Nam had to be secret, and a rebel had to hide his power until he was ready to strike. The result was a Vietnamese affinity for political action via secret organizations. These organizations, apparently innocent and conventional, often concealed a tightly-knit apparatus engaged in intrigue, assassination, and power-building.

Opposition to French policy resulted in a whole new grouping of clandestine organizations, political and nationalistic, operating in deep secrecy, staging apparently leaderless mass demonstrations, disseminating anti-French propaganda, and sometimes indulging in violence. When the French suppresses the main group of non-communist nationalists (the VNQDD) in 1930, and executed its leaders, the Communists were the only group sufficiently well organized to take over the field. The Indochinese Communist Party was officially formed in 1930. The Communist credo of united action, toughness, and discipline, appealed to the divided and demoralized nationalists. Uniquely in Viet Nam, communism came to be identified with the anti-colonial struggle for freedom.

The End of WWII in Viet Nam

During World War II, the French were forced to let Japan occupy Indochina, and in March 1945, were removed from all positions of power by the Japanese. All male Frenchmen were confined to concentration camps, and the Japanese announced to the Vietnamese Emperor Bao Dai that his Country was independent. In actuality, Japanese "advisors" took the place of French governors. Bao Dai's government floundered, lacking power and control; more than one million peasants died of famine while the Japanese were struggling against defeat in the World War II.

In August 1945 after the Japanese defeat, with the Bao Dai administration disintegrating, and the French imprisoned, the job of taking over Viet Nam was an easy one for the Viet Minh, a National Front group consisting of various nationalist groupings and led by the Indochinese Communist Party. Their plan was to take power in the name of the Vietnamese people, before the allies arrived to disarm the Japanese troops. Communist agitators inside Hanoi staged a uprising on August 17-18 and on the following day Viet Minh forces entered the capital city without firing a shot[2]. On August 25 Bao Dai handed over the Imperial Seal to the new regime, setting the stage for the rise of a new dynasty in Viet Nam. In Hanoi on September 2 a crowd of 500,000 heard the declaration of independence of the Democratic Republic of Viet Nam. Its President was Nguyên Ai Quoc, long-time nationalist, mem-

---

[2] Bernard Fall, *The Two Viet Nams* (NY: Prager, 1963), pp. 62-64

ber of the Indochinese Communist Party, and agent for the Communist International, now the new head of the DRV under the name of Ho Chi Minh (the Enlightened One).

To the average peasant in that time of famine and despair, Ho Chi Minh symbolized hope for a better future, and the return of Vietnamese independence, order, and dignity after sixty-odd years of humiliation under the French and the Japanese. Through inspiring legends and good propaganda, Ho became a living idol to the villagers. In contrast to the pretentious mandarins with their robes, luxuries, and long well-kept fingernails, Ho lived the life of an ascetic, dressing as a peasant, wearing sandals made from a discarded rubber tire, and living in an unpretentious house in Hanoi.

Ho Chi Minh tried to get official American recognition and support for his government, but was unsuccessful. He turned to his archenemy, France, and on March 6, 1946, Ho signed a treaty whereby France recognized Viet Nam as a Free State, having its own government, Parliament, army and treasury, and belonging to the Indochinese Federation (including Cambodia and Laos) and the French Union. Independence seemed to require only negotiations to dissolve the remaining links between Viet Nam and the French colonial network. On May 30, however, it became clear that the French intended to retain at least part of Viet Nam as a colony. France's Viceroy-General in Saigon, *without authorization from Paris,* recognized the Republic of Cochinchina (Viet Nam's southernmost province) as a "Free State" under a puppet government, in exactly tile same terms as the Republic of Viet Nam had been recognized on March 6 [3]. Negotiations between the Viet Minh government and France proved fruitless. Mounting tensions led the French to bombard the port of Haiphong on November 23, beginning the long war between the French Union forces and the Viet Minh that ended at Diên Biên Phu eight years later. The conflict cost French Union forces a total of 172,000 casualties, and ended a French presence that had never managed to prepare Viet Nam for self-government on the Western pattern. What Vietnamese forces there were for evolution, peaceful change, and democratic development were discredited by the French themselves in the prewar years. What defeated the French, in the end, was not so much Western communism as the power of a proud, authoritarian Vietnamese tradition which resented foreign control and domination.

The United States Involvement Until 1954

During World War II, the United States government was generally opposed to the continuation of French control over Indochina. Secretary of State Cordell Hull quoted President Franklin Roosevelt as advocating an international trusteeship over the area once the war was over. On January 24, 1944, Roosevelt said in a memorandum: "The case of Indochina is perfectly clear... France has milked it for one hundred years. The people of Indochina are entitled to something better than that."[4] The Japanese occupied Indo-

---

[3] *Ibid.,* p. 73

[4] *Memoirs of Cordell Hull,* Vol. II (NY: Macmillan, 1948), p. 1597

china in 1941, using French officers under the Vichy regime to administer the French colonies. The U.S. government under FDR refused help to the French Resistance movement which was trying to reassert Free French authority in the colonies, for FDR maintained that he was "going to do everything possible to give the people in that area their independence."[5]

In Viet Nam there was resistance to the Japanese from other quarters than the French. In the Viet Minh, nationalist and Communist guerrilla fighters were opposed to either Japanese or French occupation of their country, the U.S. had a potentially useful ally. During the winter of 1944-45 Colonel Paul Helliwell, head of the intelligence operations of the U.S. Office of Strategic Services (OSS) in South China, had a frequent visitor—Ho Chi Minh. The Viet Minh offered intelligence work, sabotage against the Japanese in Indochina, and assistance in rescuing downed American flyers. Bernard Fall, expert on Vietnamese affairs, reported that "although according to Colonel Helliwell, 'The only arms or ammunition which were ever given by OSS/China to Ho were six .38 caliber revolvers,' the fact remains that Ho and his guerrillas were soon reinforced by several OSS teams that also provided the Viet Minh guerillas with American arms and ammunition... Soon the mass missions operating in North Viet Nam and even China had acquired a number of Vietnamese aides, many of whom turned out to be good Vietnamese communists.[6]

The sympathy of the American military for the nationalist regime that the Viet Minh set up, after the defeat of Japan, aroused resentment among the French officers involved in Indochina-some of whom (General de Gaulle included) are still in office today. Such things as help for the Viet Minh guerillas, American neglect of French officers jailed by the Japanese, the establishment in October 1945 of a "Viet Nam-America Friendship Association" in Hanoi (at whose inaugural meeting U.S. Major General Philip Gallagher sang over the Viet Minh-controlled radio), and the presence of high-ranking U.S. officers at Viet Minh ceremonies not only affronted the French, but also gave Bao Dai and other noncommunist nationalists the impression that the U.S. had recognized the Viet Minh government (the Democratic Republic of Viet Nam).[7]

U.S. recognition never came, however, when the war between the Viet Minh and the French began, the United States at first remained neutral, limiting its action to mild suggestions that the French take steps toward granting independence to Indochina. In what seemed to be a struggle between a colonial power and nationalists, the American people's attachment to the principle of self-determination dictated against overt U.S. supply of France.

---

[5] General Albert Wedemeyer, *Wedemeyer Reports* (NY: Holt, Rhinehart, and Winston, 1958) pp. 340-343.

[6] Letter dated Oct. 14, 1954 from Colonel Helliwell to Bernard Fall; Bernard Fall, *Two Viet Nams*, p. 100.

[7] Bernard Fall, *op. cit.,* p. 69

Communist victory on mainland China in 1949 shattered the neutral position of the United States and ended U.S. aloofness toward the Viet Nam issue. On February 9, 1950, Senator Joseph McCarthy stepped into the national spotlight by accusing the State Department of harboring, Communists and fellow-travelers. In the American public, who wanted to know why China had been "lost," he found a ready audience. Had the U.S. helped to liberate China from the Japanese during World War II, and spent over $2 billion since then to keep the Chinese Nationalist regime afloat, only to loose all to the Communists? The State Department was on the defensive. What had seemed like a logical move in 1944—aiding Vietnamese communists and nationalists to fight Japan—became an Achilles heel to the U.S. government from 1950 on.

In May 1950, President Truman and Secretary of State Acheson reversed the FDR policy toward Indochina, and adopted a policy supporting the French effort. France at that time was arguing that its armed struggle, and the stability of the French-supported "Associated States" under Bao Dai, were the first line of defense against a militant, expansionist, Chinese communism. This made sense to the State Department. Economic and military assistance programs began on May 8.

Extension Of Military And Economic Aid
Statement by the Secretary of State, May 8, 1950

The [French] Foreign Minister and I have just had an exchange of views on the situation in Indochina and are in general agreement both as to the urgency of the situation in the area and as to the necessity for remedial action. We have noticed the fact that the problem of meeting the threat to the security of Viet Nam, Cambodia, and Laos which now enjoy independence within the French Union is primarily the responsibility of France and the Governments and peoples of Indochina. The United States recognizes that the solution of the Indochina problem depends both upon the restoration of security and upon the development of genuine nationalism and that United States assistance can and should contribute to these major objectives.

The United States Government, convinced that neither national independence nor democratic evolution exist in any area dominated by Soviet imperialism, considers the situation to be such as to warrant its according economic aid and military equipment to the Associated States of Indochina and to France in order to assist them in restoring stability and permitting these states to pursue their peaceful and democratic development.[8]

The U.S. backing of the French military campaign grew from about $150 million per year in 1950, to over $1 billion in 1954, when the U.S. bore 80% of the war costs.[9]

---

[8] Department of State *Bulletin*, May 22, 1950, p. 821.
[9] Kahin and Lewis, *The U.S. in Viet Nam*, p. 32.

Despite our massive investment in arms and aid, the French were not winning the war. The government of Viet Nam as a Free State under Bao Dai lacked popular backing, while the popular support given to the Viet Minh's struggle for independence allowed the Viet Minh regime to extend its control over increasing areas of Viet Nam. U.S. efforts to persuade the French to grant genuine independence to the French Union States of Laos, Cambodia, and Viet Nam went unheeded. Nevertheless the State Department manifested optimism about the progress of the war and the viability of Bao Dai's government. In 1953, a Department of State background paper had an optimistic ring:

> At home, where until recently the fighting was by and large limited to Viet-Nam, the young, almost fledgling, Vietnamese State is making unmistakable progress in gaining the confidence and support of its own people.[10]

Throughout this period, however, several liberal Senators, including John F. Kennedy, dissented from the State Department's analysis:

> In Indo-China we have allied ourselves to the desperate effort of the French regime to hang on to the remnants of empire. There is not broad general support of the native (Bao Dai) government among the people of that area.[11]

> John F. Kennedy, Nov. 1951

In September, 1953, France mobilized 350,000 men in her final attempt to gain a position of strength from which to negotiate with the Viet Minh. Although the French had superior numbers, artillery, planes and fortresses, they were always on the defensive, harassed and attacked by the invisible guerrillas. But the American commitment to the French cause had grown stronger; according to Robert Scigliano:

> The American commitment to the French military struggle in Indochina had become so strong by 1953 that American spokesmen were urging Vietnamese nationalists to moderate their demands for independence; Vice-President Nixon, who visited Saigon in the fall of that year, went so far as to preach the necessity of Vietnamese cooperation with the French. Indeed, as the French showed signs of willingness to end the war by negotiation, American officials redoubled their efforts to keep the fight going. In February 1954, Secretary of Defense Charles Wilson state optimistically that military victory over the Viet Minh remained "possible and probable."[12]

In the spring of 1954, the U.S. announced aid to the French totaling $1.33 billion—over one-third of the total U.S. foreign aid investment[13]. At Diên Biên Phu in April 1954, the French got the set-piece battle with the Viet

---

[10] *Indochina: The War in Southeast Asia*, Department of State Publication 4381, October 1951; revised edition, Department of State Publication 5092, August 1953.

[11] John F. Kennedy, *The Strategy of Peace* (NY: Harper, 1960), p. 60.

[12] Robert Scigliano, *South Viet Nam: Nation under Stress*, p. 196.

[13] Kahin and Lewis, *op. cit.*, p. 32.

Minh on which they had placed their hopes. Believing their artillery could destroy the Viet Minh, they invited attack on their heavily fortified base. Unexpectedly they were surrounded by an enemy that had suddenly acquired substantial artillery. The French situation grew desperate.

On March 20, 1954, General Paul Ely, then French Chief of Staff arrived in Washington to tell President Eisenhower that Indochina would be lost unless the U.S. intervened. On March 25, the U.S. National Security Council endorsed intervention, with the conditions that the venture would be undertaken with allies, and that France would give Indochina a real measure of independence so as to eliminate the issue of colonialism.

On April 3, a secret conference was called with Congressional leaders where Secretary of State Dulles called for a joint Congressional Resolution permitting the President to use American air and naval power for a massive strike to save the beleaguered French forces at Diên Biên Phu.[14] Support for U.S. unilateral action seemed to be lacking, and Dulles was told to go shopping for allies. Finding British Foreign Secretary Anthony Eden very' much opposed to military action, Dulles temporarily shelved the plan of immediate military intervention and proposed instead the creation of a Southeast Asian Treaty Organization (SEATO) for mutual security in the area.

At a meeting in Paris on April 24, however, the subject of an air strike came up again. Present were France's Foreign Minister George Bidault, Admiral Radford, Dulles, and Eden. Radford was advocating the plan, but Eden seemed still opposed. Dulles said that if the allies agreed, the President was prepared to go to Congress on the following Monday, April 26, to ask for a joint Congressional resolution authorizing such action.[15]

On Sunday, however, final word came back from London, and the word was no. England was not willing to join such an action, just before the Geneva conference was to convene to negotiate an end to the war. In a speech the next day President Eisenhower announced that a "modus-vivendi" with the Communists was to be sought at the Geneva Conference. The push for U.S. military intervention in the crisis was over. Eleven days later, Diên Biên Phu fell, and talk of settlement began at Geneva.

---

[14] Chalmers, Roberts, "The Day We Didn't Go to War," in *Viet Nam: History, Documents and Opinions on a Major World Crisis*, edited by Marvin Gettleman (NY: Fawcett, 1965), p. 96

[15] *Ibid.*, pp. 101-103.

<table>
<tr><td>Appendix

C</td><td><h1>Viet Nam Veterans Journey to Recognition: A Timeline
By Ed Gallagher, PhD</h1></td></tr>
</table>

Appendix C	Viet Nam Veterans Journey to Recognition: A Timeline By Ed Gallagher, PhD

Beginning in the late 1960s, the media covers the sorry state of the returning Vietnam War veteran through Jan Scruggs' drive to build a memorial in the middle to late 1970s, and then to Congressional hearings and approval early in 1980, ending with President Carter approving the legislation for the Viet Nam Veterans Memorial in July 1980.

1967

May 7: "The Re-Entry Problem of the Vietvets," by William Barry Furlong, *New York Times Magazine*, 05/07/67, 23, 115-21.

1968

January 12: "[Veterans] Oh, You're Back?" *Time*, 01/12/68, 15.

July 4: Opening of John Wayne's film *The Green Berets* based on the 1965 novel by Robin Moore. See Alasdair Spark, "The Soldier at the Heart of the War: The Myth of the Green Beret," *Journal of American Studies* 18.1 (1984): 29-48.

1969

May 28: Jan Scruggs is wounded near Xuan Loc.

June 27: Life magazine humanizes the "body count" by publishing the photographs of all 242 soldiers killed that week: "One Week's Dead," *Life*, 06/27/69, 20-32.

November 12: Seymour Hersh breaks the My Lai massacre story: "Officer Kept in Army in Inquiry into Killing of Vietnam Civilians," by Robert M. Smith, *New York Times*, 11/13/69, 1-2.

November 14: "'March Against Death' Begun By Thousands in Washington," by David E. Rosenbaum, *New York Times*, 11/14/69, 1.

November 15: "Wounded Unembittered by War Critics," by Nan Robertson, *New York Times*, 11/15/69, 1: 20.

1970

Jan. 21: Scruggs witnesses 12 friends killed while unloading an ammo truck.

1971

Jan.31: The Winter Soldier Investigation organized by Vietnam Veterans Against the War to publicize war crimes (reports later read into the Congressional Record by Senator Hatfield (April 6-7):

Feb. 7: "Veterans Assess Atrocity Blame: 100 Who Served in Vietnam Hold Leaders at Fault," by Jerry M. Flints, *New York Times*, 02/07/71, 17.

Apr. 19: The "March on Washington" organized by the Vietnam Veterans Against the War: "Week of Protests on War to Start," *New York Times*, 04/19/71, 5

May 26: "From Dakto to Detroit: The Death of a Troubled Hero," by Jon Nordheimer, *New York Times*, 05/26/71, A1.

1971 (Cont'd)

June 5: "Public Jobs for the Jobless," *New York Times*, 06/05/71, 1: 28.

June 7: The term "Post-Vietnam Syndrome" (later "Post-Traumatic Disorder") begins to appear: "'Syndrome' Found in Returned GIs," by Ralph Blumenthal, *New York Times*, 06/07/71, 1: 7.

Sep.: Ronald Glasser's collection of war stories, *365 Days*

1972

May 3: "Delayed Trauma in Veterans Cited," by Boyce Rensberger, *New York Times*, 05/03/72, 1: 19.

June 18: The television film *Welcome Home, Johnny Bristol* about a returning P.O.W., starring Martin Landau and Jane Alexander.

July 6: "The Next Nick Adams," by William Pelfrey, *New York Times*, 07/06/72, 1: 37.

August 21: "Postwar Shock Besets Ex-G.I.s," by Jon Nordheimer, *New York Times*, 08/21/72, 1: 1, 22-34.

September 15: Untitled article by John O'Neill, *New York Times*, 09/15/72, 37.

September 15: "The Ones Who Came Back," by Arthur Egendorf, Jr., *New York Times*, 09/15/72, 36.

October: An anthology of poetry, *Winning Hearts & Minds: War Poems* by Vietnam Veterans, by Larry Rottmann, Jan Barry, Basil T Paquet.

October 23: "President Praises Returning G.I.'s," by Linda Charlton, *New York Times*, 10/23/72, A1.

1973

Feb.: "New Profiles in Courage," by Kenneth Y. Tomlinson, *Reader's Digest*, February 1973, 126-31.

Feb. 8: House Joint Resolution 338 to honor the war dead with a grove of trees, introduced by Representative Paul Findley of Illinois, passes but goes nowhere.

Feb. 14: "Flag at Full Staff Today for Captives," *New York Times*, 02/14/73, 1: 16.

Feb. 28: "MIA Culpa," by Nicholas von Hoffman, *Washington Post*, 02/28/73, B1.

Mar. 4: *Troubled Peace, An Epilogue to Vietnam*: The Nader Report on Vietnam Veterans and the Veterans Administration by Paul Starr. Sponsored by the Center for Study of Responsive Law, 1973: "Nader Report Says V.A. Is Failing Vietnam Veterans," *New York Times*, 03/04/73.

Mar. 4: "Viet Combat G.I.'s Held Shortchanged," by Peter Braestrup, *Washington Post*, 03/04/73, 2: 25.

March 5: "The Vets: Heroes as Orphans," *Newsweek*, 03/05/73, 22-24.

March 5: "The Permanent War Prisoners," *Newsweek*, 03/05/73, 23-24.

March 8: A television broadcast of David Rabe's *Sticks and Bones* is cancelled: "Stones for 'Sticks,'" by Tom Shales, *Washington Post*, 03/08/73, E11.

March 10: "Neglected Veterans" [The Washington Merry-Go-Round: "Ultrasonic Dangers for the Unborn"]," by Jack Anderson, Washington Post, 03/10/73, D31.

1973 (Cont'd)

March 10: "Texas Group Plans Salute to Vietnam Veterans at Cotton Bowl," *Washington Post*, 03/10/73, A4.

March 12: "Forgotten Warriors?" *Time*, 03/12/73, 17-18.

March 30: Final U.S. troops withdrawn from Vietnam: "U. S. Forces Out of Vietnam," by Joseph B. Treaster, *New York Times*, 03/30/73, 81-82.

May 25: "Ex-P.O.W.'s Cheer," John Herbers, *New York Times*, 05/25/73, 1: 1.

June 2: "400 Ex-P.O.W.'s Are Given $400,000 Dallas Reception," *New York Times*, 06/02/73, 1: 8.

Nov. 20: Senator Alan Cranston puts a Veteran's Administration letter asking for legislation to deal with the personal problems of returning vets into the Congressional Record (vol 119, Part 29, 37748-49); Scruggs refers to this letter in his 1977 Congressional testimony.

Dec. 7: House Joint Resolutions #381 and #865 establish a "Vietnam Veterans Day" for March 30, 1974.

1974

March 29: "The Real Honors," New York Times, 03/29/74, A34.

March 30: Vietnam Veterans Day: "Viet Vets: A Sad Reminder, Day of Tribute Evokes Pain, Rage," by William Greider, *Washington Post*, 03/30/74, A5.

September 25: "Meanwhile, On the Hill, Lobbying and Politicking As Usual," by William V. Shannon, New York Times, 09/25/74, 1: 39.

October 29: "Ford Orders Federal Agencies to Hire 70,000 Vietnam Era Veterans by July 1," by Philip Shabecoff, *New York Times*, 10/29/74, 1: 29.

1975

April 5: "Earthquake Vietnam," New York *Times*, 04/05/75, 28.

April 14: "How Should Americans Feel?" *Time*, 04/14/75, 27.

April 21: "Seeking the Last Exit from Vietnam," *Time*, 04/21/75, 7.

April 30: Fall of Saigon: "Ford Unity Plea; President Says That Departure 'Closes a Chapter' for U.S. Helicopters Evacuate 1,000 Americans and 5,500 South Vietnamese From Saigon." by John W. Finney, *New York Times*, 04/30/75, 1-2.

May 7: President Ford declares this day the end of the Vietnam War era: "Ford Asks Nation to Open Its Doors to the Refugees," by David Binder, *New York Times*, 05/07/75, 1-2.

July 19: "TV's Newest Villain: The Vietnam Veteran," by Robert Brewin, *TV Guide*, 07/19/75, 4.

1976

Aug. 4: "The Invisible Vietnam Veteran," by James H. Webb, *Washington Post*, 08/04/76: A11.

Oct.: *Demilitarized Zones: Veterans After Vietnam* by Jan Barry and W. D. Ehrhart.

1977

Jan 3: Television movie *Green Eyes* starring Paul Winfield and Rita Tushingham.

Jan. 23: "The Old, Unhealed Wounds of Vietnam [Conversations with Three Veterans]," by William Grieder, *Washington Post*, 01/23/77, A1, 14.

Apr18: "The VA's Max Cleland: A New Kind of Battle," by Myra MacPherson, *Washington Post*, 04/18/77, B1.

May: The novel *Rumor of War* by Philip Caputo, a book the memorial competition judges were asked to read.

May 25: "Forgotten Veterans of 'That Peculiar War,'" by Jan Craig Scruggs, Washington Post, 05/25/77: A17.

June 22: Scruggs testifies at a Senate Hearing on the Veteran's Health Care Amendments Act of 1977 (Hearings before the Subcommittee on Health and Readjustment of the Committee on Veterans' Affairs, United States Senate, Ninety-Fifth Congress, first session, on S. 1693 and H. R. 6502). In his testimony, Scruggs cites his work as consistent with that of Robert J. Lifton, *Home from the War: Vietnam Veterans: Neither Victims nor Executioners* (New York: Simon and Schuster, 1973). See also Robert J. Lifton, "The Post-War War," *Journal of Social Issues* 31.4 (1975): 181-96.

Oct: The book *Dispatches* by war correspondent Michael Herr.

Oct: *A Generation of Peace*, a volume of poetry by W. D. Ehrhart.

Oct 14: The movie *Rolling Thunder* starring William Devane and Tommy Lee Jones.

Nov 4: The movie *Heroes* starring Henry Winkler, Sally Field, and Harrison Ford.

December 2: "The Class That Went to War," *Washington Post*, 12/02/77, A16.

1978

Feb. 2: The movie *The Boys in Company C* starring Stan Shaw and Andrew Stevens.

Febr.15: The movie *Coming Home* starring Jane Fonda and John Voight.

April 8: "A Plaque for Vietnam," by Josh Martin, Nation, 04/08/78, 389.

May 28: "Walking Amid History at Arlington Cemetery," by Richard Cohen, *Washington Post*, 05/28/78, B5.

May 29: "'Range of Intangibles' Said Hurting Viet Vets the Most," by Warren Brown, Washington Post, 05/29/78, A9.

May 29: "Vietnam Vets: Does Congress Finally Understand?" by Colman McCarthy, *Washington Post*, 05/29/78, A21.

June: The movie *Good Guys Wear Black* starring Chuck Norris.

June 14: The movie *Go Tell the Spartans* starring Burt Lancaster.

Aug. 2: The movie *Who'll Stop the Rain* starring Nick Nolte and Tuesday Weld.

Aug. 5: "Continuing Indifference to Vietnam Veterans," by Jan C. Scruggs, *Washington Post*, 08/05/78: A15.

1978 (Cont'd)

November 12: "Veterans Day: 'Ignored' Men of Vietnam Owed a Debt, Carter Says," by Stephanie Mansfield, *Washington Post*, 11/12/78, C1.

December: The novel *Fields of Fire* by James Webb.

December: The novel *Going After Cacciato* by Tim O'Brien.

December 8: The movie *The Deer Hunter* starring Robert Deniro and Meryl Streep.

1979

Jan. 29: "Vietnam Veterans -- Peace at Last?" *US News & World Report*, 01/29/79, 16.

Febr. 5: "Angry Vietnam Veterans Charging Federal Policies Ignore Their Needs," by Bernard Weinraub, *New York Times*, 02/15/79, A15.

March: Scruggs sees *The Deer Hunter*, after which, he says several times, he conceived the idea of a memorial.

March: Scruggs' proposal for a memorial falls flat at a meeting of forty veterans planning activities for the upcoming Vietnam Veterans Week, but he meets Robert W. Doubek, who suggests forming a corporation.

April 22: The television movie *Friendly Fire* starring Carol Burnett and Ned Beatty.

April 22: "'Friendly Fire' with Power to Penetrate," by Tom Shales, Washington Post, 04/22/79, K1.

April 23: "Heroes Without Honor Face the Battle at Home," Time, 04/23/79, 31.

April 27: Vietnam Veterans Memorial Fund is incorporated as a non-profit corporation with Scruggs as President and Doubek as Secretary.

April 28: "Vietnam Veterans Still Feel Chill from the White House," by Ward Sinclair, Washington Post, 04/28/79: A2.

April 28: "Vietnam Veterans Needs Unfulfilled," by Jack Anderson, Washington Post, 04/28/79: E37.

May 27: "Now, Vietnam Vets Demand Their Rights," by Bernard Weinraub, *New York Times Magazine*, 05/27/79: 30-33.

May 28: Scruggs holds a press conference to kick off fundraising: "Vietnam Veterans to Seek $1 Million for a Monument," *New York Times*, 05/28/79: A8.

May 28: Vietnam Veterans Week:

"Memorial Day Services, Activities Planned in Area; Veterans Ask Vietnam War Remembrance; Veterans Urge Look at Lessons Of Vietnam War," by Thomas Morgan, *Washington Post*, 05/28/79, C1.

"'All Vietnam Veterans Have a Certain Hole in Their Soul That Can Only Be Healed with Special Thanks,'" by Thomas Morgan et al., *Washington Post*, 05/29/79, C1.

"Vietnam Veterans Week: Is America Ready to Face Them?" by Myra MacPherson, *Washington Post*, 05/31/79, D1.

1979 (Cont'd)

"A Tale of Two Veterans," by Max Cleland, *Washington Post*, 05/28/79, A21.

May 30: White House dinner for Vietnam veterans: "Honoring That Extra Measure of Sacrifice," by Myra MacPherson, *Washington Post,* 05/31/79, D1.

June: As fundraising begins, some poignant letters come in with small donations, but Roger Mudd reports wryly on the *CBS Evening News* that only $144.50 has been collected, and Scruggs is made fun of by a late-night tv comedian.

June: John C. Wheeler becomes involved, meeting with Scruggs and Doubek.

Aug.: Wheeler helps convene a meeting of veterans who become the nucleus of a volunteer corps.

Aug.: A Fine Arts Commission official suggests a site for the memorial near Arlington Cemetery that Scruggs and Wheeler visit and find unacceptable.

Aug. 4: Scruggs' promotional efforts bear fruit when New Jersey Senator Charles Mathias calls and asks to see him.

Aug. 15: The movie *Apocalypse Now* starring Martin Sheen and Robert Duvall.

Aug. 19: "The Screening of Vietnam," by James Webb, Washington Post, 08/19/79: L1.

Sep.: Scruggs, Doubek, Wheeler, and three National Park Service officials meet with Senator Mathias, who picks the Constitution Gardens site, near the Lincoln Memorial.

October: Senator Warner proposes a direct mail campaign to raise funds.

Oct. 24: Meeting with National Capital Memorial Advisory Committee results in an invitation to return in January.

Oct.25: James Webb shows draft legislation to Congressman John Hammerschmidt of Arkansas, who prematurely introduces legislation in the House (Congressional Record: Vol 125, Part 23, 29680) in terms that the Vietnam Veterans Memorial Fund people feel might arouse opposition.

Nov. 8: At a press conference (designed to coincide with Veteran's Day celebrations) led by Senator Mathias, twenty-six senators announce they will back legislation introduced to build a memorial: "Vietnam War Memorial; Senate Bill Proposes Site on Mall," by Donald P. Baker, *Washington Post*, 11/9/79: C1.

Nov. 11: "We Were Young. We Have Died. Remember Us," by Jan C. Scruggs, Washington Post, 11/11/79: B4.

Nov. 11: "Vietnam Vets: Tomorrow's Leaders," by John B. Wheeler III, *Washington Post*, 11/12/79: A17.

Nov. 11: "Sad and Bitter Memories; Bitter Memories of War; Nation Honors Veterans, but Some Feel Forgotten," by Mike Sager, *Washington Post*, 11/12/79: C1.

November 13: "What the Vietnam Veteran Needs," by James Webb, Congressional Record: Vol 125, Part 24, 32250 (reprinted from *Marine Corps Gazette*)

December 1: Full-time executive director is hired by the Vietnam Veterans Memorial Fund; additional volunteer staff is recruited.

December 20: Senator Warner hosts breakfast fundraising event.

1980

Jan. 2: The VVMF opens an office.

Jan. 16: First substantial contribution: $10,000 from Gruman Aircraft.

February: H. Ross Perot makes the second substantial contribution, also $10,000: VVMF memo details Perot involvement through 12/15/81.

Feb. 14: "Planning Snags Delay Action on New Memorials," by Paul Hodge, *Washington Post*, 02/14/80, DC6.

Feb. 22: Letter from Chairman Brown to government official Ronald Peterson indicates that the Commission of Fine Arts would rather not have a specific site designated in legislation.

Feb. 22: Direct mail campaign begins: $34,000 pledged so far toward 2.5 million goal: "Vietnam Veterans Plan Memorial in Capital as Reconciliation Sign," by Richard Halloran, *New York Times*, 02/25/80: A15.

March: The Awkward Silence, a volume of poetry by W. D. Ehrhart.

Mar.5: Press conference to get House of Representatives support.

Mar. 12: Hearing before the Subcommittee on Parks, Recreation, and Renewable Resources. *The Senate. S.J. Res. 119.* March 12, 1980. Publication # 96-111.

Mar. 22: "A Vietnam Memorial," by Jan Scruggs, *Washington Post*, 03/22/80, A13.

Apr. 26: "The Making of a Monument," by Wolf Von Eckardt, *Washington Post*, 04/26/80: C1.

Apr. 30: Senate approves legislation authorizing the memorial: 96th Congress, 2nd Session. Senate. Calendar no. 709 Report 96-663.

Apr. 24: Senate passes the joint resolution 119, with an amendment. SRP.663 X96-2:S.RP 663. *Congressional Record*, Senate. April 30th, 1980. Vietnam Veterans Memorial. #9431.

May 8: "The Wounds of Vietnam," by James J. Kilpatrick, *Washington Star*, 05/08/80, A15.

May 20: The House approves the legislation: *Congressional Record*, House May 20th, 1980. Authorizing The Vietnam Veterans Memorial Fund, Inc., To Establish a Memorial. #11834.

May 22: "House Approves Bill to Establish a Memorial to Vietnam War Dead," *New York Times*, 05/22/80: A24.

May 25: "I Wish We Were More Troubled," by Tim O'Brien, *Washington Post*, 05/25/80, B3.

May 25: "After Vietnam: Voices of a Wounded Generation," *Washington Post*, 05/25/80, B1.

May 26: "Vietnam Memorial: Another Symbol of Frustration for Vets," by Ward Sinclair, *Washington Post*, 05/26/80: A3.

May 26: "Vietnam Veterans Hold Memorial," *New York Times*, 05/26/80, B9.

May 27: "Memorial Day Highlights Legacy of Different Wars; Two Memorial Day Services Contrast Legacy of Vietnam and Other Wars," by Ronald D. White, *Washington Post*, 05/27/80: C1.

1980 (Cont'd)

May 31: "Needless Obstacle," *New Republic*, 05/31/80, 7-8.

June: Paul Spreiregan is hired as a public relations strategist.

June 26: "Moving the Memorial," by Carlin Romano, *Washington Post*, 06/25/80: B8.

June 28: "About Politics: Memorializing the Vietnam War Dead," by Francis X. Clines, *New York Times*, 06/28/80: A7.

July 1: President Carter signs legislation PL 96-297 and makes remarks: "Carter Hails Veterans of Vietnam in Signing Bill for a War Memorial," by Bernard Weinraub, *New York Times*, 07/02/80: A14.

July 2: "Carter Clears Vietnam Memorial; Survey Backs More Veteran Aid," *Washington Post,* 07/02/80: A21.

July 3: "Vietnam Vets: 'This nation cares,'" *Christian Science Monitor*, 07/03/80: 28.

July 13: "The Hidden Tomb of the Vietnam Unknown," by Willy Arnheim, *Washington Post*, 07/13/80, E4.

About the Editors

Rick Ritter, MSW

I was an outreach counselor and team leader at the Ft. Wayne, Indiana Vet Center from the start of 1980 to the end of 1988. I spent nearly the whole decade working with veterans and their family members from primarily the Viet Nam era, but also from Korea and WWII. I have also worked with those involved in covert operations during the times in between, when we supposedly weren't at war with anyone.

However, the training for my work with veterans really began in 1968 when I entered the Marine Corps and spent 2-½ years on active duty prior to a medical discharge for a service-connected disability with my leg. I have told people for years that the reason I got rank so quick was because I could spell my name, when in reality when we are at war there is a higher attrition rate and rank comes much easier. I learned the most as an inpatient at Bethesda Naval Hospital (1969-70) where I spent about 5 months on an orthopedic floor full of medevacs (in this instance, a term for those persons who were wounded in combat and flown ultimately to state-side hospitals for additional medical care). I learned much there regarding trauma and I have much to thank my ward mates for from their sharing and teaching.

Working with vets and their families for the last 26 years has been an honor and a blessing. Things happen in our lives for a reason, even if we are clueless as to the why and wherefore of it. I have been blessed with meeting people and experiencing things I would have otherwise missed out on in life and my life would not have been as rich as it has been but for the veterans that I have known and worked with to date. It also gave me a periscope view of many people's lives and that has translated into a solid working knowledge of working with many other traumatized populations over the years with the veterans as the foundation for that other work—it continues today. I have said for many years that I expect to be a living memorial to those who lost their lives—Mark, Billy, Rick, Paul, Charlie, Rudy, Russ, John, Tommy, Skeet—and today I continue to work toward maintaining that commitment in its inherent imperfections.

There are many individuals and families that I can think of when I look back over the last 26 years of work with veterans and attempt to assess my work somehow —I think of the more than 25 individuals that are therapists today, or some other helping person such as massage therapist, ministers, etc. I think of the families and the individuals that have given me notes of appreciation or just a quick word passing in the grocery store or reconnecting with them when I managed the half- scale Viet Nam memorial when it came to Ft. Wayne on two different occasions.

I have been a most fortunate person to have had the contact with so many wonderful human beings—it certainly overshadows the negative factors that may have intruded at times. I hope that the 2nd edition of this book will continue to help vets and their families heal. If you change the names of the places and the dates, many have found that people experience mostly the same phenomena any war.

Paul Richards

Paul Richards was born Paul Richard Wappenstein, Jr. on December 29th, 1944 and died suddenly on April 20th, 1984; barely two months after publication of the first edition of *Made In America, Sold in the Nam.*

He served in the Marines more than 7 years and had a distinguished service record from 1963 until his honorable discharge on November 9th, 1970. Richards served his first enlistment as a Chauffer/Orderly. On April 7th, 1966 he completed training as a Radio Telegraph Operator (MOS 2533) and served with the 3rd Marines in Viet Nam for a tour in Viet Nam. During this tour, he worked part-time in Graves Registration.

He returned to the USA on March 30th, 1967 and was posted to South Bend, Indiana. Over the next few years he served for a time as a recruiter and then found himself back in Viet Nam on May 28th, 1969 in back-to-back deployments during Operations Firestone Canyon, Bold Pursuit, Mighty Play, and later on Operation Defiant Stand. He acted as an interpreter during both tours of duty in Viet Nam.

After Operation Firestone Canyon, he was promoted to Communications Chief. In late 1970 he was promoted to Company Gunny ("Gunnery Sergeant") and chose to muster out.

After leaving the Marines, Richards took odd jobs around the Pacific Northwest including his first radio job in San Francisco. In the mid-1970s he was a self-employed drywall contractor and later a headhunter for Fortune 500 companies.

He completed a 4-year degree in two years at Indiana University while working fulltime at WAKE/WJLE Radio in Valparaiso, Indiana. It was here that he really hit his stride and Paul Richard Wappenstein, Jr. became *Paul Richards.* He would be a successful News Director for several other radio stations including WTWN/WLAV (Grand Rapids, MI) and WQHK/WMEE (Ft. Wayne, Indiana). He garnered many awards for his investigative reporting including 6 awards from Associated Press and 3 awards from United Press International.

However, Paul Richards could not and would not forget his past. He served as a volunteer in the Vets Center in Ft. Wayne during the same span as Rick Ritter (1983). This experience galvanized him to bring 25 veterans together to write a book which would raise money for veterans' assistance programs and to increase public awareness of what veterans experienced in Viet Nam.

Of the first edition, Richards said, "It's basically reflections of time spent in Viet Nam. We approached it in as professional a capacity as possible, and there is a lot of talent here. It's not always pleasant reading, but war isn't a pleasant experience."

Initial goals of the book were to finance an emergency housing facility for veterans who need temporary shelter. At the time, some 20 percent of Allen County's unemployed were Viet Nam-era veterans. The initial print run was 1,000 copies and plans were laid for a second edition and a third which would have national distribution.

It has been my great pleasure to oversee the preparation of this 2nd Edition, now more than two decades later. And although I never met the man himself, I now feel an intimate connection to the hearts and minds of those who served. My only hope is that others who pick up this volume will be affected the same way.

Victor R. Volkman, Publisher
Modern History Press
July 27, 2006

Glossary

[Ed Note: although originally begun for the purpose of describing Viet Nam slang, it quickly became apparent that a wider audience could be reached by including all military terms used throughout the entire work.]

4-F: Classification given to those deemed unfit for military service (see also Draft Board).

82: 82mm mortar used by the Viet Cong.

Agent Orange: Agent Orange is the code name for a powerful herbicide and defoliant used by the U.S. military in its Herbicidal Warfare program during the Viet Nam War. Agent Orange was used from 1961 to 1971, and was by far the most used of the so-called "rainbow herbicides" used during the program. Containing dioxins, now known to be notorious carcinogen, it attacked both friend and foe alike.

AK-47: Soviet-manufactured Kalashnikov semi-automatic and fully automatic combat assault rifle, 7.62-mm; the basic weapon of the Communist forces. Known as the 'Type 56' to the Chinese, it is characterized by an explosive popping sound.

Arty: short for "Artillery".

Arc Light: code name for B-52 bomber strikes along the Cambodian-Vietnamese border. These operations shook the earth for ten miles away from the target area.

Article 15: section of the Uniform Military Code of Justice. A form of non-judicial punishment for minor offenses. The accused might or might not be granted a hearing if requested.

ARVN: Army of the Republic of (South) Viet Nam.

Bad paper: more than 560,000 less-than-honorable discharges were issued in the Viet Nam era. Bad-paper holders are not eligible for veterans' benefits until the document is upgraded to an honorable or a general discharge.

Basic (Basic Training): the initial period of training for new military personnel; involves intense physical activity and behavioral discipline. Around 9 weeks, depending on service branch and era.

B-40: a shoulder-held rocket-propelled grenade launcher used by the NVA. A variant of the Russian RPG-2, ancestor of the RPG-7.

Boat People: Events resulting from the Viet Nam War led many people in Cambodia, Laos, and especially Viet Nam to become refugees in the late 1970s and 1980s, after the fall of Saigon. In Viet Nam, the new communist government sent many people who supported the old government in the South to "re-education camps", and others to "new economic zones." These factors, coupled with poverty caused by disastrous economic reforms, caused millions of Vietnamese to flee the country. On the open seas, the boat people had to confront forces of nature, and elude pirates.

Boot (Camp): See Basic.

Buckle for Dust: to fight, as in combat.

C-Rat (C-Ration): literally "Combat Rations". Canned meals for use in the field. Each ration consisted of a canned entree, a "B2 unit" containing cheese, crackers and candy, a canned dessert, and an accessory pack. The accessory pack contained a P-38 can opener, mix for a hot beverage, salt and sugar packets, plastic spoon, chewing gum, a pack of four cigarettes and several sheets of toilet paper.

Cam On Ong: "Thank you" (Vietnamese).

CAR-15: CAR-15 has a meaning split between closely related firearms, which depends on the context. In popular usage it is a general name applied to many ultra-short and carbine variants of the Colt AR-15 rifle (adopted by the USA as the M16 rifle).

C.B.: Combat Base.

Charlie: American forces typically referred to members of the National Liberation Front as "Charlie," which comes from the US Armed Forces' phonetic alphabet's pronunciation of VC ("Victor Charlie"). See *Viet Cong*.

Chieu Hoi: translation "Open Arms". A program to actively take in defectors from the NVA. Also refers to a person who is a defector.

Claymore (M18): a directional antipersonnel fragmentation mine containing 700 steel spheres and 1.5 pounds of C-4 explosives detonated by an electrically activated blasting cap. It has a kill zone of 50 meters in a 60 degree swath to the front. Backblast is dangerous to 100 meters in the rear from secondary effects.

C.O.: Commanding Officer.

Cobra: Bell AH-1 "Cobra" was a combat workhorse in the later years of the Viet Nam war beginning with the TET Offensive of 1968. It carried a crew of two armed with 20mm cannons, TOW missiles, and 70mm rockets.

Conex: corrugated metal packing crate, approximately six feet in length.

C.P. (Check Point): A landmark used as a reference on road patrols. Usually a bridge that required a manned watch at night. CPs were manned by a squad of ARVN who lived there and assisted by an MP patrol.

CQ: (charge of quarters) An officer officially in charge of a unit headquarters at night.

Currahee: A Cherokee word meaning literally "stands alone". The word was adopted by WWII paratrooper units including the legendary 101st Airborne and aptly describes their role in combat.

D.I.: Drill Instructor.

Didi: (sometimes written as "dee dee") slang from the Vietnamese word *di*, meaning "to leave" or "to go".

DMZ (Demilitarized Zone): In military terms, a demilitarized zone (DMZ) is an area, usually the frontier or boundary between two or more groups, where military activity is not permitted, usually by treaty or other agreement. Often the demilitarized zone lies upon a line of control and forms a de-facto international border.

Dinks: racial epithet for Vietnamese. Reputedly short for "rinky dink" (worthless) or perhaps from the Vietnamese phrase "dinky dau" meaning "crazy". Same usage as gooks or slopes.

Draft Board: A Selective Service Local Board is a group of five citizen volunteers whose mission, upon a draft, will be to decide who among the registrants in their community will receive deferments, postponements, or exemption from military service based on the individual registrant's circumstances and beliefs. Members of a Draft Board are never military or law enforcement officers.

E-6: rank of Staff Sergeant (*see*) in the US Army or Marines.

Eltee: vocalization of "Lt.", as in the abbreviation for Lieutenant.

Field of Fire: The area around a weapon (or group of weapons) which can be easily and effectively reached by gun fire. Fields of fire today are mostly used in reference to machine guns.

Firebase (FSB): A Fire Support Base (FSB) is an encampment designed to provide fire support to infantry operating in areas beyond the normal range of their main base camp cannon and howitzers. FSBs were used extensively in the Viet Nam War.

Flak Jacket: During the Viet Nam War, many soldiers, Marines and Airmen received vests that would stop shrapnel, but not a bullet. In the Viet Nam climate they were hot and uncomfortable, and felt heavy and bulky. Nonetheless, they were widely adopted and the soldier in his flak vest became a symbol of the war.

Flame Tank: M67 "Zippo". Although much safer than man-carried flamethrowers, the flame tanks suffered vulnerability to anti-tank weapons on the battlefield due to the relatively short range of fire-based weaponry.

FO: Forward Observer.

Frags: fragmentation grenades.

FNG (Fucking New Guy): the New Guy was the most dangerous person to have around because he would not know the hazards and might get you killed or maimed.

Freedom Bird: the flight that would take you back to the US after your tour in Viet Nam was done.

Get Some: common expression meaning "to kill the enemy."

Gooks: racial epithet for Vietnamese.

Grunt: The term grunt is slang for an infantryman in the U.S. Army and Marines. Infantrymen are known to take extreme pride in the term. It was used especially in the Viet Nam War.

Guard Mounting: a.k.a. the Changing of the Guard, refers to a formal ceremony in which sentries providing ceremonial guard duties at important institutions are relieved by a new batch of sentries.

Gun Truck: standard cargo truck with added armor and machineguns for convoy escort.

Hearts and Minds: Hearts and Minds was a euphemism for a campaign by the United States military during the Viet Nam War, intended to win the popular support of the Vietnamese people. There is little evidence to show that it was anything other than pro-war propaganda, and rang hollow compared to anti-war publicity efforts. The eponymous film (1974) showed the inherent contradictions of the term, and the term "Hearts and Minds" remains symbolic of the fictional nature of militarist propaganda.

Hooch: building made of bamboo and covered with a thatched roof. Built on stilts to protect it from flooding.

I Corps: the northernmost military region in South Viet Nam.

Joe (G.I. Joe): the archetypal foot soldier. Coined by Dave Breger in the eponymous comic strip on June 17th, 1942.

Jungle Rot: Jungle rot is equivalent to athlete's foot and is caused by a combination of heat and moisture due to Viet Nam's tropical climate.

KIA: Killed in Action.

KP: Kitchen Patrol, e.g. washing dishes, peeling potatoes, etc.

Lifer: career military man. The term is often used in a derogatory manner.

LOCH: Light Observation / Cargo Helicopter. Typically the OH-6 Cayuse (nickname "Loach"). This two-seater was easily recognizable by its egg-shaped glass canopy and could carry six people.

LP: listening post. A two- or three-man position set up at night outside the perimeter away from the main body of troopers, which acted as an early warning system against attack.

LZ: Landing Zone, point at where infantry are inserted or extracted from the countryside.

M14: First deployed in 1962, the M14 was unwieldy in the thick brush due to its length and weight. The power of the 7.62 mm NATO cartridge allowed it to penetrate cover quite well and reach out to extended range. The M14 remained the primary infantry weapon in Viet Nam until replacement by the M16 in 1966–1968

M60: The M60 Machine Gun was introduced in 1957 by the U.S. Army. It fires the standard NATO 7.62 mm round and is used as a general support crew-served weapon. It has a removable barrel which can be easily changed to prevent overheating. The weapon has an integral, folding bipod and can also be mounted on a folding tripod.

M79: hand-held grenade launcher.

MACV: Military Assistance Command, Viet Nam.

Medevac (Medivac): Medical Evacuation of wounded, normally by helicopter.

MIA: Missing In Action.

Minigun: When the U.S. entered the Viet Nam War during early 1960s, it found it needed to arm its helicopters to provide additional firepower against enemy infantry. The Minigun, essentially an M60 machine gun with six barrels, could fire up to 4,000 rounds per minute and was soon adapted to the various helicopter mounts (including the AH-1 Cobra and UH1 "Huey").

Montagnards: (a.k.a. Mountain-Yards or just 'Yards) literally French for 'mountain dweller'. In Viet Nam they were often persecuted by the Communists. Easily identified because they are short in stature and darker than the lowland Vietnamese. In many ways, they could be compared to the Native American.

MPC: Military Payment Certificates, were used from the end of World War II until the end of the Viet Nam War. MPCs utilized layers of line lithography to create colorful banknotes that could be produced cheaply. They were issued to servicemen in the field to prevent local economies from being flooded with US dollars.

OCS: Officer Candidate School.

ODs: "Olive Drabs", the standard Army green color.

Operation Phoenix: A CIA run covert program designed to capture, kill, or otherwise neutralize the Viet Cong Infrastructure (VCI) cadres who were engaged both in recruiting and training insurgents within South Vietnamese villages as well as providing support to the North Vietnamese war effort.

PFC: Private First Class. In the US Army, PFC is the third lowest enlisted rank, just above Private and below Corporal or Specialist. Often earned after six months as a Private.

POW: Prisoner of War.

Primer cord: a thin, flexible tube with an explosive core. It is a high-speed fuse which explodes, rather than burns, and is suitable for detonating high explosives. c.f. "Primacord", a brand name for this product.

Punji Stakes: Punji stakes were bamboo stalks, about a foot long, sharpened to a point on one end. The VC stuck them in the ground, pointed end up, hoping we would step, or fall, on them. The tip of the punji stick was frequently smeared with feces, urine, poison, or other contaminants to promote infection in the wound created by the sharpened stick penetrating the soldier's skin.

QTCB: Quang Tri Combat Base.

Repl-Depl: literally, 'Replacement-Deployment'. An infantry outfit where additional training is provided just prior to deployment.

Rock Pile: The Rock Pile is the rocky hill used to be the American fire-power base in 1966. Rock Pile had no way to go up or down, therefore troops only received resupply by helicopter.

RPG (Rocket Propelled Grenade): the RPG-7 anti-tank weapon was first deployed by the Soviets in 1961. Similar in use and function as the M20 used by American forces. Still in use by Iraqi insurgents today.

RTO: Radio/Telephone Operator (RTO). One half of the Forward Observer team.

Ruck: rucksack (backpack) had to carry everything for a soldier in the field. Usually with a metal frame for stability and support.

Screaming Eagles: nickname of the 101ˢᵗ Airborne.

Seabees: the Naval Mobile Construction Battalion is known by the phonetic pronunciation of their initials (CBs = "see-bees").

Shake and Bake: sergeant who attended NCO school and earned rank after only a very short time in uniform.

Sixteen: Refers to M16 assault rifle, introduced into Viet Nam in 1967.

Sixty: Refers to M60 machine gun. It provides a higher rate of fire, greater effective range, and uses a larger caliber round than the standard-issue US assault rifle, the M16. Weighs 23 pounds, unloaded.

Staff Sergeant (SSG or SSgt): The staff sergeant is a more experienced leader of soldiers and will often have one or more sergeants under his direct leadership. SSGs are the elements from which the backbones of the US Army and Marines are made.

Steel Pot: helmet.

TET Offensive: an operation which began on lunar New Year's night, January 30ᵗʰ, 1968. Although a sound military defeat for the Communist forces, it nevertheless was an enormous propaganda victory for the NLF and PAVN.

Tetrytol: Tetrytol is a cast mixture of tetryl and TNT and is designed to obtain a tetryl mixture that may be used in burster tubes for chemical bombs, in demolition blocks, and in cast shaped charges.

VA (Veteran's Administration): U.S. Department of Veterans Affairs. Of the 25 million veterans currently alive in 2006, nearly three of every four served during a war or an official period of hostility.

Viet Cong ("VC"): from the Vietnamese term for Vietnamese Communist (Việt Nam Cộng Sản).

Ville: French word literally meaning "village". Could refer to any indigenous encampment in Viet Nam.

Index

My Tour in Hell: A Marine's Battle with Combat Trauma

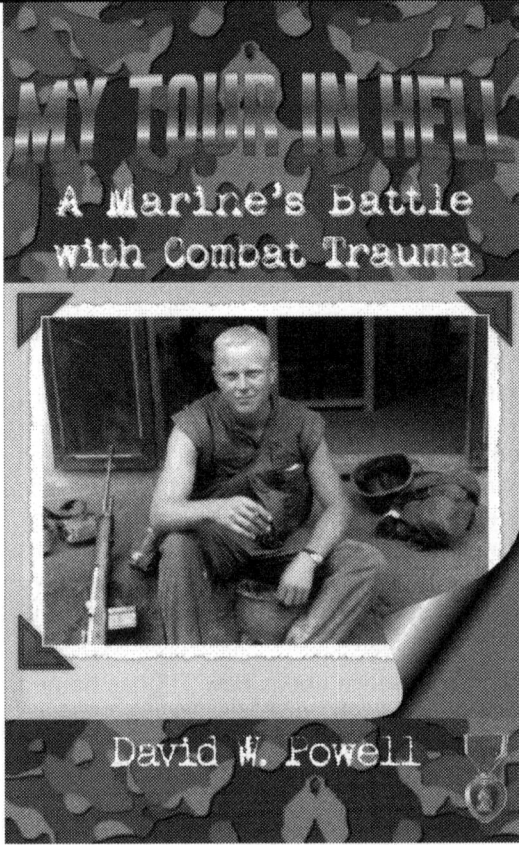

David W. Powell enlisted for a tour of duty in April 1966 with the US Marines after receiving an imminent draft notice. Believing he would be able to leverage his existing skills as a computer programmer, he never thought all they would see on his resume was his Karate expertise. Even less that he would wind up serving as a Rocket man in the jungles of Da Nang and Chu Lai for a 13 month tour in hell.

David's journey from naive civilian to battle-hardened combat veteran shows us all how fragile our humanity really is. In addition to killing the enemy on the field of battle, he was witness to countless cruelties including murder both cold-blooded and casual, cowardice under fire, and a callous disregard for life beyond most people's imagination. With each new insult, he lost a little bit of his soul, clinging to his Bible as his only solace while equally certain of his own demise.

The price he paid for what would only be diagnosed decades later as Post-Traumatic Stress Disorder was broken marriages and relationships, inability keep a job, bankruptcy, alcohol abuse, fear of his own emotions and reactions, and having to hide the service he willingly gave to his own country.

In 1989, David eventually recovered through a simple but powerful technique known as Traumatic Incident Reduction (TIR) and is now symptom-free. Not just for veterans, TIR has since been successfully applied to crime and motor vehicle accident victims, domestic violence survivors, and even children.

"His autobiographical work is a must read for veterans who remain stuck between two worlds. Healing is not forgetting; healing is making sense of the past in order to live life in the present with a restored hope for the future. Powell articulates this process very well and has given a tremendous gift to the combat veteran community of any generation."
— Father Philip G. Salois, M.S., National Chaplain, Vietnam Veterans of America

Complete details at www.MyTourInHell.com
Pub. Aug. 2006 – 204 pp. – List $26.95
ISBN-13: 978-1-932690-22-4
ISBN-10: 1-932690-22-0

Modern History Press

www.ingramcontent.com/pod-product-compliance
Lightning Source LLC
Chambersburg PA
CBHW050403110426
42812CB00006BA/1782